Keynote

INTERMEDIATE

Student's Book with the Spark platform

NGL.Cengage.com/Keynote

PASSWORD   keynoteStdt#

Paul Dummett
Helen Stephenson
Lewis Lansford

Australia • Brazil • Canada • Mexico • Singapore • United Kingdom • United States

Contents

UNIT	TED TALK	GRAMMAR	VOCABULARY
1 Working life 8–17	**A life lesson from a volunteer firefighter** Mark Bezos AUTHENTIC LISTENING SKILL Dealing with new vocabulary CRITICAL THINKING How a message is delivered PRESENTATION SKILL Being authentic	Present simple: affirmative and negative, *yes/no* questions, *wh-* questions, subject/object questions Expressions of frequency Indirect questions	Working life collocations (verb + noun) Jobs
2 Trends 18–27	**How to start a movement** Derek Sivers AUTHENTIC LISTENING SKILL Content words CRITICAL THINKING Extending an argument PRESENTATION SKILL Beginning and ending	Present simple and present continuous Present continuous	Verbs describing trends Relationships

REVIEW 1 (UNITS 1 AND 2) | **Broken Spoke** 28

UNIT	TED TALK	GRAMMAR	VOCABULARY
3 Money 30–39	**An escape from poverty** Jacqueline Novogratz AUTHENTIC LISTENING SKILL Rhythm and stress CRITICAL THINKING Reading between the lines PRESENTATION SKILL Persuasion	Countable and uncountable nouns Expressions of quantity: *much, many, a lot of, a few, a little* Extension: *very, too* and *enough*	Money
4 Success 40–49	**Don't eat the marshmallow!** Joachim de Posada AUTHENTIC LISTENING SKILL Dealing with accents CRITICAL THINKING Considering counter arguments PRESENTATION SKILL Body movement and gesture	Past simple and past continuous Past perfect	Success and rewards Prepositional phrases

REVIEW 2 (UNITS 3 AND 4) | **M-Pesa** 50

UNIT	TED TALK	GRAMMAR	VOCABULARY
5 Marketing 52–61	**3 ways to (usefully) lose control of your brand** Tim Leberecht AUTHENTIC LISTENING SKILL Understanding contrasts CRITICAL THINKING Supporting evidence PRESENTATION SKILL Using presentation slides	Comparatives and superlatives	Marketing collocations
6 Communication 62–71	**Talk nerdy to me** Melissa Marshall AUTHENTIC LISTENING SKILL Elision CRITICAL THINKING Demonstrating your argument PRESENTATION SKILL Engaging with your audience	Verb patterns with infinitive and *-ing* Infinitive and *-ing* clauses	Communication collocations Small talk phrases

REVIEW 3 (UNITS 5 AND 6) | **Morally Marketed** 72

PRONUNCIATION	READING	LISTENING	SPEAKING	WRITING
Sentence stress Intonation in questions	Skills for the 21st century	Asking about jobs	Best and worst jobs My skills Talking about jobs and studies	A formal letter Writing skill: Indirect questions
Stress in everyday phrases	Identifying trends	A conference meeting	General habits and current habits Describing trends Meetings and introductions	Formal and informal emails Writing skill: Formal and informal language
Questions with *Do you* and *Could you*	Teaching financial literacy	Everyday conversations	Standard of living and quality of life Money quiz Talking about money	A report Writing skill: Writing numbers in a report
Weak forms: *was* and *were* *had* and *hadn't* *Sorry*	Paid to succeed	Office conversations	My career path Incentives at work Giving reasons for actions	Messaging Writing skill: Prepositions in messages
Expressive intonation	The power of the crowd	Asking for opinions	Comparing the market Effective marketing Giving your views	A customer review Writing skill: Linking contrasting points
Sentence stress	Why we don't listen any more	Follow-up questions	Means of communication Communication skills Small talk	Short emails Writing skill: Reasons for writing

UNIT	TED TALK	GRAMMAR	VOCABULARY
7 Experience 74–83	**What I've learned from my autistic brothers** Faith Jegede AUTHENTIC LISTENING SKILL Weak forms CRITICAL THINKING A speaker's authority PRESENTATION SKILL Being concise	Present perfect simple Present perfect simple and past simple Extension: Present perfect continuous	Personal qualities
8 Seeing the future 84–93	**A skateboard, with a boost** Sanjay Dastoor AUTHENTIC LISTENING SKILL Prediction CRITICAL THINKING Evaluating claims PRESENTATION SKILL Signposting	Predictions with *will* and *might* Decisions with *going to* Reported speech	Describing devices

REVIEW 4 (UNITS 7 AND 8) | **One World Play Project** 94

UNIT	TED TALK	GRAMMAR	VOCABULARY
9 Being effective 96–105	**How to tie your shoes** Terry Moore AUTHENTIC LISTENING SKILL Word boundaries CRITICAL THINKING Understanding the main argument PRESENTATION SKILL Demonstration	Zero and first conditional Imperatives in conditionals	Being effective Practical solutions (adverbial phrases)
10 The environment 106–115	**How we can eat our landscapes** Pam Warhurst AUTHENTIC LISTENING SKILL Understanding fast speech CRITICAL THINKING Recognizing tone PRESENTATION SKILL Being straightforward	The passive Phrasal verbs	Phrasal verbs Food adjectives

REVIEW 5 (UNITS 9 AND 10) | **Pavegen** 116

UNIT	TED TALK	GRAMMAR	VOCABULARY
11 Leaders and thinkers 118–127	**Life at 30,000 feet** Richard Branson AUTHENTIC LISTENING SKILL Fillers in conversation CRITICAL THINKING Fact or opinion PRESENTATION SKILL Dealing with questions	Modal verbs (1): *must, mustn't, have to, don't have to, need to, don't need to, can* Modal verbs (2): *should* and *shouldn't*	*make* and *do*
12 Well-being 128–137	**How to succeed? Get more sleep** Arianna Huffington AUTHENTIC LISTENING SKILL Discourse markers CRITICAL THINKING Adapting an argument to an audience PRESENTATION SKILL Using humour	Second conditional Extension: Third conditional	Well-being adjectives

REVIEW 6 (UNITS 11 AND 12) | **CHG Healthcare** 138

Grammar summaries 140 | Audioscripts 164 | Communication activities 171

PRONUNCIATION	READING	LISTENING	SPEAKING	WRITING
Weak forms: *have*, *has* and *been* Linking words	France's new CV law	A job interview	Life experiences Diversity at work Describing skills and interests	A CV Writing skill: Verb forms
want and *won't* Contraction *'ll*	Our pick – new gadgets	Phrases in telephoning	Transport options Can I live without it? Leaving messages	Short emails Writing skill: Reported speech
Word stress	Getting the basics right	Practical instructions	Practical solutions Offering a good service Giving instructions	An email to a visitor Writing skill: Giving directions
Stress in passive forms Intonation in questions	Big rise in greenhouse gas emissions	In a restaurant	Survey: How 'local' are you? Expressing an opinion Explaining what's on a menu	A description of a system Writing skill: Explaining results
Positive and negative questions	Words of wisdom	Problem solving	Dilemmas Life advice Analysing problems and suggesting solutions	Posting advice on a forum Writing skill: Features of online posts
Contraction *'d* Stress in suggestions	Health and well-being news	Time wasting	Well-being and productivity Proposals for well-being Discussing options	A reply to an enquiry Writing skill: Listing options

TED Talk transcripts   173

1 Working life

BACKGROUND

1 You are going to watch a TED Talk by Mark Bezos called *A life lesson from a volunteer firefighter*. Read the text about the speaker and the talk. Then work in pairs and answer the questions.

1. What job did Mark Bezos have before and what jobs does he have now?
2. How do people in the USA feel about firefighters?
3. What motivates Mark Bezos?

TEDTALKS

MARK BEZOS worked in advertising for many years and now works for a charity organization, Robin Hood, which fights poverty in New York City. He is also a volunteer firefighter in Westchester County, New York, where he lives. Firefighting is a highly respected job in the USA. Mark Bezos is continuously amazed and motivated by the acts of heroism – big and small – that he sees every day.

Mark Bezos's idea worth spreading is that every act of generosity matters – even the small ones.

Reconstruction work, Hassan II Mosque, Casablanca

KEY WORDS

2 Read the sentences (1–7). The words in bold are used in the TED Talk. First guess the meaning of the words. Then match the words with their definitions (a–g).

1 Firefighting is his **vocation**. He wanted to be a firefighter from the age of twelve.
2 He was **jealous** of his colleague's new office.
3 She's the **homeowner** – it's her house and she's lived there for twenty years.
4 Poor people can get meals from a local **soup kitchen**.
5 In my job as a firefighter, I am **witness** to a lot of accidents.
6 When the firefighters arrived, the kitchen was **in flames**.
7 My mother is a retired doctor, but she still works as a **volunteer** in an old people's hospital.

a someone who does a job for no pay
b on fire
c a person who owns a house or flat
d a job or career that you feel fits your aims in life
e feel negatively about someone who has something you want
f someone who sees an event
g a place where free food is served to people in need

AUTHENTIC LISTENING SKILLS Dealing with new vocabulary

When you listen to authentic speech, you will hear many new vocabulary items. Don't try to understand every word.

- Listen for words that are stressed.
- Listen for words that the speaker repeats.
- Stay relaxed and keep listening.

3a 🎧 1 Look at the Authentic listening skills box. Listen to three sentences from the TED Talk. Underline the words that are repeated and circle the words that are stressed.

1 Back in New York, I am the head of development for a non-profit called Robin Hood.
2 When I'm not fighting poverty, I'm fighting fires as the assistant captain of a volunteer fire company.
3 Now in our town, where the volunteers supplement a highly skilled career staff, you have to get to the fire scene pretty early to get in on any action.

3b 🎧 2 Read sentence 4. Which words will be stressed? Which words are repeated? Then listen and check.

4 I am witness to acts of generosity and kindness on a monumental scale … but I'm also witness to acts of grace and courage on an individual basis.

1.1 A life lesson from a volunteer firefighter

TEDTALKS

1 ▶ **1.1** Mark Bezos tells a story about a time he went to help at a fire. Watch the TED Talk. Choose the lesson (a–c) that you think Mark Bezos wants us to learn.

    a We should always help our friends and family first.
    b Small acts of kindness are as important as big ones.
    c First be successful in your job and then go out and help others.

2 Work in pairs. What example did Mark Bezos give to illustrate this lesson? Discuss with your partner.

3 ▶ **1.1** Watch the first part (0.00–1.06) of the talk again. Choose the correct option to make true sentences.

    1 Mark Bezos is a *professional / volunteer* firefighter in his town.
    2 At his first fire he was the *first / second* volunteer to arrive.
    3 When Mark Bezos found the captain, he was speaking to *another volunteer / the homeowner*.
    4 It was the middle of the *day / night* and it was raining.

▶ profit /ˈprɑfɪt/ **N AM ENG**
▶ profit /ˈprɒfɪt/ **BR ENG**
▶ gotten /ˈgɑt(ə)n/ **N AM ENG**
▶ got /gɒt/ **BR ENG**

4 ▶ 1.1 Read the sentences. Then watch the second part (1.06–2.46) of the talk again. Complete the sentences with one word per space.

1 The captain asked the other volunteer to rescue a _dog_ from inside the house.
2 Mark Bezos felt _jealous_ that the other volunteer could tell people he saved a living animal.
3 The captain asked Mark Bezos to go into the house and _carry/bring_ back some shoes.
4 He carried the shoes back downstairs and gave them to the _homeowner_.
5 A few weeks later, the homeowner sent a letter thanking the fire department, in particular for saving her _shoes_.

5 ▶ 1.1 Watch the third part (2.46 to the end) of the talk again. Answer the questions.

1 What has Mark Bezos learned about the acts of kindness and generosity that he sees? _all are imp._
2 Mark Bezos's two-word message for his audience is 'Don't _wait_.' What does he mean by this?
3 What is one example of the kind of help we can give to others?

6 Work in pairs. Discuss other ways that people can help their communities. What could *you* do?

VOCABULARY IN CONTEXT

7 ▶ 1.2 Watch the clips from the TED Talk. Choose the correct meaning of the words.

8 Work in pairs. Complete the sentences in your own words.

1 There's a pretty good chance that next year I will …
2 I'm pretty much done … (*-ing*) …
3 The three things that matter most to me are …

CRITICAL THINKING How a message is delivered

9 Work in pairs. Read the conclusion or 'message' of Mark Bezos's talk. How did he get this message across? Choose the best answer (a–c).

'Don't wait until you make your first million to make a difference in somebody's life. If you have something to give, give it now.'

a with different examples
b with visuals / pictures
c with a simple story

10 Read this comment* about the TED Talk. Then discuss the questions.

1 What does the viewer like about the way Mark Bezos delivered his message?
2 Do you agree with her?

Viewers' comments

R Rachel – I like this talk – a short, everyday story with a simple lesson. It was a small gift from Mark Bezos which could make a big difference in many people's lives.

*The comment was created for this activity.

PRESENTATION SKILLS Being authentic

11 Work in pairs. What kind of person do you think an audience most likes to see giving a presentation: a confident person, a knowledgeable person, a funny person, a sincere person? Of these qualities, which is most appealing to you, and why?

12 Look at the Presentation tips box. What kind of person does it suggest people like to listen to?

> **TIPS**
>
> When you give a talk, it's important to be yourself and for your personality to come through. Follow these steps:
> 1 Write your talk yourself. Use words and expressions that you would normally use so that your words convey your personality.
> 2 Speak from the heart. Talk about things that you know about and believe in.
> 3 Don't worry if you are nervous. An audience sometimes warms more to someone who is nervous than someone who is full of confidence. They want you to succeed.
> 4 Relax your body. Try to move and gesture as you normally do.

13 ▶ 1.3 Watch the clip from the TED Talk. Then answer the questions.

1 Does the audience 'warm' to Mark Bezos? How can you tell?
2 Which points (1–4) from the Presentation tips box do you think Mark Bezos follows in his talk?

14 You are going to give a two-minute mini-presentation. Make some brief notes to present what you do for a living or what you are studying. Explain some surprising things about your job or studies – what people may not know about it – and/or the aspects of your job or studies that you like or dislike.

15 Work in pairs. Give your presentation. Use the advice from the Presentation tips box and be yourself!

▶ offer /ˈɑfər/ **N AM ENG**
▶ offer /ˈɒfə(r)/ **BR ENG**
▶ opportunity /ˌɑpərˈtunəti/ **N AM ENG**
▶ opportunity /ˌɒpə(r)ˈtjuːnəti/ **BR ENG**

1.2 What makes a good job?

WHAT DO OCCUPATIONAL THERAPISTS DO?

1 **ASSIST** people with injuries or disabilities
2 **HELP** people to recover
3 **TRAIN** people to do everyday tasks again

WHERE DO OCCUPATIONAL THERAPISTS WORK?

At the patient's home   At the therapist's clinic/hospital

OCCUPATIONAL THERAPY IN NUMBERS

Number of occupational therapists in the UK 2015

35,902

Salary
£21,388–£40,000

 Training time
3 YEARS

Average time in patients' homes
50%

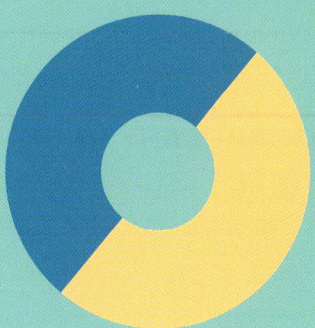

GRAMMAR Present simple

1 Work in pairs. What makes a good job? Put the points (a–g) in order of importance for you. Then discuss your priorities.

a a good salary
b respect of others in society
c job security
d a low level of stress
e a high level of training
f the satisfaction of helping other people
g a mental or physical challenge

2 Look at the infographic. What do you think an occupational therapist helps patients to do? Give examples. Which of the points (a–g) in Exercise 1 do you think are true for this job?

3 🎧 3 Listen to an occupational therapist talking about her job. Answer the questions.

1 What is the satisfying part of the job?
2 What is the more routine part of the job?
3 Do you like the sound of the job? Why? / Why not?

4 Read the sentences (1–6) in the Grammar box. Answer the questions (a–d).

PRESENT SIMPLE

1 I **work** as an occupational therapist.
2 The patient **comes** to your clinic.
3 What **do** you **do** exactly?
4 **Does** that **give** you a lot of satisfaction?
5 I **don't spend** all my time with patients.
6 **Who comes** to see you at the clinic?

a Do the verbs in bold describe a permanent or a temporary situation?
b When does an affirmative verb have a final -s?
c What is the auxiliary (not main) verb in questions and negative sentences?
d What is the difference between question 3 and question 6?

Check your answers on page 140 and do Exercises 1–2.

5 Complete the sentences using the correct form of the present simple.

1. What jobs _____ (occupational therapists / help) people with?
2. A: How long _____ (they / spend) with each patient?
   B: Well, _____ (it / depend) on the patient.
3. How many patients _____ (a therapist / see) each day?
4. How far _____ (you / have) to travel each day?
5. How much _____ (an occupational therapist / earn)?
6. A: Which _____ (person / help) people with physical injuries: a physiotherapist or an occupational therapist?
   B: They both _____. But a physiotherapist _____ (not / help) you to do specific jobs.

GRAMMAR Expressions of frequency

6 Read the sentences in the Grammar box. Answer the questions (1–3).

EXPRESSIONS OF FREQUENCY

Adverbs of frequency

I *usually* advise them about equipment.
People in these situations *often* have no confidence.
I *always* try to make them feel more confident.
They are *always* really grateful.
I *rarely* get home before 6.30 in the evening.

Adverbial phrases

Most days I visit people in their homes.
I write reports and attend meetings *every day*.

1. Where do adverbs of frequency (*usually, often,* etc.) go in relation to the main verb?
2. Where do adverbs of frequency go in relation to the verb *be*?
3. Where do adverbial phrases (*most days, every day, in the evening*) go in the sentence?

Check your answers on page 140 and do Exercises 3–5.

7 Put the words in the correct order to make sentences.

1. by 8.00 in the morning / 'm / usually / I / at work
2. rarely / my boss / checks / my work
3. sometimes / he / on the train / works
4. always / my emails / before I send them / check / I
5. don't / people in my country / late / work / usually
6. on Fridays / wear / casual clothes / people / often
7. tidy / once a month / I / my desk
8. home with me / never / I / take / in the evenings / work

Pronunciation Sentence stress

8a 🎧 4 Listen and check your answers to Exercise 7. Are the expressions of frequency stressed or not?

8b Work in pairs. Practise saying the sentences from Exercise 7 with the correct stress.

9 Look at your answers to Exercise 7 again. Change the expression of frequency and other words if necessary so that the sentences are true for you. Use these expressions of frequency to help you.

always	every day	most days	often
once a week	rarely	sometimes	
three times a year	twice a month	usually	

10 Work in pairs. Discuss your day. Ask and answer the questions. Use expressions of frequency.

- When do you leave for work / college and get home?
- What regular activities do you find rewarding / fun / boring / stressful?
- Who do you talk to when you are at work / college?
- How often do you socialize with work colleagues / fellow students?

I leave the house at 7.00 a.m. and I don't usually get home before 7.00 p.m.

SPEAKING Best and worst jobs

11 **21st CENTURY OUTCOMES**

Work in groups. Look at the list of best and worst jobs. Discuss the questions.

1. Explain to each other what each person does.
2. Say why you think this is a good or a bad job.

A: *A translator translates documents from one language to another.*
B: *Why do you think it's the best job?*
A: *Well, they probably have a good salary and I imagine the work is usually interesting.*

BEST AND WORST JOBS IN THE UK
2013 survey

	Best jobs	Worst jobs
1	Translator	Miner
2	Web developer	Courier
3	Surgeon	Builder's labourer
4	Lawyer	Journalist
5	Vet	Sous chef*
6	Pilot	Electrician
7	Physiotherapist / Occupational therapist	Lorry driver
8	Architect	Waiter

*A second or assistant chef

21st CENTURY OUTCOMES INFORMATION LITERACY Evaluating data

1.3 Have you got what it takes?

READING Skills for the 21st century

1 Work in pairs. Look at the list of work skills. What do you think each one means? Discuss with your partner.

   a Interpersonal skills
   b Working independently
   c Bilingualism
   d Technological knowledge
   e Critical thinking
   f Teamwork
   g Organizational skills
   h Management skills

2 Read the article. Answer the questions.

   1 Which of the skills in Exercise 1 does the author say are important? *interpersonal skills (l.1-11) critical (l.21) technological knowledge (l.22) teamwork (l.12)*
   2 What other skills does the author mention? *lines 2-5, 23, 24, 26, 28*

   organise study (l.27)

3 Read the article again. Choose the correct option (a–c) to complete the sentences according to the article.

   1 People need to understand other groups and other cultures because:
      a it will help them get a better job.
      b it is everyone's personal responsibility to do this.
      (c) everyone in the world is connected today. *l.1-2*

   2 The article says that 21st century employees want to work for organizations that:
      a offer them a good career.
      (b) benefit the community or people in general. *l.7-9*
      c care about their employees.

   3 Good interpersonal skills help you to:
      a make progress in your career.
      b choose the best way to communicate with people.
      (c) deal with all kinds of people and situations. *l.15-17*

   4 Thinking critically is important because:
      (a) there is so much information to process. *l.19-20*
      b technology moves so fast.
      c a lot of information is visual.

   5 The article says that employers in the 21st century expect their employees to:
      a have many different skills and interests.
      b relax and have some fun.
      (c) work fast and make good decisions. *l.27-30*

4 Do you agree with the ideas in the article? Do you think the skills for the 21st century are different from the skills people used at work in the last century? Discuss with your partner and give reasons. *agree/disagree sides of the classroom?*

5 Find these words in the article. Then choose the correct meaning (a–c).

   1 **appreciate** (line 5)
      a think about these differences
      (b) welcome these differences
      c ignore these differences

   2 **inspire** (line 8)
      a pay people well
      (b) make people enthusiastic
      c communicate with people

   3 **collaboration** (line 12)
      (a) working together
      b working independently
      c giving people instructions

   4 **conflict** (line 16)
      a people you work with
      b a difficult decision
      (c) a serious disagreement

   5 **huge** (line 20)
      (a) very big
      b big
      c unusual

   6 **stand back from** (line 32)
      a relax after
      b leave
      (c) look at from a distance

VOCABULARY Working life collocations (verb + noun) — *combinations*

6 Find verbs in the article that collocate with these nouns.

   a _have_   a career — *find in text first*
   b _understand_ cultural differences, technology
   c _do_   a job
   d _attend_   meetings
   e _speak_   on the phone
   f _deal with_   a difficult situation, conflict
   g _get_ , _process_ information
   h _prioritise_ tasks
   i _have_   fun

7 Complete the conversation with the correct verbs. Then check your answers with the collocations in Exercise 6.

A: I know you're a lawyer. But what do you ¹ _do_ exactly?
B: I work in the music industry. We ² _deal with_ legal conflicts about music.
A: Do you meet a lot of pop stars, then?
B: Not really. I sometimes ³ _speak_ on the phone to the artists, but I usually ⁴ _attend_ meetings with other lawyers.

14

A: Is it interesting?
B: It's very interesting. But there's a lot of information to 5 _process_. The music industry is changing fast and you have to 6 _understand_ the new technology and the different ways that people listen to music now via the Internet. It's hard work, but we 7 _have_ a lot of fun too.
A: How did you get into it?
B: My first idea was to 8 _have_ a career as a musician, but that didn't really work out.

SPEAKING My skills

8 **21st CENTURY OUTCOMES**

Think about the work skills in Exercise 1 and the skills mentioned in the article. Write down:
- four skills that are important to you in your work or studies
- two things that you want or expect from your employer

9 Work in small groups. Compare your lists from Exercise 8. Do you need similar skills at work or in your studies? Do you want or expect similar things from your employer? Why are these skills important in your work or studies?

SKILLS for the 21st Century

What are the skills that people need to have in today's workplace? What does this mean for the careers that they have? And their lives in general? What does it mean for the companies that employ them? We asked Imogen Roberts, an expert in 21st century skills. Here is a selection of her answers.

A THE BIG PICTURE | 'We live in a global economy and we are part of a global community. So people need to know how different countries and groups relate to each other. They need to understand cultural differences and to appreciate these. Everyone has a responsibility to society and to the environment. So a question that 21st century employees often ask is: Does my company or organization help society? Does it inspire me? If the answer is 'no', they look for other work.'

B COMMUNICATION | 'In today's workplace, interpersonal skills are very important. This is because many of the jobs we do involve collaboration. So when you attend meetings, speak to people face-to-face or on the phone, or communicate with them by email, you need to build good relations. People are not always easy to work with and sometimes in your work you have to deal with conflict and difficult situations.'

C LEARNING | 'We get information now in many ways and these ways are changing constantly. Today's worker has to process huge amounts of written and visual information. So they have to think critically about this information and they need to understand technology and to choose the best way to communicate with it. They also have to be creative and, above all, they have to want to learn.'

D PRODUCTIVITY | 'The 21st century world moves fast. So you need to be quick and you need to be efficient. Employers expect this, so employees need to be organized and they need to be able to prioritize tasks – to distinguish between what is important and what is not – so they work more productively. At the same time, companies have to recognize that work is not everything: people want time to stand back from their work and they want time to relax and have fun.'

21st CENTURY OUTCOMES   PROFESSIONAL DEVELOPMENT   Understanding and reflecting critically on your skill set

1.4 What do you do?

VOCABULARY Jobs

1 Look at the jobs. Match the jobs with the photos (A–F). Which words describe someone who is learning a job?

engineer
law student
medical researcher
plumbing apprentice
sales assistant
trainee nurse

A _____

B _____

C _____

D _____

E _____

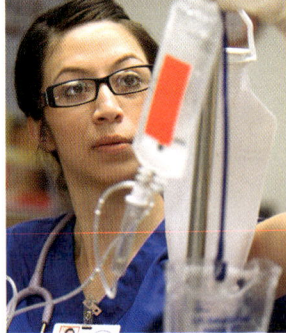
F _____

2 🎧 **5** Listen to how the jobs in Exercise 1 are pronounced. Then practise saying them with a partner.

LISTENING Asking about jobs

3 🎧 **6** Listen to a conversation in which Jake is asking Martha about her job. Answer the questions.

1. What is Martha's job?
2. What stage of her career is Martha at?
3. Does she like her job?

4 🎧 **6** Listen to the conversation again. Complete the questions that Jake asks.

	Question
1 Job	What _____ ?
2 Company / Organization	Who _____ ?
3 Location	_____ based?
4 Job description	_____ involve?
5 Size of organization	Is _____ then?
6 Type of contract	What _____ ?
7 Like / Dislike	Do _____ ?

5 Complete Martha's answers to the questions in Exercise 4. Compare your answers with your partner.

Pronunciation Intonation in questions

6a 🎧 **7** Listen to the questions in Exercise 4. Notice how the intonation rises (↗) or falls (↘) at the end of the question. What rule can you make?

6b Work in pairs. Act out the conversation between Martha and Jake. Pay attention to your intonation in the questions.

SPEAKING Talking about jobs and studies

7 Make notes about your job or studies. Then ask your partner about their job or studies and complete the table. Use the questions in Exercise 4 and the expressions from the Useful language box on page 17 to help you.

	My partner
1 Job / Studies	
2 Company / Institution	
3 Location	
4 Job / Course description	
5 Size of organization / institution	
6 Type of contract / course	
7 Like / Dislike	

TALKING ABOUT JOBS AND STUDIES

I'm a … / I work as a … / I study …
I … and I have to …
I work for …
I study at …
I'm / The company is based in …
It's a temporary / permanent / part-time / full-time contract.
It's a part-time / full-time / three-year course.
It's great. / It's not very interesting. / It's hard work.

WRITING A formal letter

8 Work in pairs. Read the advertisement. Imagine you are going to apply for this job. What questions do you have about it? What information is missing?

WANTED

SPORTS EQUIPMENT DEMONSTRATORS

We are looking for enthusiastic and fit people to tour schools with us in the UK and demonstrate our range of indoor and outdoor sports equipment.

Temporary position – South-east area – Good rates of pay

---

9 Read the letter. Does the writer have the same questions about the job as you?

Dear Sir / Madam,

I saw your advertisement for Sports Equipment Demonstrators in the *Daily Record* and I am interested in applying. However, before I make my application I need to check two important points.

1 The advertisement says the job is based in the South-east, but it does not give the exact location. Can you tell me where it is?

2 It also says that this is a temporary position, but it does not specify the length of the contract. I'd like to know how long the contract lasts and if there is a possibility of extending the contract at the end of this period.

I look forward to hearing from you.

Yours faithfully,

Stefan Krantz

---

10 Read the letter again. Put the functions (a–d) in the order they appear in the letter.

a Explain to the reader what you want to happen next
b Refer to the job advertised
c Describe the information you need
d Explain the reason for writing

Writing skill Indirect questions

11a Look at the indirect questions from the letter in Exercise 9. Complete the direct question.

1 Can you tell me where it is?
Where _____ ?

2 I'd like to know how long the contract lasts.
How long _____ ?

3 I'd like to know if there is a possibility of extending the contract at the end of this period.
_____ of extending the contract?

See page 140 for more information about indirect questions, and do Exercise 6.

11b Rewrite the direct questions as more polite indirect questions.

1 'What kind of work is it?'
Can you tell me _____ ?
2 'Where are you based?'
Could you tell me _____ ?
3 'Is it a big company?'
Can you tell me _____ ?
4 'What does the work involve?'
I'd like to know _____ .
5 'How long does the interview usually take?'
Do you know _____ ?
6 'How often do buses go to the business park?'
Can you tell me _____ ?

12 **21st CENTURY OUTCOMES**

Read the job advertisement. Write a letter asking for more information. Ask two indirect questions.

▼ FILM EXTRAS

We are looking for people to be part of a new film we are shooting later this year. This will be one or two weeks' work. No acting experience necessary.

Apply to the Assistant Casting Director, Harvard Studios

---

13 Work in pairs. Exchange letters. Check that your partner's letter includes these points:

- a reference to the advertisement
- the reason for writing
- two indirect questions about the job
- what the reader should do next

2 Trends

BACKGROUND

1 You are going to watch a TED Talk by Derek Sivers called *How to start a movement*. Read the text about the speaker and the talk. Then work in pairs and discuss the questions.

1 What is Derek Sivers famous for?
2 Do you think Derek Sivers is a 'leader' or a 'follower'?
3 What about you? Give an example or a reason for your answer.

TEDTALKS

DEREK SIVERS is best known as the founder of CD Baby, one of the first sellers of independent music on the Internet. His latest company, Wood Egg, advises people on how to build companies in Asia and the Far East. So he knows about starting a movement.

Derek Sivers's idea worth spreading is that while leaders get the credit for starting a movement, the first followers are often the driving force.

Fans of the British comedy group Monty Python attend the celebration of the International Silly Walk Day, Czech Republic

KEY WORDS

2 Read the sentences (1–5). The words in bold are used in the TED Talk. First guess the meaning of the words. Then match the words with their definitions (a–e).

1 You need **guts** to stand up and give a talk to 2,000 people.
2 People think he is a **nut** because he does things differently.
3 In times when everyone tries to be the same as others, people who do things differently really **stand out**.
4 No one else at the time thought this was a good idea – his was a **lone** voice.
5 When she first decided to be a racing driver, people **ridiculed** her, because it was a man's sport. But now that she drives for a famous team she has everyone's respect.

a a crazy person (*slang*)
b single, alone
c courage (*colloquial*)
d laughed at, treated as a joke
e be noticeable in a crowd

AUTHENTIC LISTENING SKILLS Content words

When you listen to authentic speech, you may not hear and understand every word. Generally, you hear the important or content words more clearly, because they are stressed. Try to construct the meaning from these content words.

3a 🎧 8 Look at the Authentic listening skills box. Read the first sentence of the TED Talk (the content words are underlined). Listen and practise saying the sentence with your partner.

1 So, ladies and gentlemen, at TED we talk a lot about leadership and how to make a movement.

3b 🎧 9 Listen to the second sentence from the talk. Complete the sentence with the content words. The other content words are underlined.

2 So let's _____ a movement happen, start to finish, in under _____ minutes and dissect some _____ from it.

19

2.1 How to start a movement

TEDTALKS

1 ▶ 2.1 Watch the TED Talk. Answer the questions.

  1 Who are the different people that are involved in a movement?
  2 According to Derek Sivers, which person is the most important?

2 ▶ 2.1 Watch the first part (0.00–1.02) of the talk again. Choose the correct option to complete the description of the first two people who start the movement.

  1 The leader needs *an idea / guts* to stand out and be *ridiculed / followed*.
  2 The first follower shows everyone else how to *follow / lead*.
  3 The leader treats the first follower as *a friend / an equal*.
  4 The first follower transforms the man who started dancing from a *nut / nobody* into a leader.

3 ▶ 2.1 Watch the second part (1.02–1.55) of the talk again. Complete the notes with these words.

  crowd   followers   movement   ridiculed   risky

  • When three people join in, it becomes a ¹_____.
  • As more followers join, they copy the other ²_____.
  • Now that you have a movement, it is less ³_____ to join in.
  • Then all the people who like to be with the ⁴_____ join in too, because they could be ⁵_____ if they don't.

▶ notice /ˈnoʊdɪs/ **N AM ENG**
▶ notice /ˈnəʊtɪs/ **BR ENG**
▶ calling /ˈkɔlɪŋ/ **N AM ENG**
▶ calling /ˈkɔːlɪŋ/ **BR ENG**

4 ▶ **2.1** Watch the third part (1.55 to the end) of the talk again. Choose the correct option (a–b) to answer the questions about the lessons we can learn from the talk.

1 What is the most important thing for a leader to do?
   a have a good idea
   b treat the first followers as equals

2 Who usually gets the credit for starting a movement?
   a the leader
   b the first follower

3 Who is the person who deserves to get the credit, according to Derek Sivers?
   a the leader
   b the first follower

4 What does Derek Sivers say ordinary people should not be afraid of?
   a joining a new movement
   b starting your own movement

VOCABULARY IN CONTEXT

5 ▶ **2.2** Watch the clips from the TED Talk. Choose the correct meaning of the words.

6 Work in pairs. Complete the sentences in your own words.

1 When you learn a language it is crucial to …
2 When you are starting a new job, you should never underestimate …
3 Sitting on the fence can be a good idea sometimes. For example, …
4 A good boss nurtures …

CRITICAL THINKING Extending an argument

7 Work in pairs. Answer the questions.

1 What did you learn from the talk about leaders?
2 What's courageous about following?
3 When might it take courage not to follow someone?

8 Read this comment* about the TED Talk. What is the viewer saying about following others? Can you think of a similar example from your own experience?

> **Viewers' comments**
>
> **S** **Sun Kim** – I like this talk, but I think it sometimes takes more courage not to follow the crowd. Some people at my school had a hard time because they weren't part of the in-crowd. They went their own way. One guy I know made his own music and now he is a very successful musician.

*The comment was created for this activity.

PRESENTATION SKILLS Beginning and ending

9 Work in pairs. What ways can you think of to begin and end a talk? Discuss your ideas.

1 Beginning
2 Ending

10 Look at the Presentation tips box. Compare the tips with the answers you gave in Exercise 9.

> **TIPS**
>
> In a talk, you're taking your audience on a journey. You should know where you want to take them (beginning, middle and end). Ideas include:
>
> **Beginning**
> - Introduce yourself and say why you are talking about this topic
> - Begin strongly: say something that gets the audience's attention (for example a personal story)
> - Give an overview of what you are going to say
>
> **Ending**
> - Make a conclusion – share what you have learned from your experiences
> - Emphasize your main idea one last time, simply and powerfully
> - Thank the audience for listening

11 ▶ **2.3** Watch the clips from the TED Talk. How did Derek Sivers begin and end his talk?

12 Work in pairs. Think of a group that you belong to (a club, an interest group, an online community) and how you can persuade people that it is a good group to join. Prepare the opening and closing lines of your presentation.

13 Work with a new partner. Take turns to give the beginning and ending of your presentation.

▶ guy **N AM ENG**
▶ guy or bloke **BR ENG**

2.2 Who are you following?

TWITTER FACTS AND FIGURES 2014

Active registered Twitter users
645,750,000

New Twitter users signing up every day
135,000

Number of Twitter employees
2,000

Twitter users
Individuals   Companies   Governments

Twitter annual advertising revenue
- 2013 $405,500,000
- 2012 $259,000,000
- 2011 $139,000,000
- 2010 $45,000,000

Popular trending topics
Football World Cup
Ice bucket challenge
Ebola

The most followed brand on Twitter
YouTube (40m)

The most followed celebrity on Twitter
Katy Perry (51.6m)

5 days – Number of days it takes for 1 billion tweets

9,100 – Number of tweets that happen every second

40% – Percentage of Twitters who don't tweet but watch other people tweet

GRAMMAR Present simple and present continuous

1 Work in pairs. Read the definition of Twitter and answer the questions.

> Twitter is a social networking site where users send and read short 140-character text messages called 'tweets'.

1. Do you use Twitter?
2. Do you follow anyone on Twitter? Why? / Why not?

2 Look at the infographic. Answer the questions.
1. How many people around the world use Twitter?
2. How fast is the number of users growing?
3. What is the name for topics that are popular on Twitter?
4. Who follows Twitter to see what these topics are?

3 Read the text in the Grammar box. Answer the questions (1–2).

PRESENT SIMPLE AND PRESENT CONTINUOUS

*Twitter users **comment** about different topics and events in the world. At this very moment, millions of people **are looking** at Twitter to find out about trending topics. Companies, governments and famous people also **follow** Twitter every day. They want to know, 'What **are** people **saying** about me?'*

1. Which verbs in bold describe something that is generally true?
2. Which verbs in bold describe events which are happening now or around now?

Check your answers on page 142 and do Exercise 1.

4 Look at the infographic again. Complete the sentences with the present simple and present continuous.

Twitter ¹ _____has_____ (have) over 645 million users and new people ² __are joining__ (join) all the time. These users ³ _____ (send) over one billion tweets every five days. At this very moment 9,000 people in the world ⁴ _____ (send) a tweet. 40% of Twitter users ⁵ _____ (not / tweet), but they ⁶ _____ (look) at other people's tweets. The most followed things on Twitter are pop singers and YouTube. 51.6 million people ⁷ _____ (follow) Katy Perry and 40 million people ⁸ _____ (follow) YouTube. Twitter's advertising revenue ⁹ _____ (also / grow) rapidly. Twitter ¹⁰ _____ (employ) 2,000 people, but it ¹¹ _____ (recruit) more people at the moment because of its growth in popularity.

5 Read the sentences (1–3) in the Grammar box. Match the sentences with the uses of the present continuous (a–c).

PRESENT CONTINUOUS

1 He**'s working** from home this week.
2 Twitter **is becoming** more popular.
3 A: What **are** you **doing**? B: I**'m writing** a message.

We use the present continuous to describe:

a events that are happening now
b temporary situations
c trends (situations that are in a process of change)

Check your answers on page 142 and do Exercises 2–7.

6 Work in pairs. Read the sentences. Identify the use of the present continuous (a–c) from the Grammar box.

1 People are working longer hours than in the past.
2 Excuse me. I'm looking for the Post Office.
3 Are you waiting for someone?
4 I'm working in Bristol today.
5 The Earth's climate is becoming warmer.
6 I'm training for the London marathon – it's next month.

7 Read the sentences. Decide if the sentences contain correct uses of the present continuous. Write *correct* (C) or *incorrect* (I). Correct the incorrect uses.

1 The price of petrol is going up and up.
2 Kate is thinking that her salary is too low.
3 She's half-Swiss. Her father is Dutch and her mother is coming from Geneva.
4 I'm cycling to work this week, because my car is at the garage.
5 He loves his car! He is cleaning it every week.
6 The retirement age is rising because people live longer than in the past.

8 Write sentences to complete the conversation. Use the present simple and present continuous.

A: ¹ How often / you / use / Twitter?
B: ² I / read / other people's tweets every day, but I / not / tweet.
A: And what is Twitter good for?
B: Well, I'm a scientist and ³ I / usually / use / Twitter for my work. ⁴ It's very important for me to know what / happen / in my field currently.
A: ⁵ So who / you / follow / at the moment?
B: ⁶ Right now / I / follow / a conversation between two scientists in Canada about the environment.
A: And what about other subjects?
B: ⁷ Sometimes / I / look / at what famous people / say / at the moment about things in the news. ⁸ This week a lot of people / talk / about the situation in the Middle East.

9 Work in pairs. Look at these time phrases and adverbs. Which time phrases and adverbs do you expect to see with a) the present simple and b) the present continuous?

| at the moment | currently | every day | now |
| sometimes | this week | usually | |

10 Discuss where you would put each time phrase from Exercise 9 in these sentences.

1 We meet to practise our English together. (present simple)
2 I am learning English in evening classes. (present continuous)

SPEAKING General habits and current habits

11 **21st CENTURY OUTCOMES**

Look at the topics. Think about what you do generally in each area, and what you are doing at the moment. Then discuss in small groups. Explain if you are doing something different from what you normally do.

Topics
- what your work is / what your studies are
- what you read
- what food you eat or like eating
- what exercise you do
- what social media you use
- how you relax in your free time

I study engineering at university. At the moment I'm preparing for my exams.

I generally eat a lot of fast food, but at the moment I'm trying to eat healthy food.

2.3 The next big thing

READING Identifying trends

1 Work in pairs. Look at the predictions of 'the next big thing'. Say if these people were right and if so, give examples.

1 In 1968, the science fiction writer Arthur C Clarke predicted that in 2001 people would read newspapers on computers.
2 In 1900, the civil engineer John Elfreth Watkins predicted that in one hundred years photographs would be telegraphed around the world.
3 Ray Kurzweil, the inventor, predicted that in the early 21st century, learning and classrooms would be dominated by computers.

2 How are people able to spot future trends like these? Discuss with your partner.

3 Read the article. Are the author's ideas the same as your ideas from Exercise 2?

4 Complete the summary with words and phrases from the article. Then compare your summary with a partner. Did you include the same information?

There are three ways to spot future trends. First, you can ¹_____. The author, Naisbitt, did this. He ²_____ devoted to a topic in the ³_____. This isn't possible now because there is ⁴_____. The next way is looking for ⁵_____, not just in ⁶_____. The third thing is to pay attention to ⁷_____ in their ⁸_____ time.

5 Find examples in the article that illustrate each of the three ways of spotting a trend.

6 Find six different adjectives in the article which describe trends. Which adjectives:

1 refer to a trend that has appeared recently? (two adjectives)
2 refer to the size of the trend? (one adjective)
3 refer to the time of the trend? (two adjectives)
4 refer to who is affected by the trend? (one adjective)

7 Can you think of an example of the following?

1 a general trend in the way that people pay for the things they buy
2 a current trend in exercise or diet

VOCABULARY Verbs describing trends

8 Read the sentences (1–6). Match the verb or verb phrase in bold with its opposite.

becoming less common
decreasing
falling
getting worse
getting poorer
shrinking

1 The economy is **growing** fast.
2 The number of young people smoking is **increasing**.
3 The quality of food in restaurants is **improving**.
4 Obesity* is **becoming more widespread.**
5 The average age of the population is **rising.**
6 The middle class are **getting richer.**

*Being very overweight

9 Work in pairs. Discuss which trends (1–6) from Exercise 8 are true of your country.

10 Complete the sentences with the verbs and verb phrases from Exercise 8. Sometimes more than one answer is possible.

1 The population is _____ older.
2 The market for electric cars is _____ by eighty per cent each year.
3 It's _____ more difficult to find a cheap holiday.
4 The weather is _____.
5 The habit of working from home is becoming more _____.

SPEAKING Describing trends

11 **21st CENTURY OUTCOMES**

Work in small groups. Each choose one of the areas below. Write a sentence describing a trend in this area. Then discuss your trends and the possible reasons for them.

- food and eating habits
- holidays and travel
- transportation
- working habits
- health and medicine

More and more people in my city are cycling to work. I think this is mainly because the traffic is so bad.

IDENTIFYING TRENDS

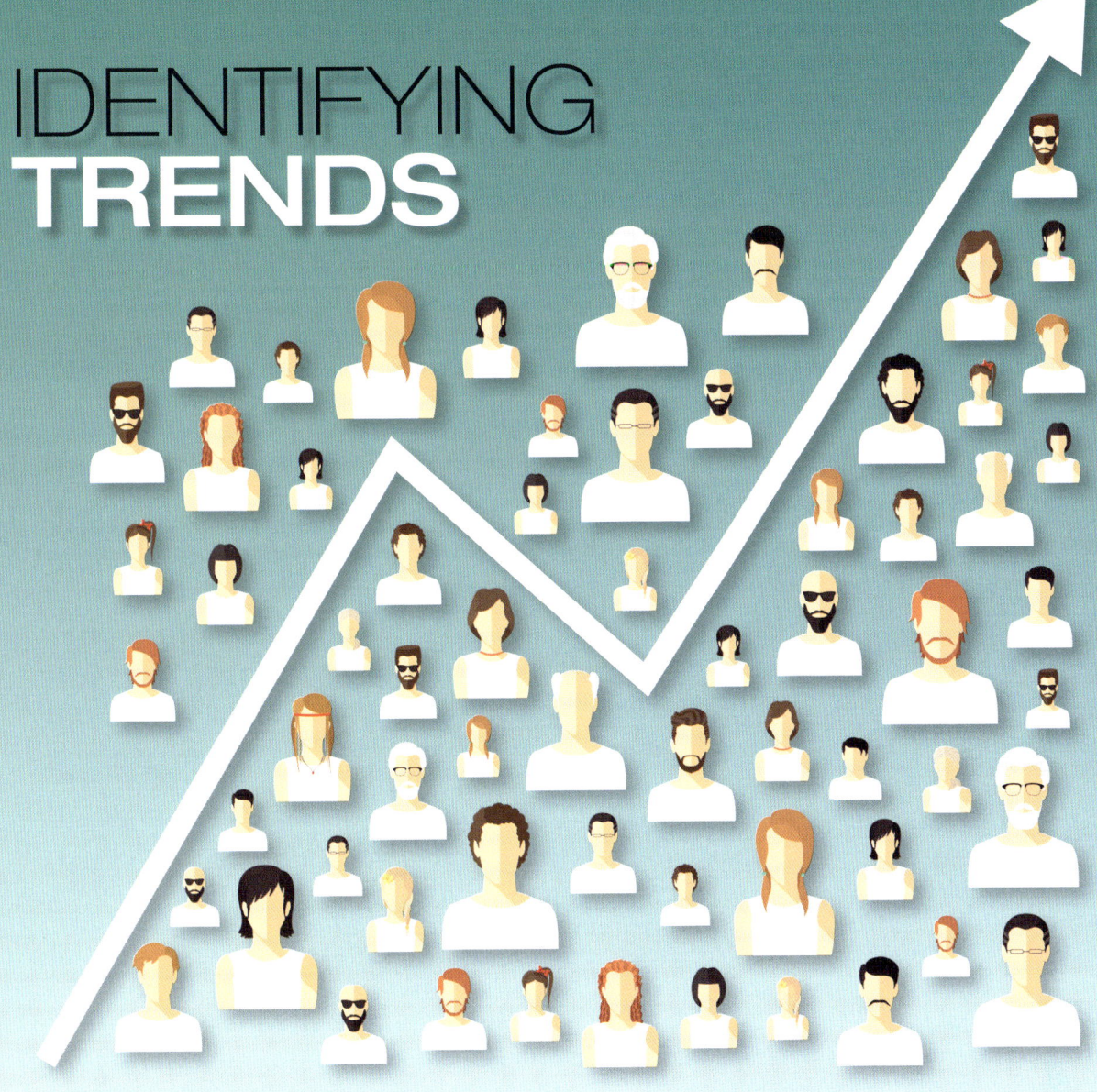

EVERY COMPANY wants to know what the next major trend is going to be in their sector so that they can plan for the future and take advantage of it. But how can we know what the next big thing is before others find out? Alan Kay, the American computer scientist, once said 'The best way to predict the future is to invent it.' Well, that's good advice if you are an inventor, but most of us have to use other methods.

Perhaps the best guide to future trends is to look and listen to what is happening now. When John Naisbitt wrote his famous book, *Megatrends*, in 1982, he did exactly that. He looked through newspapers and measured the amount of space that was devoted to particular topics. When he saw that a topic was receiving more and more attention in the newspapers, for example environmental issues, he noted this as an emerging trend. It is more difficult to use Naisbitt's method nowadays, because there is so much more information to read. Because of the Internet, the amount of published information has increased by around three thousand per cent since the 1980s. But keeping your eyes and ears open is still important.

The next thing is looking for general trends, outside your own sector. If you see new trends in your sector, then you are probably too late to take full advantage of them. Looking for trends in everyday life in general can be more useful. Imagine, for example, that your company makes everyday clothes. You notice the two following trends: 1) people are becoming more and more active; and 2) companies are teaming up with other companies to make more interesting offers to consumers. Two ways of exploiting these current trends immediately come to mind: making clothes that can serve as both everyday and active wear and/or teaming up with an established maker of sports clothes to create a new range of clothing.

Finally, it's important to notice how people are playing, particularly if they are playing enthusiastically. Trends in consumer behaviour are not always driven by things that make us more efficient. Often they originate in people's hobbies and things they do to have fun. Apple was founded by two members of the Homebrew Computer Club, a group of hobbyists who played around with computers in the 1970s and 80s. And the whole social networking phenomenon – Facebook, etc. – was built on people sharing photographs or personal information in their free time.

---

emerging (adj) new, in early stages of growth
originate in (v) begin with

21st CENTURY OUTCOMES   **CRITICAL THINKING** Drawing conclusions about general trends

2.4 How are you doing?

VOCABULARY Relationships

1 Look at these words. Then complete the table.

assistant	boss	business partner	colleague
friend	husband	IT expert	manager
other half	partner	technical guru	wife

People you work with	People you (probably) don't work with

2 Find the three informal expressions from the words in Exercise 1: one meaning 'manager', one meaning 'expert' and one meaning 'partner'.

3 Work in pairs. Discuss how you would greet three of the people in Exercise 1 differently.

| bow | handshake | kiss | nod of the head |
| 'hello' | smile | | |

In Japan, it's common for people to bow as a way of showing respect to another person.

LISTENING A conference meeting

4 🎧 10 Listen to a conversation between three people at a conference: Jim, Theresa and Franco. Who knows each other and who is meeting for the first time?

	Know each other	First meeting
a Jim and Theresa		
b Jim and Franco		
c Theresa and Franco		

5 🎧 10 Listen to the conversation again. Choose the correct phrases to complete the extracts. Are the phrases Jim uses formal or informal?

1 Jim: Hello, Theresa. Good to see you. *How are you doing? / How do you do?*

2 Theresa: *Things are going very well, thanks. / Pleased to meet you.* What brings you here?

3 Theresa: Good luck with that. By the way, *may I introduce you to Franco / this is Franco*, my marketing assistant.

4 Jim: Hi, Franco. *Pleased to meet you. / Good to meet you.* I'm Jim Hyland.

5 Franco: *How do you do? / Pleased to meet you, Jim.*

6 Jim: *How's it going? / How do you find it?* Is Theresa working you very hard?

7 Theresa: Well, we have a meeting to go to now. But *it was a pleasure to meet you / great to see you* and see you tomorrow.

Pronunciation Stress in everyday phrases

6 🎧 11 Listen to the phrases from Exercise 5 and repeat them. Pay attention to the stress.

SPEAKING Meetings and introductions

7 Work in groups of three. Take turns to play the roles below (A, B and C).

Student A: You are at a restaurant with your new boss, Student C. You worked with Student B at your previous company, ADG.

Student B: You see Student A at a restaurant. Student A worked at your company, ADG, but left a year ago.

Student C: You recently joined the company, ADG. You are having lunch with one of your employees, Student A.

Act out a conversation like the one in Exercise 4. Use the expressions in the Useful language box on page 27 to help you.

MEETINGS AND INTRODUCTIONS

More formal

How do you do?
Pleased to meet you.
May I introduce you to … (Franco)?
How are you? (second meeting)
It was a pleasure to meet you.

Informal

Hi, I'm … (Jim).
How's it going?
Good / Nice to meet you.
This is … (Sarah).
How are you? / How are you doing? (second meeting)
It was great to meet you.

Possible responses

How do you do?
Pleased to meet you too.
Pleased to meet you, … (Franco).
Very well, thanks. And you?
It was nice to meet you too.

Possible responses

Good to meet you, … (Jim). I'm … (Franco).
Yeah, good, / not bad, thanks.
You too.
Hi, … (Sarah). I'm … (Faisal).
Fine, thanks. / Good, thanks.
Nice to meet you too.

WRITING Formal and informal emails

8 Read the two emails (A and B). Which email is more formal and which email is informal?

A

TO: *Click here to add recipients*   CC:
SUBJECT:

Hi Jim

Good to see you at the conference last week. We're having a party to say goodbye to Isabelle Jacobs, who's leaving at the end of the month (details attached). Just wondered if you'd like to come.

Look forward to hearing from you.

All the best

Theresa

B

TO: *Click here to add recipients*   CC:
SUBJECT:

Dear Jim

It was good to see you at the conference last week. The company is organizing a farewell party for Isabelle Jacobs, who is leaving at the end of the month. I just wondered if you would like to come. (The details are attached.)

I look forward to hearing from you.

Kind regards

Theresa

Writing skill Formal and informal language

9a Work in pairs. Underline the differences between the two emails.

9b Look at the pairs of words and expressions. Which expressions (a or b) are more formal?

1 a thanks   b thank you
2 a the following week b the week after
3 a I think   b I reckon
4 a a good time   b a convenient time

10 Read the email to a customer. Rewrite the email using more formal language. Then compare your email with a partner.

TO: *Click here to add recipients*   CC:
SUBJECT:

Hi Paul

Thanks for your email about visiting our showroom to look at bathrooms. No problem. Just need to know when's a good time for you. We're having some building work in the showroom next week, so I reckon the week after's probably better.

Look forward to hearing from you.

All the best

Tim

(Customer Services)

11 **21st CENTURY OUTCOMES**

Write a formal reply to the email. Thank Tim and suggest when you will visit the showroom.

12 Exchange emails. Check that your partner has:

- used full sentences
- used verbs in their full (not contracted form)
- organized their email into four clear sections
- included an appropriate greeting at the beginning and end
- used vocabulary that is not too informal

21st CENTURY OUTCOMES   COMMUNICATION Using email to inform, using the appropriate register

Review 1 | UNITS 1 AND 2

LISTENING

1 Work in pairs. Read the text about Broken Spoke. Discuss the questions.

1 Who goes to Broken Spoke?
2 What do visitors to Broken Spoke do there?

2 🎧 12 Listen to an interview with one of the founders of Broken Spoke. Answer the questions.

1 Is Broken Spoke a business or a charity?
2 What does she hope that Broken Spoke does for people?
3 What is the main problem for the business?

3 🎧 12 Complete the notes. The first letter is given for you. Then listen again and check your answers.

Main activities: training courses, selling bicycle
¹ p_____ , drop-in ² w_____

Reasons for starting: cycling is ³ h_____ ,
it builds a ⁴ c_____ , people share knowledge,
it helps the ⁵ e_____

Similar projects: in the UK, the ⁶ U_____ and around the world. The ⁷ b_____ model works.

GRAMMAR

4 Put the expression of frequency in the correct place in the sentence.

1 Broken Spoke is open to customers. (three days a week)
2 There is someone to help you immediately. (often)
3 You have to wait ten or fifteen minutes. (sometimes)
4 Broken Spoke has a large number of parts for bikes. (always)
5 They don't have trouble finding the part that you need. (usually)
6 They see lots of different kinds of bike problems. (every day)
7 They like people to leave without solving their problem. (never)

5 Complete the comments about Broken Spoke with the present simple and present continuous form of the verbs.

1 *A volunteer worker says:*
'I ¹ _____ (have) a job at the moment: I'm unemployed. But I ² _____ (go) to Broken Spoke twice a week to help out. It's my first month here so I ³ _____ (learn) how to do basic bicycle repairs. At first, there weren't many customers, but it ⁴ _____ (get) busier and busier, as more people hear about it.'

Broken Spoke

THE BROKEN SPOKE BIKE CO-OP is a DIY (do-it-yourself) bicycle workshop based in Oxford in the UK. It teaches people of all ages and backgrounds how to ride and repair bicycles. They also work with homeless people or people in difficult situations. Broken Spoke gives these people an old bicycle that someone has thrown away and helps them to renovate it. By doing this, the staff are promoting cycling as a form of transport in the community.

co-op (n) co-operative
renovate (v) to repair something and make it look new again

2 A customer says:

'I ⁵_____ (have) an old bicycle that I ⁶_____ (try) to rebuild. When I ⁷_____ (not / have) the right tool for a particular job, I ⁸_____ (visit) the workshop. One of the staff ⁹_____ (find) the right tool for me and then ¹⁰_____ (explain) to me how to do the job. It's fantastic. At the moment I ¹¹_____ (fit) new brakes on the bike.'

3 A journalist says:

'This kind of social enterprise ¹²_____ (become) more and more popular nowadays. We ¹³_____ (see) more and more businesses like this opening up around the country. I think that's because everyone benefits. Customers ¹⁴_____ (like) it, not just because they ¹⁵_____ (pay) less for their bicycle repairs, but because they ¹⁶_____ (learn) something at the same time. The volunteers benefit because Broken Spoke ¹⁷_____ (teach) them important work skills.'

VOCABULARY

6 Choose the correct options to complete the text.

When the economy is not ¹ *rising / growing*, jobs are harder to find. The chance of ² *doing / having* a career with only one company is small. It is difficult to find a job as a ³ *trainee / trainer* or an apprentice, because companies don't want to risk ⁴ *increasing / improving* the number of staff. So how do young people deal ⁵ *to / with* this new reality?

One way is to volunteer to ⁶ *make / do* a job for someone. In this way, you can learn important work skills, like how to ⁷ *attend / prioritize* tasks. Another possibility is to create your own business or social enterprise. Organizations like Broken Spoke are becoming more ⁸ *common / often*. Young people realize they will not ⁹ *get / go* rich this way, but they know that they can help people and ¹⁰ *make / have* fun at the same time.

DISCUSSION

7 Work in pairs. List the ways that the Broken Spoke business model is making a positive contribution to society.

8 Compare your answers from Exercise 7 with another pair. Then build a similar business model for one of these organizations. Explain to the rest of the class how it works.

Our café has three main activities. We sell drinks and food, we …

1 a café
2 a flower shop
3 a sports club or gym

SPEAKING

9 Read the conversation between Jim and Ursula. Then complete the conversation using the prompts.

Jim: Hello, I'm Jim.
Ursula: ¹ *How / you / do, Jim?* ² *I / be / Ursula.*
_____

Jim: ³ *Pleased / meet / you, Ursula.* ⁴ *you / work / here?*
_____

Ursula: Yes. ⁵ *I / currently / work / as / trainee architect* – just for six months. ⁶ *I / be / still / a student, really.*
_____
_____

Jim: Oh, I see. ⁷ *Where / you / study?*
_____

Ursula: ⁸ *My college / be / base / Nice / France.*
_____

Jim: ⁹ *And how / you / find the work here?*
_____

Ursula: It's great. ¹⁰ *It / be / very interesting company / work for.*
_____

Jim: Oh, I'm glad to hear that. ¹¹ *Well, / be / pleasure / meet you, Ursula.* Good luck with the job.
_____

Ursula: Thanks. ¹² *Nice / meet / you too.*

WRITING

10 Read the letter to a company asking for more information about a job. Rewrite the underlined words and expressions using more formal language.

TO: *Click here to add recipients*   CC:
SUBJECT:

¹ Hello,

² Just seen your advertisement for a trainee chef in the ³ paper and ⁴ I'm interested in applying. But I'd like to check ⁵ a couple of things before I make my application.

1 The advertisement says that it helps if applicants have some previous experience of cooking, but I ⁶ don't have any experience. Is that a problem?

2 The advertisement ⁷ doesn't give details of the hours and pay. ⁸ Where can I find this information?

⁹ Look forward to hearing from you.

¹⁰ All the best

Zoe Naismith

11 Exchange letters with your partner. Did you make the same changes?

29

3 Money

The mother of the bride at a wedding celebration, Lagos, Nigeria

TEDTALKS

JACQUELINE NOVOGRATZ is the founder of Acumen, a non-profit organization that funds projects to improve the lives of poor people.

Jacqueline Novogratz's idea worth spreading is that we can change the way the world fights poverty. Instead of giving money (traditional top-down aid), Acumen supports local organizations that improve communities and provide services to poor areas – such as lighting, clean water and housing. In this way, she says people can 'solve their own problems'.

BACKGROUND

1 You are going to watch an edited version of a TED Talk by Jacqueline Novogratz called *An escape from poverty*. Read the text about the speaker and the talk. Then work in pairs and discuss the questions.

1. What kind of aid (help) do poor countries in the world receive? Who gives this aid?
2. What kind of things does Acumen help people with?
3. How is Acumen's approach to helping poor people different from other types of aid?

KEY WORDS

2 Read the sentences (1–6). The words in bold are used in the TED Talk. First guess the meaning of the words. Then match the words with their definitions (a–g).

1. They live in a small **shack** in a **slum** in Nairobi.
2. When she got a **sewing machine**, she was able to make and sell clothes and improve her family's income.
3. Acumen specializes in 'patient capital': giving people long-term **loans** to start businesses.
4. If you put in $100, I will **match** this amount with $100 of my own money.
5. Many poor people cannot hope to get a **mortgage** and buy their own house.
6. I am hoping to find a job where I can **counsel** people who are in financial difficulty.

a money that you borrow from a bank to buy a property
b money that someone lends you (i.e. you must pay it back in the future)
c a very poor residential area of a city with few or no services
d give advice to someone
e put two things together so that they balance each other
f a small low-quality house, usually made of wood or metal
g a machine for making clothes

AUTHENTIC LISTENING SKILLS
Rhythm and stress

One element in understanding fast speech is becoming familiar with the rhythm and stress of English. Learning stress patterns in words can help you enormously.

Learn to recognize words by listening for the syllables that are stressed (because the syllables that aren't stressed are difficult to hear).

af*ford*   *preg*nant   *some*body   responsi*bili*ty*

*Notice that long words often have a secondary stress: one stressed and one lightly stressed syllable.

res‚ponsi'bility

3a 🎧 **13** Look at the Authentic listening skills box. Listen to two extracts from the TED Talk. Notice the syllables that are stressed in the first extract. Then listen again and underline the syllables that are stressed in the words in italics in the second extract.

1. I've been working on issues of poverty for more than twenty years.
2. And yet the *complexity* of *poverty* really has to look at *income* as only one *variable*. Because really, it's a *condition* about choice, and the lack of *freedom*.

3b 🎧 **14** Listen to these words from the talk. Underline the syllables that are stressed.

A	B	C
freedom	experience	generation
doctor	development	definition
girlfriend	family	condition
business	customer	decision
income	opportunity	organization

3.1 An escape from poverty

TEDTALKS

1 ▶ **3.1** Watch the edited version of the TED Talk. How did Jane from Mathare Valley escape from poverty? Answer the questions. Then compare your answers with a partner.

1 What happened to Jane's husband?
2 What is Jane's job now?
3 Where is her new house?

2 ▶ **3.1** Watch the first part (0.00–1.53) of the talk again. Choose the correct option to complete the sentences.

1 We often look at poverty in dollar terms. But really poverty is about a lack of choice and *money / freedom*.
2 Jacqueline Novogratz got an understanding of poverty in the Mathare Valley *slums / farms* in Kenya.
3 In Mathare Valley, *a quarter of / half* a million people live in little tin shacks, often eight or ten people to a room.
4 Jane, who lived in Mathare, had two dreams: to be a *doctor / mother,* and to marry a good man.
5 She got married when she was eighteen and had *one child / two children,* but then her husband left her.
6 She was left with no money and no *home / skills*.

▶ mom **N AM ENG**
▶ mum **BR ENG**
▶ girlfriend **N AM ENG**
▶ friend (female) **BR ENG**

3 ▶ **3.1** Watch the second part (1.53–3.12) of the talk again. Complete the summary with these words.

buys   makes   lends   save   sells

In 2001, Jane's life changed. She heard about an organization called Jamii Bora. Jamii Bora ¹_____ money to people if they can match it with the same amount of their own money. Jane worked for a year and was able to ² _____ fifty dollars. With this money she bought a sewing machine. Now she ³ _____ second-hand clothes and makes dresses that she ⁴ _____ to women for their daughters' celebrations. Now Jane ⁵ _____ more than four dollars a day, so she isn't so poor any more, but she still lives in Mathare.

4 ▶ **3.1** Watch the third part (3.12–4.00) of the talk again. Complete the sentences. Use one word in each space.

1 With money from Acumen and other organizations, Jamii Bora built a low-cost _____ development outside Nairobi.
2 They designed it for _____ like Jane.
3 Jane had to give them _____ dollars.
4 Then Jamii Bora matched Jane's mortgage to what she paid in _____ for her shack.

5 ▶ **3.1** Watch the fourth part (4.00 to the end) of the talk again. Are the sentences true (T) or false (F)?

1 The dreams Jane had as a little girl have come true.
2 Jane is happy that she had children.
3 Jane is sad that she did not become a doctor.
4 Jacqueline Novogratz believes that it's important for people like Jane to make decisions and choices for themselves.

VOCABULARY IN CONTEXT

6 ▶ **3.2** Watch the clips from the TED Talk. Choose the correct meaning of the words.

7 Work in pairs. Complete the sentences in your own words.

1 The building was originally a school, but they turned it into …
2 A shop that does good business in my town is …
3 The most important milestone in my life was …

CRITICAL THINKING Reading between the lines

8 Work in pairs. Which of the statements (a–c) about poverty do you think Jacqueline Novogratz agrees with?

Poverty is:

a a problem which we can't do anything about.
b a problem which individuals can solve with the right support.
c a problem which rich people can solve by giving money to poor people.

9 Read this comment* about the TED Talk. Do you agree with the comment? Why? / Why not?

> **Viewers' comments**
>
> **Thibault** – It's a nice story, but for me, it's suggesting that people in poverty can always help themselves. I don't think that's true – sometimes the only answer is to give direct aid.

*The comment was created for this activity.

PRESENTATION SKILLS Persuasion

10 Work in pairs. Look at the Presentation tips box. Which tip is the most effective in your opinion? Why?

> **TIPS**
>
> If you want to persuade people, here are some suggestions for making your argument more effective:
> • Stay focused on your one big idea.
> • Use facts and real-life examples so the audience is confident that you know what you are talking about.
> • Use stories that engage the audience emotionally with what you are saying.

11 ▶ **3.3** Watch the clip from the TED talk. What facts and real-life examples did Jacqueline Novogratz use to persuade you she knew what she was talking about?

12 Work in pairs. You are going to present a short introduction to a talk.

Student A: Turn to page 171.
Student B: Turn to page 172.

13 Take turns to present your introduction. Include two facts. Begin like this: *I would like to talk today about a serious problem in the world …*

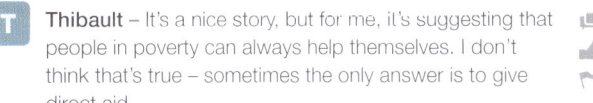

▶ Sweet 16 **N AM ENG**
▶ 16th birthday celebration **BR ENG**
▶ jewelry **N AM ENG**
▶ jewellery **BR ENG**

3.2 The money in your pocket

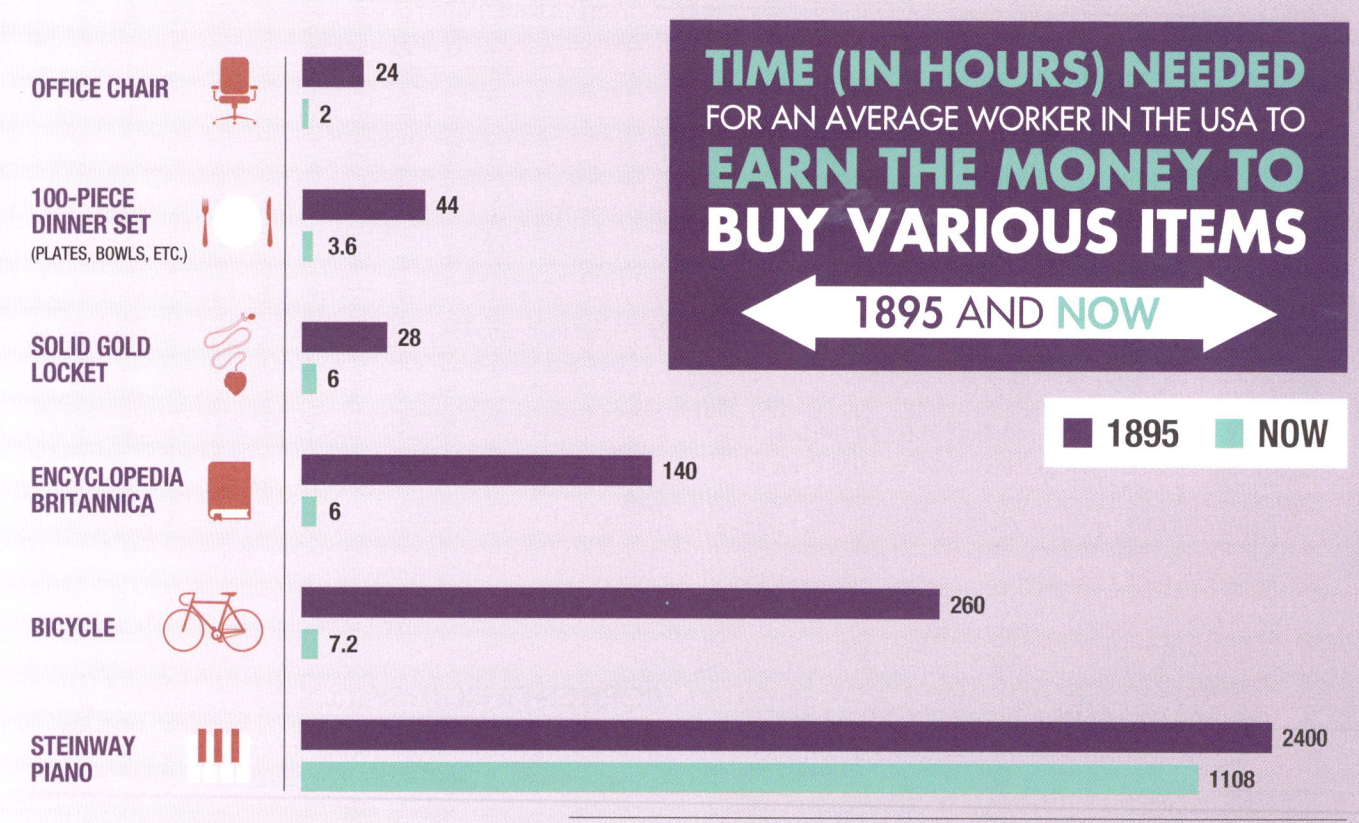

standard of living (n) how much money and material comfort people have

GRAMMAR Countable and uncountable nouns

1 Work in pairs. Discuss the questions.

1 Do people in your country have a higher or lower standard of living than fifty years ago?
2 Do you think that people's standard of living will go up or down in the next fifty years? Why?

2 Look at the infographic and answer the questions.

1 Which items are easy for an average worker to buy now that were difficult to buy in 1895?
2 Which item was easiest for a person to buy in both 1895 and now?
3 Which item is still very difficult for a worker to afford now?

3 🎧 **15** Listen to an interview about the changes in our standard of living. Answer the questions.

1 According to the presenter, how should we feel about our economic situation?
2 According to Professor Long, how does our standard of living compare to that of a king who lived 300 years ago?
3 Does Professor Long say that our standard of living is going up or down?

4 Read the sentences in the Grammar box. Answer the questions (1–2).

COUNTABLE AND UNCOUNTABLE NOUNS

In 1895 a **person** had to work 24 **hours** to earn the **money** to buy an office chair.

1 Look at the words in bold. Which word is:
  a a singular countable noun?
  b a plural countable noun?
  c an uncountable noun?

a(n), the, some and any

We haven't had **any** good news about **the** economy lately, but here is **some** positive information – **some** facts that will perhaps make you feel better about **the** money in your pocket.
In the studio today, we have **an** economist, Professor David Long.
People who didn't have **any** hopes of buying **the** things that we can afford today.

2 Complete the rules (a–b) with *a(n), the, some* and *any*.
  a We use _____ and _____ before a singular countable noun.
  b We use _____, _____ and _____ before an uncountable or a plural countable noun.

Check your answers on page 144 and do Exercises 1–4.

5 Choose the correct option to complete the sentences.

1 I feel lucky to have *a / some* job.
2 We bought some nice *furniture / chair* at a garage sale last weekend.
3 I don't have *some / any* money to spend on new clothes.
4 I read *a(n) / some* interesting information about people's standard of living twenty years ago.
5 Some people can't afford to eat *a / —* meat every day.
6 He has a good *advice / suggestion* for saving money.
7 Money *doesn't / don't* have the same value now as it did in the past.
8 The problem is: I don't have *any / a(n)* time to spend my money.

6 Work in pairs. Rewrite the sentences in Exercise 5 so that the other option fits grammatically. Use these words.

| a | dollars | fact | have |
| meal | opportunity | some | ~~work~~ |

1 I feel lucky to have some work.

7 Put these notes into full sentences. Use the correct form of the verb and add *a, an, the, some* or *any* where necessary.

1 I / have / job / in / bank.
 I have a job in a bank.
2 There / be / three / questions / I want to ask you.
3 Do you have / information / about / train / to London?
4 I'd like to buy / writing paper and / envelopes.
5 I'm sorry. I don't have / advice / for you.
6 Do you have / time / for / drink / before you leave?
7 There / be / furniture shop in / city centre. They have / nice things.

GRAMMAR Expressions of quantity: *much, many, a lot of, a few, a little*

8 🎧 **16** Listen to an extract from the interview with Professor Long. Are the sentences true (T) or false (F)?

1 120 years ago most people did not own many things.
2 They spent a lot of time not working.
3 People now have to work only a short time to afford an office chair.
4 The economics of many countries in the world are growing slowly.

9 Read the sentences in the Grammar box. Answer the questions (1–3).

EXPRESSIONS OF QUANTITY: MUCH, MANY, A LOT OF, A FEW, A LITTLE

They didn't have **much** *food.*
120 years ago people didn't have **many** *possessions.*
There are still **a lot of** *poor people in the world.*
120 years ago a book cost **a lot of** *money.*
A few *countries have very low economic growth.*
They only had **a little** *time for leisure.*

1 Which expressions of quantity go before a countable noun?
2 Which expressions of quantity go before an uncountable noun?
3 Which expression can be used before both a countable and an uncountable noun?

Check your answers on page 144 and do Exercises 5–7.

10 Choose the correct options to complete the conversations.

1 A: How *much / many* people live in your town?
   B: There are 100,000 permanent residents, but there are also *a little / a few* students.
2 A: Do you do *much / many* exercise?
   B: No, not at the moment. But I want to join a sports club. There are *much / a lot of* clubs around here.
3 A: Do you have any work to do this weekend?
   B: I have *a little / a few*. I have to make *a little / a few* phone calls too.
4 A: How *much / many* money do you have on you?
   B: I have one £5 note and *a little / a few* coins.

SPEAKING Standard of living and quality of life

11 **21st CENTURY OUTCOMES**

Work in pairs. Ask each other *How much / How many* questions about the following things.

1 sleep you get each night
2 hours you work or study per day
3 vehicles you own
4 stress you have in your work or studies
5 pairs of shoes you have
6 fast food you eat each week
7 hours you spend outdoors each day
8 time you spend with friends and family each week

12 Work with a new partner. Tell them about your partner's quality of life.

Jerzy has a lot of stress in his job and he doesn't get much sleep each night. But he enjoys himself at the weekend.

3.3 How to manage your money

READING Teaching financial literacy

1 Work in groups. Answer the questions

1 What does it mean to be 'good with money'? Tick (✓) the ideas you agree with.
   a saving money for the future
   b not spending much money
   c making your money grow
   d spending money wisely
   e getting the most for your money
   f being rich
2 Are you good or bad with money? In what way?
3 Did your parents teach you lessons about money?
4 Did you learn any financial skills at school?

2 Is it important for schools to teach financial skills to children? Why? At what age?

3 Read the article about teaching financial literacy to children. Find answers to the questions in Exercise 2.

4 Read the first two paragraphs of the article again. Complete the facts. Use one word in each space.

1 The story of the *Three Little Pigs* has traditionally been read for _____ .
2 Professor Glaeser uses it to teach _____ skills.
3 Young people today generally use _____ to buy things.
4 Money seems less real because many transactions are done _____ .
5 The other problem is that you can easily _____ money when you need it.
6 It's a _____ to make financial lessons fun.

5 Read the last two paragraphs of the article again. Match the teaching tools (1–4) with the descriptions (a–d).

1 The Magic Magpie
2 MyBnk quiz
3 Monopoly
4 Supermarket Sweep

a teaches you how to save money when buying things
b shows that you can't always be kind if you want to make money
c shows the importance of being careful with money
d shows how much money you can earn or save in your life

6 Work in pairs. Answer the questions.

1 What do you think of the teaching ideas in Exercise 5?
2 Can you think of any other fairy stories that could have a financial message?

VOCABULARY Money

7 Choose the correct options to complete the descriptions of three people's financial situations.

1 Graham got a lot of money from his parents. He *borrowed / invested* it in a house and he still has £80,000 savings in the bank. But he doesn't *afford / earn* much from his job.
2 Florence was a student for seven years and now she has a lot of debts. She *borrowed / saved* money from the bank – a loan of £40,000 – to pay for her studies and she still *lends / owes* the bank £35,000. But she is working now as a qualified dentist and has a good salary.
3 Louis doesn't have a regular income. He *saves / spends* a lot of money buying old cars. Then he restores them to make them like new again. When he sells one, he *makes / affords* good money. At other times, he can't *spend / afford* to pay the rent.

8 Look at the descriptions in Exercise 7 again. Find nouns to do with money. Match the nouns with their meaning (1–5).

1 money that you save
2 money that you owe people
3 money that someone lends you
4 money that you get regularly from a job
5 money that you get from work or investments

9 Work in pairs. Write sentences about yourself using five different words or expressions from Exercises 7 and 8. Then discuss your sentences.

A: *I want to go to a festival in England this summer, but I can't afford it.*
B: *Can you make money selling things on eBay?*

SPEAKING Money quiz

10 **21st CENTURY OUTCOMES**

Work in pairs. Look at the statements (1–8). Do you agree, partly agree or disagree? Give examples to support your opinion.

1 Money is for spending today. Who knows what will happen tomorrow?
2 It's important to save at least 10% of your salary each week.
3 If I can't afford something, I'm happy to borrow the money.
4 I'm always looking for new ways to make money.
5 I like to shop around for the best price before I buy something.
6 I only like buying things that are a good investment for the future.
7 Spending large amounts of money makes me feel nervous.
8 Having a regular income is better than having a lot of money one day and a little the next.

11 How are your attitudes different to your parents' attitudes to money?

Teaching
FINANCIAL LITERACY

In the children's story, *The Three Little Pigs,* each pig builds his house out of different materials: one from straw, one from sticks and one from bricks. The big bad wolf comes along and blows down the houses of straw and sticks and eats the first two pigs. The brick house, however, is too strong, and in the end the wolf can only get in through the chimney. The last pig is waiting at the bottom and cooks the wolf in his cooking pot. Most parents read this story to their children for enjoyment. But Edward L. Glaeser, an economics professor at Harvard, uses it as a financial teaching tool. The story, he says, shows children the benefits of investing your money wisely.

Glaeser is part of a growing movement in favour of teaching basic financial skills to children from an early age. Why is this so important now? For two reasons. First, the use of plastic (credit cards) and online banking makes money seem less real to today's generation. Secondly, borrowing is easier. So, there is more danger that people will spend more than they can afford and get into debt. For Glaeser, and other educators like him, the challenge is to make learning about finance more fun, to find media that children can enjoy and learn from at the same time. *Education Weekly* looked at a range of these, from fairy stories to quizzes and games.

Daniel Britton, who claims that 97 per cent of teachers support financial education, has written several financial fairy tales. In *The Magic Magpie,* the main character – who wants to get rich quickly – gets her brother, who is careful with money, into trouble with a giant. There's a quiz from 'MyBnk' which tries to engage children with questions about how much celebrities earn. It also asks questions like: *If you saved £2.50 every day from the age of fourteen in a savings account with 8% interest, you'd save £1 million by the age of 70! True or False?*

Then there are games: board games like 'Monopoly' (teaching you not to be sentimental in business) or the 'Game of Life' (teaching you about key financial decisions like whether to take a loan to buy a house). There are also classroom-based games, like 'Supermarket Sweep'. In this game, students have a shopping list and a limited time to research where they can buy the items, online or in-store, for the cheapest price. This teaches them essential money-saving skills.

brick (n) a small clay block used in building
sentimental (adj) easily emotional or sad about things
straw (n) dried plant stalks

21st CENTURY OUTCOMES **FINANCIAL LITERACY** Making good financial decisions

3.4 Have you got any change?

LISTENING Everyday conversations

1 Look at the photos (1–5). Match the photos with the questions (a–e).

   a Is service included?
   b Could you lend me £5 to get some lunch?
   c Do you have change for a £10 note?
   d Do you charge commission?
   e Can I have a receipt, please?

2 🎧 17 Listen to five everyday conversations about money and check your answers from Exercise 1.

3 🎧 17 Complete the conversations (1–5) with these words. Then listen to the conversations again and check your answers.

bill	buys	coins	free	here
note	pay	rate	that	

1 A: I'd like $200 in Swiss Francs, please. What's the _____ today?
    B: OK. $200 _____ you 181 Swiss Francs.
    A: Do you charge commission?
    B: No, it's commission-_____ .

2 A: OK. _____'s $16.80, please
    B: Thanks. _____'s $20. Please keep the change.
    A: Thank you.
    B: Oh, and can I have a receipt, please?

3 A: Excuse me. Do you have change for a £10 _____?
    B: Sorry, I don't, but you can get _____ from the change machine.
    A: OK. Thanks.

4 A: Thanks, that was delicious. Could you bring us the _____?
    B: Certainly … Here you are.
    A: Thanks. Is service included?
    B: No, it isn't.

5 A: Could you lend me £5 to get some lunch?
    B: Sure.
    A: I'll _____ you back when I go to the bank.
    B: OK – no hurry.

SPEAKING Talking about money

Pronunciation Questions with *Do you* and *Could you*

4a 🎧 18 Listen to the questions. Notice how the underlined words are pronounced. Then practise saying the questions.

   1 <u>Do you charge</u> commission?
   2 <u>Do you have</u> change for a £10 note?
   3 <u>Could you bring</u> us the bill?
   4 <u>Could you lend me</u> £5 to get some lunch?

4b 🎧 19 Listen to four more questions. Which underlined words from Exercise 4a did you hear?

5 Work in pairs. Look at the photos and questions in Exercise 1. Then act out conversations for these situations. Use the expressions in the Useful language box to help you.

1 You want to change $200 into euros. You want small notes.
2 You want to pay the restaurant bill. You and your friend will pay half each.
3 You want to pay the taxi fare ($17). You only have a $100 note.
4 You need to borrow $20. You will not see the other person for two weeks.

TALKING ABOUT MONEY

Can I have the bill, please?
Is service included?
Keep the change.
That's $20.
Can I have a receipt, please?
Could you lend me £10? I'll pay you back tomorrow.
Do you have change for a $10 note?
I'd like to change $200 into Swiss Francs.
What's the rate today?
Do you charge commission?

WRITING A report

6 Read the report and answer the questions.

1 Are the sentences long or short?
2 Does the report contain more facts or more opinions?
3 Does the report end with the most recent action or the next step?

TO:
FROM:
DATE:
RE: Restaurant Location Proposal

The city has a population of 115,000 and 1.1 million tourists visit every year. There are 62 restaurants serving these people. Twenty-two of them serve local food and the remaining forty are international. About 45% of these are Italian or pizza restaurants. The average cost of a meal is $10.80. At the moment only three restaurants specialize in French food, so I think there is a real opportunity for us here. I have a meeting with the business advisor at the city council at 2 p.m. on Friday 17th October. I will report back again after that.

Writing skill Writing numbers in a report

7a Read the report in Exercise 6 again. For each type of number (1–8), is the number written as a number (N) or as a word (W)?

1 Numbers with a decimal point
2 Numbers below 20
3 Numbers over 20 (not at the beginning of a sentence)
4 Numbers at the beginning of a sentence
5 Round numbers (thirty, forty, fifty, sixty)
6 Prices
7 Dates and times
8 Percentages in a report

7b Read the report in Exercise 6 again. Notice the position of commas and full stops in the numbers and times. Write the correct punctuation in these numbers.

1 930am   3 $12 99
2 450   4 30000

7c Read the short report about Slovenia. All the numbers are written in words. Write them as numbers where necessary.

SLOVENIA is a beautiful country to visit. It is a small country with a population of two point one million. About fifty-five per cent of the country is covered by forest. It joined the European Union on the first of May two thousand and four and enjoyed a period of fast economic growth between two thousand and four and two thousand and seven. There are many things for visitors to do and generally it is not an expensive country. Fifty dollars a day is probably a good amount to budget for.

One thing you should certainly do is visit the caves at Postonja. A day trip from Llubljana costs forty-three dollars and the visit takes around two hours.

8 **21st CENTURY OUTCOMES**

Write a similar report about Ireland using the notes and figures below.

Place:	Ireland
Population:	4.6 million (25% in the Dublin area)
Economy:	Joined EU in 1973; economy grew fast 1995–2007
Things to do:	Beautiful countryside to visit; buy a Dublin sightseeing pass: entrance to 32 different museums and sights, cost €60 for a 2-day pass
Cost:	Dublin expensive – $150 per day minimum

9 Work in pairs. Exchange reports. Check that your partner has:

- given appropriate facts
- used short sentences
- written the numbers correctly

4 Success

Celebrations at the summit of Bertha's Tower, Queen Maud Land, Antarctica

TEDTALKS

JOACHIM DE POSADA was a writer and motivational coach from Puerto Rico. He helped companies and teams to find deep and lasting reasons to succeed. His books (in Spanish and English) include *How to Survive Among the Piranhas* and *Don't Eat the Marshmallow … Yet*.

Joachim de Posada's idea worth spreading is that self-discipline can be an important predictor of future success. In his talk, he explains how a 'marshmallow test' demonstrates this idea.

BACKGROUND

1 You are going to watch a TED Talk by Joachim de Posada called *Don't eat the marshamallow!* Read the text about the speaker and the talk. Then work in pairs and discuss the questions.

1. Who did Joachim de Posada help in his work and what did he help them to do?
2. In what other areas of life are coaches employed to help and encourage people?
3. Do you know what piranhas and marshmallows are? What do you think the titles of his books mean?

KEY WORDS

2 Read the sentences (1–6). The words in bold are used in the TED Talk. First guess the meaning of the words. Then match the words with their definitions (a–f).

1. Asking a child to wait for a sweet is **equivalent to** asking an adult to wait for a cup of coffee.
2. I believe in the **principle** that success comes from hard work.
3. Don't give up – you'll feel a great sense of **gratification** when you solve the problem.
4. You need a lot of **self-discipline** to learn something by yourself.
5. I got top **grades** in maths and science at school because I studied hard.
6. Maths has many **applications** in everyday life – in computing, in business, in managing your own money.

a marks or scores at school (e.g. A+, C−)
b the same as
c a rule or basic idea that you follow
d the ability to control yourself and apply yourself to your work
e pleasure or satisfaction
f uses

AUTHENTIC LISTENING SKILLS Dealing with accents

When you travel or work abroad, or if you work in a multinational company, you will often hear foreign or regional accents in English. It's helpful to know which individual vowel and consonant sounds non-native speakers pronounce differently from native speakers. When you have identified these, practise – and enjoy! – listening to examples of this accent.

3a 🎧 **20** Look at the Authentic listening skills box. Then listen to this sentence from the TED Talk, firstly pronounced by a native British English speaker and then by Joachim de Posada, a native Spanish speaker. Compare the pronunciation of the underlined sounds.

'If, after I <u>come</u> back, this marshmallow is here, you will get <u>a</u>n<u>o</u>ther one.'

3b 🎧 **21** Read the sentences. Then listen to how Joachim de Posada pronounces the underlined words. How would a native British speaker pronounce them? Discuss with your partner.

1. They were in <u>trouble</u>.
2. <u>Some</u> of them dropped out.
3. So I went to <u>Colombia</u>.
4. And it was very <u>funny</u>.
5. In <u>other</u> words, …

4.1 Don't eat the marshmallow!

TEDTALKS

1 ▶ **4.1** Watch the TED Talk. Answer the questions. Then discuss your answers with a partner.

   1 What were the children not supposed to do in the marshmallow test?
   2 Did most of them succeed or not?
   3 According to Joachim de Posada, which children were more successful fifteen years later?

2 ▶ **4.1** Watch the first part (0.00–1.24) of the talk again. Choose the correct options to complete the description of the marshmallow test.

The marshmallow test was the idea of a professor of ¹*psychology / economics* at Stanford University. He put children aged ²*two / four* alone in a room with a marshmallow. He told them that if they didn't eat the marshmallow, he would give them ³*a prize / another marshmallow* when he returned. Then he left them for ⁴*five / fifteen* minutes. ⁵*One / Two* out of three children ate the marshmallow.

3 ▶ **4.1** Watch the second part (1.24–2.47) of the talk again. Complete the sentences with one word or number in each space.

   1 According to Joachim de Posada, the most important principle for success is self-_____.
   2 Fifteen years later _____ per cent of the children that hadn't eaten the marshmallow were successful, according to Joachim de Posada.
   3 But a lot of the kids who ate the marshmallow were in _____: they had bad _____.
   4 Joachim de Posada wanted to know if Hispanic kids would react in the same way. So he repeated the experiment in _____.

▶ pants **N AM ENG**
▶ trousers **BR ENG**

▶ grades **N AM ENG**
▶ marks **BR ENG**

4 ▶ **4.1** Watch the final part (4.44 to the end) of the talk again. Complete the answers to these questions about the lessons we should learn from this experiment.

1 What did the last girl in the video do?
2 What does Joachim de Posada think this tells us about her?
3 What does Joachim de Posada suggest that a salesperson can do to sell more things to a customer?
4 Where are they teaching children the principle of 'learning to wait'?
5 According to Joachim de Posada, where should they be teaching this principle and why?

VOCABULARY IN CONTEXT

5 ▶ **4.2** Watch the clips from the TED Talk. Choose the correct meaning of the words.

6 Work in pairs. Complete the sentences in your own words.

1 I didn't make it to …
2 One reason a lot of people drop out of university is …
3 When I finish studying, I'd like to go into …
4 You meet people from all walks of life in …

CRITICAL THINKING Considering counter arguments

7 When people present arguments for an idea, they sometimes fail to consider the arguments against that idea. Read the main argument of the TED Talk. Then discuss with a partner the possible arguments against this.

'Learning to wait and having self-discipline are key factors for success in life.'

8 Read these comments* about the TED Talk. Compare your ideas from Exercise 7 with the ideas in the comments. Discuss which comment(s) you agree with.

> **Viewers' comments**
>
> **Michael** – When I think of my own experience, this experiment doesn't work. I remember once saving some chocolate in my drawer at home. When I went back to it a month later, it was bad. Sometimes waiting is not a good thing – particularly in business. You can miss an opportunity if you wait too long.
>
> **Sanjay** – There's a big problem here. What if the promise of the second marshmallow is broken? Then the kid gets nothing.
>
> **Leonie** – This is about control, not self-control. The children who wait are the ones who do what they are told. It doesn't encourage kids to be independent and creative.

*The comments were created for this activity.

PRESENTATION SKILLS Body movement and gesture

9 Work in pairs. Discuss the questions.

1 How can body movement and gesture help communication?
2 When do body movement and gesture not help communication?

10 Look at the Presentation tips box. Compare your ideas from Exercise 9 with the tips in the box.

> **TIPS**
>
> If used correctly, body movement and gestures can help you get your message across during a talk.
>
> 1 Move around the stage to keep the audience's attention, but not too much.
> 2 Use gestures to make a point strongly.
> 3 Use gestures if they help to explain an action you are describing.
> 4 Keep your body open. Try not to cross your arms or legs so you appear confident and relaxed.

11 ▶ **4.1** Watch the TED Talk again. Which of the techniques from the Presentation tips box did Joachim de Posada follow in his talk?

12 ▶ **4.3** Watch the clip from the talk. What gestures did Joachim de Posada use to explain these ideas?

1 'If, after I come back, this marshmallow is here, you will get another one.'
2 'We'll bring you coffee in two hours.'
3 'As soon as the door closed …'
4 'Two out of three ate the marshmallow.'
5 'Could not wait.'
6 '… one out of three would look at the marshmallow and go like this …'
7 'The ability to delay gratification.'

13 Work in pairs. You are going to explain the marshmallow experiment. Make notes about the key points.

14 Work with a new partner. Take turns to explain the marshmallow experiment in your own words. Use movement and gesture to help explain the ideas.

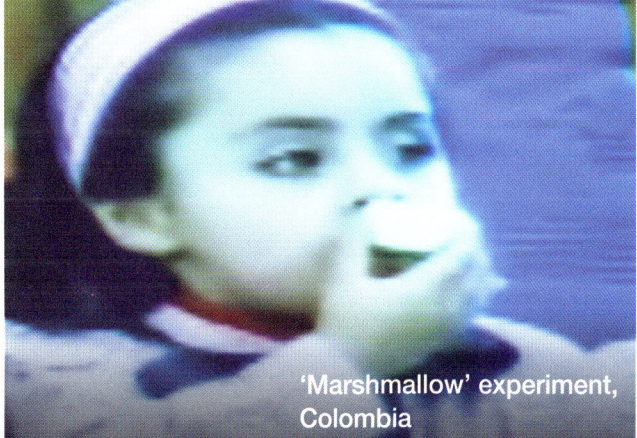

'Marshmallow' experiment, Colombia

▶ cash register **N AM ENG**
▶ till **BR ENG**

4.2 The road to success

WHO IS SIMON SINEK?

1973 — Born 1973 Wimbledon, England

1976–86 — Lives and goes to school in different countries (South Africa, Hong Kong)

1987–91 — High school, New Jersey, USA

1992–95 — Brandeis University; studies anthropology, becomes interested in human behaviour

WHERE DID HE STUDY?

1996 — London; starts training to be a lawyer; leaves law school early

1997 — Moves to New York; gets a job in an advertising company

WHAT DID HE DO AFTER LEAVING SCHOOL?

2002 — Sets up his own marketing company

2002–06 — Works very hard and builds the company; but starts asking 'Why am I doing this?'

WHEN DID HE START HIS OWN COMPANY?

2009 — Publishes *Start with Why: How Great Leaders Inspire Everyone to Take Action*

2010 — Book is very successful

WHEN DID HE WRITE HIS FIRST BOOK?

2015 — Teaches graduates at Columbia University; successful public speaker, telling companies and organizations to start with 'Why'

WHAT DOES HE DO NOW?

GRAMMAR Past simple and past continuous

1 Work in pairs. Discuss which of these statements you agree with.

1 Going to university isn't right for everyone.
2 It's never too late to change career.
3 You can't be happy in life if you are not happy in your work.
4 It's not *what* you do that's important in your career, it's *why* you do it.

2 Look at the infographic about the career of Simon Sinek. Answer the questions.

1 What was his first job and what does he do now?
2 Which ideas in Exercise 1 are true for him?

3 Read the text in the Grammar box. Answer the questions (1–2).

PAST SIMPLE AND PAST CONTINUOUS

*Simon Sinek was born in England in 1973. As a child, he **lived** and **went** to school in different countries. He **graduated** from High School in New Jersey in 1991. Sinek then **went** to Brandeis University to study anthropology. While he **was studying**, he **became** very interested in human behaviour. In 1996, he **started** studying law in London, but he **decided** that he didn't want to be a lawyer and so he **didn't finish** law school. He **left** London and **moved** to New York, where he **got** a job in an advertising company in New York.*

1 Which verbs describe the main events of Simon Sinek's life in sequence, one after another?
2 Which verb describes a background action in progress when another event took place?

Check your answers on page 146 and do Exercises 1–2.

4 Complete the rest of Simon Sinek's story. Use the correct form of the past simple and past continuous.

In 2002, Sinek ¹_____ (set) up his own company. He ²_____ (work) hard and ³_____ (build) the company. But while he ⁴_____ (work) so hard, he ⁵_____ (not / feel) happy. Then he ⁶_____ (ask) himself the question 'Why am I doing this job?' When he ⁷_____ (find) the answer – 'to inspire other people in their work' – his whole life ⁸_____ (change). In 2009 he ⁹_____ (publish) a book about his ideas, *Start with Why*. The book ¹⁰_____ (be) very successful and now Sinek talks about his ideas to different organizations.

5 Choose the correct options to complete the sentences.

1 I *was becoming / became* interested in journalism while I *was studying / studied* communications at university.
2 We *were moving / moved* to Manchester because the cost of living in London *was going / went* up and up.
3 He *was going / went* for the interview but he *wasn't getting / didn't get* the job.
4 I *was leaving / left* my job because I *wasn't liking / didn't like* the company.
5 He *was interrupting / interrupted* us while we *were having / had* an important discussion.
6 Their living room ceiling *was falling / fell* down. Luckily they *weren't sitting / didn't sit* in the room at the time.

Pronunciation Weak forms: *was* and *were*

6 🎧 **22** Listen to the pronunciation of *was* and *were*, *wasn't* and *weren't* in these sentences. Which words are stressed and which are not? Then practise saying them.

1 I learned to speak Spanish while I was working in Spain.
2 Did you decide to be a politician while you were studying?
3 Sorry. What did you say? I wasn't listening.
4 We weren't expecting you, but we're very happy you came.

7 Complete the sentences in your own words. Then compare your sentences with a partner.

1 I decided to change job because …
2 I met a lot of interesting people when …
3 I took a part-time job while …
4 … when I was travelling.
5 … because I was keen to have a change.
6 … while I was working as a waiter.

GRAMMAR Past perfect

8 Read the description of a singer, Yvonne Cortez. What was her first job? What does she do now?

Yvonne Cortez had a talent for singing from an early age. She is now a professional singer. But her career was not straightforward. She left school at seventeen and got a job as a door-to-door salesperson.

9 🎧 **23** Listen to an interview with Yvonne Cortez. Answer the questions.

1 Why didn't Yvonne go to college after she left school at seventeen?
2 Did she hope to become a professional singer at that point? Why? / Why not?

10 Read the sentences in the Grammar box. Answer the questions (1–3).

PAST PERFECT

Why did you decide to leave school at seventeen?
*Well, I guess like a lot of kids, I **had studied** for long enough.*
*I **had done** some concerts at school and a lot of people **had said** I was good.*
*I **hadn't thought** about it as a career.*
So I took a job as a door-to-door salesperson.

1 Look at the underlined verb and the verbs in bold. Did these actions happen before (B) or after (A) Yvonne left school?
2 Which tense is used to talk about events before the main event (Yvonne leaving school)?
3 How is this tense formed?

Check your answers on page 146 and do Exercises 3–6.

Pronunciation *had* and *hadn't*

11 🎧 **24** Listen to the sentences with *had/hadn't* from the Grammar box. How is *had* pronounced? Then practise saying them.

12 Choose the correct options to complete the sentences.

1 When I went to university, I *didn't decide / hadn't decided* what future job I wanted.
2 When I got my first job, I knew a little about work, because I *had / had had* part-time jobs as a teenager.
3 I got to work an hour late on my first day, but luckily my boss *didn't arrive / hadn't arrived* yet.
4 In the experiment, some children *didn't eat / hadn't eaten* the marshmallow. These children did well at school later on.
5 I never thought about 'having a career'. I just *took / had taken* jobs that interested me.
6 I decided to apply for a summer job picking fruit because my brother *did / had done* it before and loved it.

SPEAKING My career path

13 **21st CENTURY OUTCOMES**

Work in pairs. Make a time line of your own education and working life up to now. Then describe the events to your partner and the reasons for your career path.

When I was studying at university, I started writing for the university newspaper. I hadn't done any journalism before, but I really liked it. Then I …

COMMUNICATION Explaining reasons for actions

4.3 I didn't do it for the money

READING Paid to succeed

1 Read the statement about motivation. What do the words in bold mean? Think of an example for each and discuss with your partner. Do you agree with the statement?

> There are two basic ways to motivate people to do things. You can **reward** them if they do well or you can **punish** them if they do badly.

2 Work in pairs. Look at the list. Discuss how your parents or school motivated you to do these things and if it worked.

- behave well at school
- get good results at school
- help with jobs around the home
- practise a musical instrument or sport

I had to practise the violin for twenty minutes every day. When I had finished, I could go out and play with my friends.

3 Read the article. Choose the statement (a–c) that best summarizes Professor Stephen Gorard's idea for motivating children.

a Pay students for getting good results in their exams.
b Pay students for attending school every day.
c Pay students for learning good study habits.

4 Choose the correct option (a–c) to complete the sentences.

1 Middle-class children are more motivated to do well at school because:
 a their parents encourage them to work hard.
 b they understand why a good education is important.
 c their parents have the money to send them to good schools.

2 Professor Gorard's system works by:
 a making students pay money if they do badly.
 b getting richer students to give money to poorer students.
 c giving money to students who come to school and work hard.

3 The Chicago example shows that:
 a offering money to school children can be a good idea.
 b offering money for good exam results can improve their marks.
 c offering money for results doesn't make children better students.

4 David Day thinks that praising students is a better way than offering financial reward because:
 a it improves the student–teacher relationship.
 b it helps students to become more motivated.
 c it costs more, but it is also more effective.

5 Find the words (1–5) in the article. Then match the words with their similar meanings.

goals   hard work   results   reward   rich

1 well-off _____
2 pay-off _____
3 efforts _____
4 targets _____
5 scores _____

VOCABULARY Success and rewards

6 Choose the best option to complete the sentences. Look at the text again, if you are not sure.

1 We *reward / motivate* people who work hard.
2 It is normal to give financial *incentives / money* to sales people, but not to school children.
3 The best way to *motivate / pay* people is to tell them that they did a good job.
4 I always *praise / offer* my children when they do something good.
5 I failed my driving test the first time, but I *passed / achieved* it the second time.
6 They *set / offered* a target of 90% attendance and he achieved 95%.
7 She *passed / succeeded* in her goal of becoming a lawyer.
8 I failed to *achieve / succeed* everything I wanted to, but I am not unhappy.

7 Complete the text with words from Exercise 6. You may need to change the form.

In 2014 a newspaper asked readers this question: 'Is it a good idea to ¹_____ your child with money if they ²_____ their exams?' These were some of the answers.

'I don't see any problem with it. Anything that ³_____ them to do well is a good thing.'

'I think it sends the wrong message. It's like saying, we'll only love you if you ⁴_____.'

'I think it's a good idea. Children don't really understand that doing well at school will help them to ⁵_____ their other goals in life.'

'No, it isn't. You have to ⁶_____ your children for trying even if they ⁷_____ to achieve their target.'

'Financial ⁸_____ are a bad idea. It makes people think that money is the only important thing in life.'

8 Work in pairs. Which view(s) in Exercise 7 do you agree with?

SPEAKING Incentives at work

9 21st CENTURY OUTCOMES

Work in small groups. Look at the list of incentives that employers use. Discuss which ones:

a cost the company the most
b are the most effective
c you personally respond to best

10 Can you think of any other cheap and effective incentives for employees?

Incentives

- praising an employee for doing a good job
- telling an employee their work isn't good enough and that you know they can do better
- giving an employee a bonus (extra money) for achieving their targets
- giving a bonus to the whole team for achieving their targets
- arranging a party or day out for employees
- giving an employee more responsibility and a new job title

PAID to succeed

It's not always easy for children from less well-off backgrounds to understand why they should study hard at school. A child from a middle-class background can see the benefits of a good education when they look at their parents' lives – a satisfying job, a nice house, an expensive car. But for a child from a poor background, the pay-off is not so obvious. For this reason, some sociologists have suggested rewarding children financially if they do well at school so that they can see an immediate return for their efforts. Professor Stephen Gorard of Durham University in the UK is one of these.

Professor Gorard recommends that schools set up a fund of approximately US$200 for each poor student. The school then sets targets for students' attendance, homework and reading time. Each time a student fails to achieve these targets, they lose a part of this money.

Gorard's conclusions are based on research carried out by various institutions in Australia, Britain and the US. The research also looked at whether offering money in return for passing exams was a good idea, but concluded that it wasn't. One high school in Chicago offered first year students up to $2,000 in exchange for good test results, but the incentive did not work: test results did not greatly improve. The reason for this, according to Professor Gorard, was that, although the children wanted the cash, they did not know the right steps to take to succeed in their exams.

In contrast, Gorard's own experiments showed that when schools rewarded students for attendance, good behaviour, reading and completing their homework, their reading and maths scores improved. In other words, results were improved by rewarding good study habits.

But others think that paying students is wrong. David Day, a UK school principal, said that the results did not justify the cost. He believes that praising students for good performance is a better way to motivate than by financial reward. He found that when teachers told students they were happy with their work, the students naturally became more self-motivated.

21st CENTURY OUTCOMES BUSINESS LITERACY Thinking about what motivates employees

4.4 Sorry, I did my best

VOCABULARY Prepositional phrases

1 Match these phrases with their meanings (1–5).

be in a hurry   be on a call   be out of practice
have a day off   have an off day

1 do something you haven't done for a long time
2 have no time to do things
3 have a day when you don't perform well
4 have a holiday
5 be speaking to someone on the telephone

2 Work in pairs. Discuss the questions.

1 When was the last time you:
  a had a day off?
  b had an off day?
2 Can you think of something you recently did in a hurry?
3 What are you out of practice with?
4 Is it rude to be on a call when you arrive to see someone?

LISTENING Office conversations

3 🎧 **25** Listen to six short conversations in an office. Complete the subject of each conversation.

1 _____ a letter
2 booking a _____
3 writing a _____
4 _____ a letter
5 ordering some _____
6 booking some _____

4 🎧 **25** What happened in each conversation? Discuss with your partner. Then listen again and write the number of the conversation (1–6) next to the reason (a–f) the speaker gave.

a Did the best job I could.   d Did not know priorities.
b I didn't feel right.   e Was under pressure.
c Made an independent   f Made a quick decision.
  decision.

5 Match the reasons (a–f) in Exercise 4 with expressions in the Useful language box.

GIVING REASONS FOR ACTIONS

Asking for explanations

Why did you / didn't you *post / speak to / book* …?
Did you *post / speak to / book* …?

Giving reasons

It seemed a good idea at the time.
I did my best.
I did it without thinking / checking.
I didn't realize it was urgent / my job.
I'm a bit out of practice.
I was on a call.
I was in a hurry.
It was my day off.
I was having an off day.

Pronunciation *Sorry*

6a 🎧 **26** Listen to three different ways (1–3) of saying *sorry*. Match the ways with the function (a–c). Then practise saying *sorry* in these ways with your partner.

1 Sorry? ╱   a showing you are sad
                       something happened
2 No, sorry. ─   b asking someone to repeat
                       something
3 Oh, sorry. ╲   c refusing without emotion

6b 🎧 **25** Listen again to the way people said *sorry* in the conversations in Exercise 3. Which way (1–3) did they use?

SPEAKING Giving reasons for actions

7 Work in pairs. Act out conversations about three of the situations below. Use the expressions in the Useful language box to help you.

- Leaving a meeting early
- Advertising a job online
- Buying a new coffee machine for the office
- Buying tickets for a concert
- Fixing a door that doesn't close

WRITING Messaging

8 Read the text messages (1–9). Are they a message of congratulation (C), a message of sympathy (S) or a message of explanation (E)?

1
> Sorry to hear you missed out on the job. But you did really well to get that far.

2
> Shame about the tickets. Perhaps get some on eBay?

3
> Apologies for not coming to the party – I wasn't feeling well. Hope to see you soon.

4
> Great news about your exams. Well done on your results. You deserved it after all your work.

5
> Congratulations on the promotion! Not surprised, but very pleased for you!

6
> Can't come to training tonight, as I promised Lottie I'd help with her homework.

7
> Brilliant news! When's the happy day?

8
> Thanks for your message. Afraid I'll be 20 minutes late because of long meeting.

9
> Bad luck about your car. Hope the damage wasn't too bad.

9 Work in pairs. Discuss what caused the writer to write each message.

10 We sometimes miss out words in text messages to keep them short. What words are missing in these phrases?

1 Hope to see you soon.
2 Can't come to training tonight.
3 Shame about the tickets.
4 Great news about your exams.

Writing skill Prepositions in messages

11 Complete the sentences with the correct preposition: *about*, *for* or *on*. Look at the messages in Exercise 8 again to help you.

1 Bad luck _____ the flat. I'm sure you'll find another one.
2 Good news _____ the tickets – I got the last two! Thanks _____ telling me.
3 Congratulations _____ finishing the marathon. We're all really pleased _____ you.
4 I'm afraid we can't join you on Sunday, because Tina's parents are visiting. Apologies _____ that and hope to see you soon.
5 Well done _____ getting into Bristol University. That's brilliant!
6 Shame _____ the party being cancelled. Hope to see you soon anyway.

12 **21st CENTURY OUTCOMES**

Work in pairs. Look at the following subjects (a–c). Write messages to each other for each subject. Then add one more subject of your own choice and write another message.

a your partner has passed their driving test
b you need to go to the doctor and can't attend a meeting
c your partner lost their passport and couldn't go on holiday

13 Exchange messages. Check that your partner has:

- written a clear message
- used appropriate phrases to congratulate, show sympathy or give an explanation
- missed out appropriate words to keep the message short
- used prepositions correctly

Unit 4 Success

21st CENTURY OUTCOMES EFFECTIVE COMMUNICATION Writing appropriate messages

Review 2 | UNITS 3 AND 4

READING

1 Read the article about M-Pesa. Answer the questions.

1. What does M-Pesa mean?
2. What is the revolution M-Pesa has started?
3. What are the two adjectives beginning with 'c' that describe the benefits of M-Pesa's system?
4. Where do users of M-Pesa deposit and collect money?
5. What is the extra benefit of M-Pesa's success?

M-PESA

Paying for things using your mobile phone – a taxi, for example – is easier in Kenya than it is in almost any other country. About 75 per cent of Kenyans have mobile phones and 80 per cent use them to make payments. The service behind this revolution is M-Pesa. (*M* means 'mobile' and *Pesa* is Swahili for 'money'.)

M-Pesa was founded by Safaricom and Vodafone in 2007 for two reasons. The first was that people needed a cheap way to receive loans and make payments. The second was that people needed a convenient place where they could receive and transfer money. Kenya is a rural country and does not have a large network of banks. So instead, customers can take their cash to one of M-Pesa's 65,000 service points or 'outlets'. These outlets are usually in petrol stations or small shops. Customers then transfer money by text message to another outlet where the person they want to receive the money can collect it. Kenyans also use the system to pay for bus tickets and school fees, to pay their rent and to send money home when they are working abroad.

M-Pesa is so successful that the company now operates in Tanzania, South Africa, Afghanistan, India and Romania. But there is another benefit. Becoming a world-leader in a new technology has motivated a new generation of Kenyan entrepreneurs. They are looking for other ways that new technology can help people in developing countries.

GRAMMAR

2 Choose the correct options to complete the summary of how the M-Pesa system works.

Because there are not ¹ *much / many* banks in Kenya, M-Pesa has outlets in ² *a lot of / much* shops and petrol stations. Customers can deposit ³ *a / —* money at these outlets and then use their phones to transfer the money to another outlet. They do this with ⁴ *a / some* simple text message. 'It's fantastic,' says one user. 'Exchange ⁵ *a little / a few* numbers with other people, and you can pay for anything in seconds. You don't need ⁶ *no / any* cash and there are ⁷ *no / any* long journeys to towns that have ⁸ *a / some* bank.'

3 Complete the description using the correct past tense form of the verbs.

The idea for transferring money by text message originally ¹_____ (come) from researchers at a Telecoms organization called Gamos in 2002. They ²_____ (notice) that people in Uganda and Ghana ³_____ (send) phone minutes to friends and relatives in place of money. The friends and relatives then ⁴_____ (use) these minutes or ⁵_____ (sell) them to other people. In 2004, the researchers ⁶_____ (meet) representatives from Vodafone. People at Vodafone ⁷_____ (already / start) to look at mobile phone banking. In 2007, they ⁸_____ (launch) M-Pesa.

VOCABULARY

4 Choose the correct options to complete the sentences about M-Pesa.

1. In the past, it was expensive for people to *lend / borrow* money from the bank.
2. About 60 per cent of Kenyans *earn / afford* less than $5 a day and are paid in cash by their employer.
3. A study by the University of Edinburgh showed that household *income / salaries* increased by five to thirty per cent when people used M-Pesa.
4. M-Pesa didn't have to *spend / invest* in new buildings because they used existing shops and petrol stations.
5. Some people even use M-Pesa as a place to put their *debts / savings*.
6. The company *rewards / praises* people for transferring small amounts by giving them the best rates.
7. M-Pesa is a social enterprise because it helps ordinary people *succeed / achieve* their financial goals.
8. M-Pesa offers users free registration as a(n) *incentive / praise* to join.
9. When M-Pesa came to Romania, it *set / offered* a target of creating 2,000 outlets in its first year.
10. Some people say that M-Pesa will only *pass / succeed* in countries where not many people have bank accounts.

5 Complete the account of a person seeing M-Pesa in practice with these words.

achieving	afford	lent	loan
made	payment	save	succeeding

I went to visit a group of women who started a fruit and vegetable business with a ¹_____ from the bank. Every month someone from the bank visits them to see if the project is ²_____. First they check that the group are repaying the money. Each woman tries to ³_____ enough money each month to repay their share of the loan. Then they make the ⁴_____ by mobile phone. This month one woman couldn't ⁵_____ to pay, but the others ⁶_____ her the money. The farm was going well and the women are ⁷_____ their goal of selling more fruit and vegetables each month. This month they ⁸_____ $850 between the ten of them.

DISCUSSION

6 Work in pairs. Discuss the questions.

1. Do you use your mobile phone to do banking and make payments? Why? / Why not?
2. What countries is M-Pesa present in? What do you think these countries have in common?
3. Can you think of any other examples of technology that is adapted to suit a particular country or situation?

SPEAKING

7 Jonny is travelling to Kenya to meet colleagues in his company's office in Nairobi. Read the conversations. Then complete the conversations using the prompts.

1. **At the airport** (J – Jonny, C = Cashier)
   J: Hello. ¹*I / like / change €200 / Kenyan shillings*. ²*What / rate / today?*
   _____
   C: It's 110 shillings for 1 euro.
   J: OK. ³*you / charge / commission?*
   _____
   C: Yes, two per cent.
   J: That's fine. ⁴*I / have / receipt / please?*
   _____

2. **At a café** (J = Jonny, W = Waiter)
   J: Sorry. ⁵*I / be / hurry*. ⁶*I / have / bill / please?*
   _____
   W: Yes, here you are. It's 230 shillings.
   J: ⁷*service / included?*
   _____
   W: No, sir.
   J: Here's 300 shillings. ⁸*Please / keep / change*.

3. **With a local Kenyan colleague** (J = Jonny, W = Wilson)
   W: So, Jonny, what did you do on your day off yesterday?
   J: I went on a city tour, but the guide spoke Swahili.
   W: How is your Swahili these days?
   J: ⁹*I / bit / out / practice*. ¹⁰*But I / do / best*.

4. **At the offices in Nairobi** (J = Jonny, D = David)
   J: I tried to contact you earlier, David. Did you get my message about printing the new contracts?
   D: Oh, yes. Sorry. ¹¹*I / be / on / call*. But I got the message.
   _____
   J: So, did you print them?
   D: No, sorry. ¹²*I / not / realize / it / be / urgent*.
   _____

8 Work in pairs. Act out the conversations with your partner.

WRITING

9 Work in pairs. Write three short text messages to your partner about these subjects.

1. Someone offered you an exciting new job in Kenya.
2. Ask if your partner can meet you after work for a coffee.
3. You missed your flight home. Say why.

10 Read your partner's messages. Write a short reply to each one.

11 Compare your answers. Did you use the same phrases to congratulate, explain and show sympathy?

5 Marketing

A video-art project ('Inside Out') by artist JR, Times Square, New York, USA

TEDTALKS

TIM LEBERECHT was born in Germany, but now lives in San Francisco. He is Chief Marketing Officer of global design and innovation firm *frog*, which has developed and marketed products and services for Apple, AT&T, BMW, Disney, GE, HP, Intel, SAP, Siemens and Sony among others.

Tim Leberecht's idea worth spreading is that you can build a stronger brand with a more loyal following if you hand over control to your customers or employees.

BACKGROUND

1 You are going to watch an edited version of a TED Talk by Tim Leberecht called *3 ways to (usefully) lose control of your brand*. Read the text about the speaker and the talk. Then work in pairs and discuss the questions.

1 Do you follow any companies or brands on social media? Which ones?
2 Do you ever make comments about companies or brands on social media? Are they positive or negative?
3 How can customers' comments on social media affect a brand? Can you think of an example?

KEY WORDS

2 Read the sentences (1–6). The words in bold are used in the TED Talk. First guess the meaning of the words. Then match the words with their definitions (a–g).

1 We **collaborated with** our customers to develop a product they liked.
2 I'm very **loyal** to *Levi's*. I never buy any other **brand** of jeans.
3 It was very **generous** of the company to donate sports equipment to the school.
4 **Hyperconnectivity** means that people can be contacted anywhere anytime.
5 People want to see more **openness** from companies so that they know what they are buying.
6 Companies have to try to build long-term relationships, not just focus on making money in the **short-term**.

a being connected through many different digital media.
b for a short period of time
c faithful, showing support for one person or organization
d not closed; allowing others to see what you are doing
e worked with
f kind and giving
g a particular name of a company or product that is well known to customers

AUTHENTIC LISTENING SKILLS
Understanding contrasts

Certain words and phrases introduce contrasts. When you listen, try to be aware of these words, so you will know that you are about to hear a contrasting idea. Here are the most common examples:

but, however, although, in spite of this

3a 🎧 **27** Look at the Authentic listening skills box. Read the two pairs of contrasting ideas (1–2) from the beginning of the TED Talk. Then listen and complete the extracts.

1 A recent survey said that 27 per cent of bosses believe their employees are inspired by their firm. _____, in the same survey, only four per cent of employees agreed.
2 Companies are losing control of their customers and their employees. _____ are they really?

3b 🎧 **28** Read two more sentences from the talk. Then listen and complete the contrasting ideas.

3 Buyers could determine the price, but _____ _____.
4 It may have jeopardized short-term sales, but it _____ loyalty.

3c 🎧 **29** Now listen to all four sentences and practise saying them.

5.1 3 ways to (usefully) lose control of your brand

TEDTALKS

1 ▶ 5.1 Tim Leberecht is interested in how companies communicate with customers and employees. Watch the edited version of the TED Talk. Write down as many of the companies and products Tim Leberecht mentions as you can.

Company	Product
1 the band Radiohead	a new album

2 Work in small groups and compare your notes from Exercise 1. Discuss why one of these companies or products was interesting to Tim Leberecht.

3 ▶ 5.1 Watch the first part (0.00–1.18) of the talk again. Choose the correct option to complete the sentences.

1 Companies are losing *control / customers*, but are they really?
2 Management teams are increasingly *connected to / disconnected from* their staff.
3 Your brand is what other people *think / say* about you when you are not in the room.
4 Hyperconnectivity and transparency allow *customers / companies* to be in that room now, 24/7.

4 ▶ 5.1 Read the examples (1–6) of companies giving more and less control. Then watch the second part (1.18–3.36) of the talk again. Match the examples with the companies (a–f).

1 Customers had control of the price of the product.
2 Customers could buy the product if they promised to do something kind for someone.
3 The company asked customers not to buy its products during the peak shopping season.
4 Employees could set their own work schedules and salaries.
5 Customers didn't know the destination of their trip.
6 Customers received surprise gifts.

a Patagonia outdoor clothing
b Radiohead album
c Semco
d Anthon Berg chocolates
e KLM airline
f Nextpedition travel

▶ traveler N AM ENG
▶ traveller BR ENG
▶ behavior N AM ENG
▶ behaviour BR ENG

5 ▶ **5.1** Complete the sentences with these words. Then watch the third part (3.36 to the end) of the talk again and check your answers.

connect   help   open   smile   true

1 Research suggests that employees feel more productive when they _____ others. At *frog*, Tim Leberecht's company, they have 'speed-meet' sessions to _____ old and new employees.
2 Hyperconnectivity means companies have to be open in their behaviour. So the only thing they can do is to stay _____ to themselves.
3 Instead of worrying about how _____ they should be, they must just _____ and be open to all possibilities.

VOCABULARY IN CONTEXT

6 ▶ **5.2** Watch the clips from the TED Talk. Choose the correct meaning of the words.

7 Work in pairs. Complete the statements in your own words.

1 I sometimes purchase used … but I don't like purchasing used …
2 The two peak holiday seasons in my country are …
3 At the end of the day, the important thing in work is to …

CRITICAL THINKING   Supporting evidence

8 When people present a theory or an idea, they often give examples to support that idea. Work in pairs. Read the examples (a–c). How did the examples support Tim Leberecht's message that 'Companies can give their employees and customers more control or less.'

a Radiohead allowed customers to decide the price of their new album.
b *Frog* holds 'speed-meet' sessions where new employees have to talk to old employees.
c The clothing company Patagonia encouraged customers to look for used clothes on eBay.

9 What do you think of the ideas in Exercise 8? Do you think they are effective ideas?

10 Read this comment* about the TED Talk. Does the viewer agree that companies are more open and are giving customers more control? Do you agree with him?

> **Viewers' comments**
>
> **M** **Mike** – I'd like to believe this is a new open conversation, but I don't. It's just marketing. Saying to customers 'Don't buy this jacket' is actually a way of encouraging them to buy it.

* The comment was created for this activity

▶ clothier **N AM ENG**
▶ clothing company **BR ENG**

PRESENTATION SKILLS   Using presentation slides

11 Work in pairs. Why do speakers use visuals like slides in a presentation? What makes presentation slides effective? Or ineffective?

12 Look at the Presentation tips box and compare your answers from Exercise 11. What are the most important things to remember about using visuals?

> **TIPS**
> • Visuals should be bright, clear and simple.
> • No one should have to 'read' your slides – they should be instantly comprehensible. If you use words, write in simple phrases.
> • Your slides are not there to help you remember what to say, they are there to help your audience understand. So they should add to what you say, not just repeat it word for word.
> • Don't read from your slides and don't turn your back on your audience to look at them.

13 ▶ **5.3** Watch the clips from the TED Talk. How many words did Tim Leberecht typically use in his presentation slides? What else was on each slide?

14 Work in pairs. Read this idea. Discuss how you could present it visually. Then prepare your slide(s).

One way to engage your customers is to monitor social networks to see who is having a bad day. Then the company can make this person's day better by sending them a surprise gift.

15 Work with another pair. Present your slide(s). Did you use similar images and words?

5.2 What are you looking for?

CAR COMPARISON CHECKER

Do you usually choose a car because of its brand? That's not a good idea. Look at the facts and figures first. Ask yourself what you are looking for: A car that is safe and practical? The car that is the cheapest to buy? A car with more features than your current car? A car that is not as expensive to run as your current car? A car that is more comfortable than your current car? Or the car with the best performance? Use the information to decide before you look at the full report and find out what make each of these cars is.

	A	B	C
FEATURES	★★★★	★★	★★★
PRACTICALITY*	★★	★★★	★★★★
PERFORMANCE	★★★★	★★	★★★
COMFORT	★★★	★★★	★★★★
SAFETY	★★★	★★	★★★★
RUNNING COSTS	$$$	$$	$$
PRICE	$$$$	$$	$$$

* e.g. room for enough people; space to carry large objects

GRAMMAR Comparatives and superlatives

1 Work in pairs. Discuss the questions.

  1 Do you compare the market when you buy the following things? How do you get the information you need?
   a clothes
   b computers
   c phones
   d cars

  2 In which areas – (a–d) or another area – are you loyal to a particular brand?

2 Look at the infographic from a car magazine and read the text. Why does the infographic not tell you the make or brand of the cars?

3 Read the text in the infographic again. Find the car (A, B or C) that answers each question.

4 Read the sentences (1–4) in the Grammar box. Answer the questions (a–c).

COMPARATIVES AND SUPERLATIVES

1 *It's a safe and practical car.*
2 *It's the cheapest car to buy.*
3 *It has more features than my current car.*
4 *It's more comfortable than my current car.*

a Which sentences compare one car with another car?
b Which sentence compares one car with all the other cars?
c Which sentence doesn't make a comparison?

Check your answers on page 148 and do Exercises 1–6.

5 Complete the sentences using the words in brackets. Use the information in the infographic to help you.

1. Car C is _____ of the three cars. (safe)
2. Car C is _____ than Car A. (comfortable)
3. Car A is _____ to run of the three cars. (expensive)
4. Car B has _____ performance of the three cars. (bad)
5. Car A is _____ of the three cars. (practical)
6. Car C has a _____ price than Car A, but it isn't _____ Car B. (low, low)

6 Look at the infographic again. Which car do you think is the best? Why? Discuss with a partner.

7 Look at the infographic below. Complete the facts about cars in the UK with these words.

as   as   as   least   less   more   most   most   the   than

1. One in three men spend longer looking for a new car _____ for a girlfriend.
2. _____ women than men feel emotionally attached to their cars.
3. The _____ popular name for a car in the UK is 'Betty'.
4. Black, white and silver are _____ most common colours for cars in the UK.
5. Drivers of black cars are the _____ likely to have an accident and drivers of silver cars are the _____ likely.
6. Fifty per cent of car drivers spend _____ money on holidays each year than on their cars.
7. British people do not spend _____ much time socializing with friends _____ they spend driving.
8. Fifty per cent of people buying a new car buy the same brand _____ they had before.

8 Do any of the facts in Exercise 7 surprise you? Why? Are any of them true for you?

9 Read the question. Then choose the correct option to complete each response.

Imagine you have to buy a new camera. How do you decide which one to buy?

1. I always look for the one that has the *more / most* features for *a / the* cheapest price.
2. I just buy the same brand *as / than* I had before.
3. I read all the customer reviews to see what people say is the *better / best* one.
4. I go to the shop to look at them. Then I go online to see if I can find a better price *than / as* in the shop.
5. I don't worry about it too much. Cameras aren't very different *than / from* each other.
6. I think the *more / most* important thing is to find a reliable camera. I don't mind if it's a little *more / less* expensive than the others.

10 Work in pairs. Discuss which statement(s) in Exercise 9 describe(s) what you normally do when you want to buy something new.

SPEAKING Comparing the market

11 21st CENTURY OUTCOMES

Work in pairs.

Student A: Turn to page 171.
Student B: Turn to page 172.

Ask each other questions to complete the table.

12 Make comparisons between the two hotels and tell each other which hotel you prefer. Give reasons.

I think I prefer the Astra Hotel because it's quieter.

WE LOVE OUR CARS

50% of people think their **relationship** is **harder to maintain** than their car

24% of British men **value** their **cars above** family **pets**

53% of Brits have **named** their car **BETTY**

33% of men spend **longer** looking for a new **car** than a **girlfriend**

60% of **women** and **41%** of **men** have felt emotionally **attached** to their **car**

25% of Brits **cried** when they **parted** with their **car**

1 BETTY 2 BETSY 3 BESS 4 BERTIE 5 DAISY 6 BERTHA 7 MEG 8 CHARLIE 9 HERBIE 10 BOB

ACCIDENTS BY CAR COLOUR

 HIGH RISK    LOW RISK

British people spend more time driving than socializing

50% of people are loyal to brand

50% of car drivers spend more on cars than holidays

TOP 10 BRITISH CAR NAMES

21st CENTURY OUTCOMES   INFORMATION LITERACY Using facts to make judgements and express preferences

5.3 Help is out there

READING The power of the crowd

1 Work in pairs. Discuss the questions.

1 When was the last time you bought something because of an advertisement you saw? What was it?
2 When was the last time you stopped using a product or service because you saw or read some negative publicity?

2 Read the article. Choose the options (a–c) that best describe the main ideas in the article.

1 These days marketers are trying to:
 a use social media to deal with customers' problems.
 b advertise through the Internet to particular groups of people.
 c involve their customers in product development and promotion.

2 They are doing this so that:
 a they spend less money on advertising.
 b their products will be more successful.
 c they won't have bad publicity.

3 Read the article again. Match the paragraphs (1–5) with the headings (A–E).

A Your advertisement isn't welcome here
B An advert made by customers
C A prize for joining in
D An open conversation
E Co-operating to improve products

4 Complete the sentences with a word from each paragraph.

1 These days customers often _____ online about their experiences of products and services.
2 When companies put advertisements on social media sites, customers feel it is an _____.
3 Crowdsourcing and co-creation are when companies _____ to other people for help with their business.
4 Lay's competition was successful because a lot of people _____ their ideas for new crisp flavours.
5 The key to a successful product or campaign is to _____ your customers in a conversation with you.

5 Do you agree with sentences 2 and 5 in Exercise 4? Why? / Why not?

Yes, I think it's a good idea for companies to talk directly to their customers because ...

VOCABULARY Marketing collocations

6 Complete the sequence using these verbs.

| develop | do | launch | listen |
| measure | promote | run | understand |

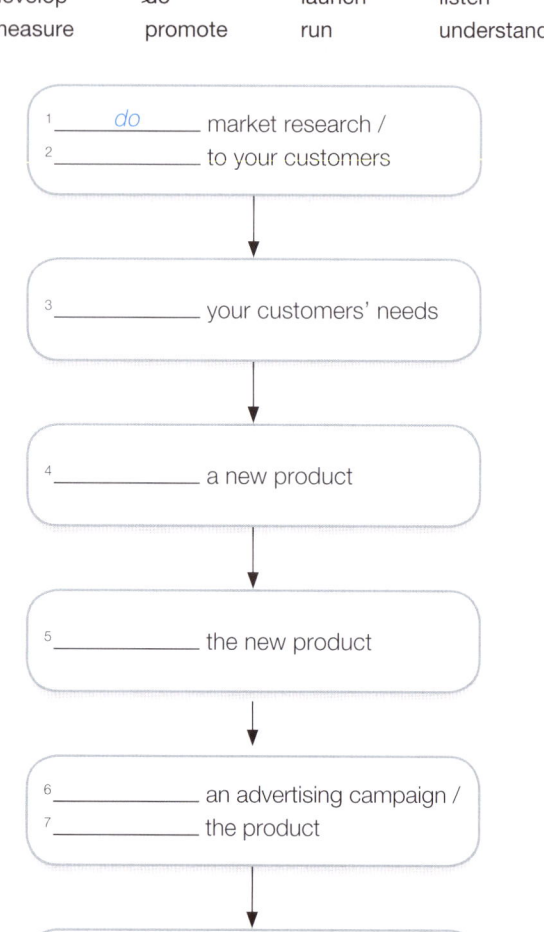

1 *do* market research /
2 _____ to your customers

3 _____ your customers' needs

4 _____ a new product

5 _____ the new product

6 _____ an advertising campaign /
7 _____ the product

8 _____ customer satisfaction

7 Work in pairs. Discuss which parts of the sequence in Exercise 6 the companies (Lay's and Ford) did, according to the article.

8 Choose the best option to complete the sentences. Then compare your answers with a partner.

1 The best way to measure customer satisfaction is to *ask customers / look at sales results*.
2 The most effective way to promote a new product is to *advertise on TV / get people talking about it*.
3 *August / January* is not the best time to launch a new product.
4 It's cheaper to run an advertising campaign *on the Internet / on TV*.
5 You can understand your customers' needs better if you *are a customer yourself / listen to them*.

SPEAKING Effective marketing

9 **21st CENTURY OUTCOMES**

Work in small groups. Each choose an example of at least three of the following kinds of promotion or recommendation that have caught your attention (either in a positive or negative way). Then discuss and compare your experiences.

We got a flyer through our door from a guy called Mr Fix It. We had a lot of things in the house that needed repairing, like a door that didn't close and a tap that dripped water. So we telephoned him and …

Promotion or recommendation
- a **flyer** that someone put through your door or gave you in the street
- a funny **viral video** (e.g. on YouTube)
- a personal (**word-of mouth**) **recommendation** from someone you met
- a **TV advertisement**
- a **newspaper** or magazine **advertisement**
- a **competition**
- a **special offer** sent to your email

THE **POWER** OF THE CROWD

1 When we look for a new car or washing machine, most of us now first search online for customers' reviews of similar products. In online chatrooms and on social media, we discuss our recent holiday and travel experiences, the books we like or the music we are listening to. This is an age of openness, where consumers chat freely to each other about their experiences of products and services, and more and more companies are realizing that it is better to be part of these conversations than to be outside them.

2 When companies first started using social media to market their products, they simply placed their advertisements on social networking pages in the same way that they placed an advertisement on TV or in a newspaper. But users of social media responded badly to this, because it felt like an interruption, as if someone was butting in on their private conversation. These days marketers realize that they need to be more sensitive in how they join in the conversation. Moreover, they are aware that these customers can actually help them in their marketing.

3 'Crowdsourcing' has been around for almost a decade. It is the idea that, via the Internet, companies can appeal to groups of people to help them with their business. This can be financial, technical or marketing help. In marketing the idea has evolved into something called 'co-creation', where companies and customers work together to design and promote better products.

4 In 2012 the crisp manufacturer Lay's ran a competition called 'Do Us a Flavor' in which they invited people, through Facebook, to create a new flavour for their crisps. Many people submitted their ideas and a group of food experts shortlisted three of these. Facebook fans then voted for the best idea. The company paid the winner $1 million, so this was not a way of saving money, but they could be confident that their marketing effort had created a product that people would like.

5 In another example of co-creation, Ford invited people to help with an advertising campaign. They asked spectators to film its new car as professional racing drivers drove it through the streets of Key West in Florida. They then put the clips together and made the first-ever spectator-filmed advertisement. In both these examples, marketers were able to engage consumers in a conversation and attracted user support for a product before it was actually launched.

21st CENTURY OUTCOMES EFFECTIVE COMMUNICATION Evaluating different means of communication

5.4 What do you think of it?

LISTENING Asking for opinions

1 Complete the table with these adjectives.

all right   amazing   awful   dreadful   fantastic   so-so

Great	OK	Terrible
_____	_____	_____
_____	_____	_____

2 Work in pairs. Use the adjectives in Exercise 1 to describe things in these categories (a–c). Think of at least one example for each category.

- a food
- b music
- c film / TV

a My mum's cooking is fantastic. My sister's cooking is OK. But my cooking is terrible.

3 🎧 **30** Listen to five conversations. Complete the subject of the conversation and the speaker's opinion of each subject.

- a good (G)
- b probably good (P)
- c OK (OK)
- d no opinion (N)

Subject	Opinion
1 Olly's _____ restaurant	_____
2 _____ in Brighton	_____
3 Giant _____	_____
4 Vietnamese _____	_____
5 Tarantino's new _____	_____

4 🎧 **30** Look at the Useful language box on page 61. Listen to the conversations again and tick (✓) the phrases that the speakers used to give their opinion or comment on the subject.

5 Work in pairs. How did each speaker explain their answers? Complete the descriptions with these adjectives.

fantastic   heavy   interesting   limited
special   spicy   strong

1 The menu is very _____, but the food is _____.
2 Brighton is more _____ than many places.
3 Giant bikes are quite _____, but they're really _____.
4 In most Asian restaurants you can ask them to make the food less _____.
5 The new Tarantino film isn't anything _____.

Pronunciation Expressive intonation

6a 🎧 **31** Listen to the sentences. Notice the difference in intonation when the speaker makes a positive or a negative point.

1 It's a wonderful book.
2 I don't think the food is great.
3 The weather was cold, but we had an amazing holiday.
4 It's a very beautiful walk, but it's quite long.
5 What a fantastic talk that was!

6b Work in pairs. Practise saying the sentences with an expressive or flat intonation.

1 The film is great – I'd recommend it!
2 In my experience, there isn't much to see there.
3 It's a fantastic museum, but it's very expensive.
4 I love his new song – it's really catchy.

SPEAKING Giving your views

7 Work in pairs. Act out conversations about three of these things. Use the expressions in the Useful language box to help you.

1. a restaurant in your town
2. a recent (blockbuster) film at the cinema
3. a new TV series / programme everyone is talking about
4. a well-known holiday resort
5. a particular type of food (e.g. Greek food)
6. a particular make of car

GIVING YOUR VIEWS

Asking for information

Do you know if something is …?
Do you know anything about …?
What do you think of …?
Is … a good …?

Giving opinions

I love it. / I'd recommend it.
It's great / good / OK.
I think / don't think it's …
In my experience …
It depends on …

Commenting

I don't know. / I couldn't tell you.
I imagine …

WRITING A customer review

8 Read the two reviews of the same laptop computer. Answer the questions.

1. Write a list of the positive and negative points in each review.
2. Which points did the reviewers agree on?
3. What is the conclusion of each reviewer?

Writing skill Linking contrasting points

9a Read the reviews again. Notice how the writers of the reviews balance good and bad points. Find four more similar sentences or pairs of sentences.

It's not the most attractive laptop on the market, but it works well.

9b Underline the words or phrases in the reviews used to link contrasting points. Then answer the questions.

1. Which linking words/phrases join two clauses in a sentence?
2. Which linking words/phrases can come at the beginning of a new sentence?

9c Rewrite the contrasting points using the linking words and phrases given.

1. The screen is a bit small, but it's a good product. (Although)
2. It's excellent quality, but it isn't cheap. (Having said that)
3. The instruction manual is hopeless, but the shop assistants were very helpful. (However)
4. Although I normally like this company, I was disappointed by this product. (but)

10 `21st` **CENTURY OUTCOMES**

Write a review of a product or service that you bought recently. Include the following points:

- your rating of the product and a title
- good points and bad points about the product
- linking phrases that connect these contrasts
- a conclusion

11 Work in pairs. Exchange reviews with your partner. Check that your partner has included all the points in Exercise 10. Would you buy the product or service based on this review?

CUSTOMER REVIEWS

★★★★ **Nice computer**

This laptop is fast, simple to use and, so far, problem-free. It's not the most attractive laptop on the market, but it works well and that's the most important thing. I had a Sony before, which was beautiful, but it was also twice as expensive.

Someone says in another comment on this website that the screen isn't great. However, I disagree. I watch movies on it and the quality seems fine to me. My only gripe is that the webcam is not very good quality. Having said that, the sound is excellent. Overall, it's very good value for money.

Would recommend.

★★★ **Good, I think**

I bought this laptop four weeks ago. Although the guy in the shop gave me lots of help with it, I am still trying to learn how to use it! But it seems good. It's light and very fast. It's also a very good price. I'm sure that when I learn how to use it properly, it will be better than my old laptop.

gripe (n) complaint

6 Communication

BACKGROUND

1 You are going to watch a TED Talk by Melissa Marshall called *Talk nerdy to me*. Read the text about the speaker and the talk. Then choose the best options to complete the summary.

> Melissa Marshall is an academic. Her specialist subject is
> [1] *science / communications*. She believes that scientific
> innovations are very important for our [2] *future / work* and
> wants to help scientists to explain their [3] *ideas / jobs* to us.

TEDTALKS

MELISSA MARSHALL works at the Department of Communication Arts & Sciences at Penn State University. She specializes in teaching speaking skills to engineering students and has also lectured at Harvard Medical School, the New York Academy of Sciences and Cornell University. She believes that the future depends on the innovations of scientists and engineers and is passionate about helping them describe their work.

Melissa Marshall's idea worth spreading is that even complex and technical topics can be easy to understand and exciting if they are communicated in the right ways.

Temple talk, Jaipur, Rajasthan, India

KEY WORDS

2 Read the sentences (1–6). The words in bold are used in the TED Talk. Match the words in bold with their definitions (a–f). Then ask and answer the questions with a partner.

1 Why is science important for us in our daily lives? How is it **relevant** to me?
2 Do you find it difficult to understand scientists when they use a lot of specialist words and scientific **jargon**?
3 How can scientists make their work more **accessible** to the general public so we can all understand it?
4 Do you find it helps when people use an **analogy** to explain things?
5 Did you think that people at school who were keen on science and computing were **nerdy**?
6 Can science **tackle** the world's big problems like climate change?

a expressions used by a particular professional group
b a comparison that helps people to understand something
c easy to understand
d connected to the subject being discussed
e deal with (a problem)
f very knowledgeable about a technical area and with a mind fixed only on this area

AUTHENTIC LISTENING SKILLS Elision

When it is difficult to say two consonant sounds together – one at the end of a word and one at the beginning of the next word – we elide the sounds by cancelling the first one. This makes it more difficult for the listener to separate the individual words. It is common to elide /t/ and /d/ when they are at the end of a word.

next please = /neks/pliːz/   it could be = /ɪ/kʊ/biː/
I can't come = /aɪ/kɑːn/kʌm/   you and me = /juː/ən/miː/

3a 🎧 32 Look at the Authentic listening skills box. Then listen to these extracts from the TED Talk. Underline the sound in the extract that is elided (cancelled).

1 … saw **that door** to a whole new world.
2 … the key to opening that door is **great communication**.
3 **First question** to answer for us: so what?
4 … drop the **bullet points**.

3b 🎧 33 Listen to three more extracts from the talk. Complete the extracts with the words you hear.

5 … when she went down that _____
6 Our scientists and engineers are the ones that are tackling our _____
7 … the engineers that I've _____

6.1 Talk nerdy to me

TEDTALKS

1 ▶ 6.1 Watch the TED Talk. Answer the questions. Then discuss your answers with a partner.

  1 What is the amazing new world that Melissa Marshall wants us to see?
  2 How is she trying to make this possible?

2 ▶ 6.1 Watch the first part (0.00–1.36) of the talk again. Choose the correct options to complete the description.

When Penn State University asked Melissa Marshall to teach a communications class to [1] *English / engineering* students, at first she felt [2] *surprised / scared*. But as she looked into their world she was [3] *amazed / amused* by their ideas and she wanted others to see this [4] *wonderland / dreamland*. She believes this is important because scientists and engineers are trying to solve the world's biggest challenges in energy, our environment and [5] *welfare / health care*.

3 ▶ 6.1 Look at the steps Melissa Marshall believes scientists must take. Then watch the second part (1.36–3.33) of the talk again. Complete the sentences. Use one word in each space.

  1 They must tell us why science is _____ to us.
  2 They must try not to use _____ when they talk.
  3 They must follow Einstein's principle: 'Make everything as simple as possible, but no _____.'
  4 They must not use lots of _____ points in their presentations.
  5 Instead they should use single sentences on their slides and _____ to help us understand.

▶ students /ˈstʌd(ə)nts/ **N AM ENG**
▶ students /ˈstjuːd(ə)nts/ **BR ENG**

▶ new /nu/ **N AM ENG**
▶ new /njuː/ **BR ENG**

4 ▶ 6.1 Watch the third part (3.33 to the end) of the talk again. Complete the equation using these words. Then discuss with a partner what you think Melissa Marshall means.

equal (=)   divide (÷)   multiply (×)   subtract (−)

'Take your science, ¹ _____ your bullet points and your jargon, ² _____ by relevance, meaning share what's relevant to the audience, and ³ _____ it by the passion that you have for this incredible work that you're doing, and that is going to ⁴ _____ incredible interactions …'

VOCABULARY IN CONTEXT

5 ▶ 6.2 Watch the clips from the TED Talk. Choose the correct meaning of the words.

6 Work in pairs. Complete the sentences in your own words.

1 The key to good communication is …
2 When you use gestures in another country, beware of …
3 Not speaking English well is a barrier to …

CRITICAL THINKING Demonstrating your argument

7 When you give advice or make recommendations, it often helps to show how you follow this advice yourself. Work in pairs. Discuss how Melissa Marshall followed her own recommendations in preparing and giving her talk.

8 Read this comment* about the TED Talk. According to this viewer, who else should follow their own advice? Do you agree? What other professions might this be especially important for?

Viewers' comments

R Ryu – I think this is very true and Melissa Marshall gives a good example of how to present ideas. It's a good lesson for teachers and for anyone who instructs others: doctors who tell us how to be healthy, employers who tell us how to work efficiently, bankers who tell us to be careful with our money, etc.

*The comment was created for this activity.

9 Talk about an example from your experience of a professional who you thought was a good communicator.

PRESENTATION SKILLS Engaging with your audience

10 A presentation seems like a one-way form of communication, but a skilled presenter will make it seem like a conversation. Work in pairs. Discuss how good presenters can do this.

11 Look at the Presentation tips box. Compare your ideas from Exercise 10. Were your ideas similar?

> **TIPS**
> To have a more personal, two-way conversation with your audience:
> - Make eye contact with them.
> - Smile – and use humour where appropriate.
> - Use relaxed and friendly body language.
> - Ask questions (as if you are in a real conversation).
> - Talk enthusiastically – let your personality come through.

12 ▶ 6.3 Watch the clip from the TED Talk. Which of the techniques from the Presentation tips box did Melissa Marshall use?

13 You are going to explain a particular idea or concept. Make some brief notes to present an idea or concept from your work, area of study or an interest/hobby. You want to help others to understand this idea/concept.

14 Work in pairs. Give your presentation. Use the techniques from the Presentation tips box to engage with your audience.

▶ can't /kænt/ **N AM ENG**
▶ can't /kɑːnt/ **BR ENG**
▶ area /ˈeriə/ **N AM ENG**
▶ area /ˈeəriə/ **BR ENG**

6.2 How do you communicate?

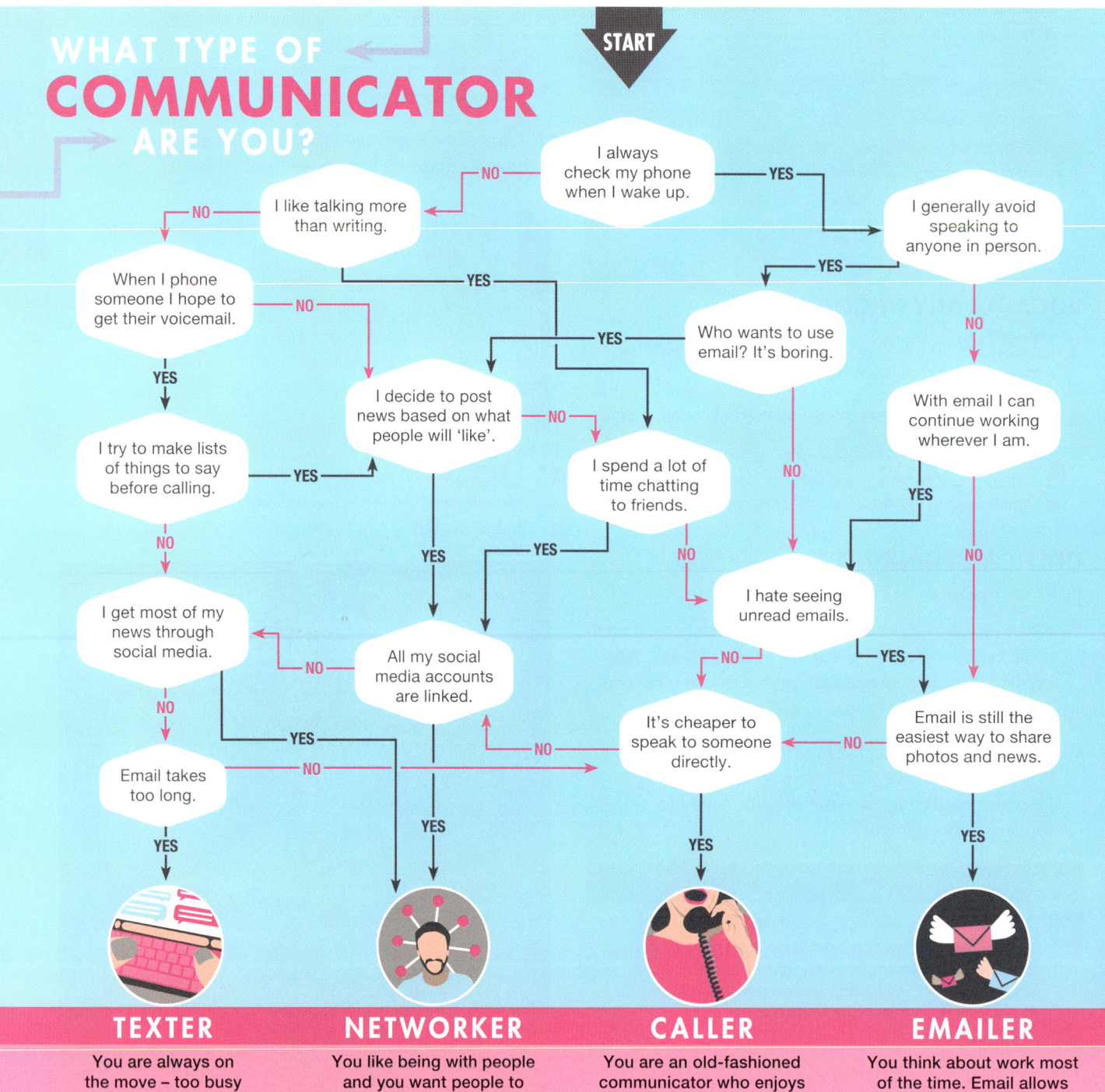

GRAMMAR Verb patterns with infinitive and *-ing*

1. Work in pairs. Make a list of the different ways of communicating with people. Divide them into a) written and b) spoken communication.

2. Work with another pair. Compare your lists from Exercise 1. Which of these ways is the most personal way of communicating? And the least?

3. What kind of communicator are you? Do the quiz and find out.

4. Do you agree with the result? Why? / Why not?

5 Read the sentences in the Grammar box. Answer the questions (1–3). Then look at the quiz again and find two more examples of verbs that are followed by:

a *to* + infinitive
b *-ing* form

VERB PATTERNS WITH INFINITIVE AND *-ING*

I generally **avoid** speaking to anyone in person.
I **try** to make lists of things to say before calling.
Email **allows** you to keep up-to-date.
I **hate** seeing unread emails.
Who **wants** to use email?

1 Which verbs in bold are followed by *to* + infinitive?
2 Which verbs in bold are followed by the *-ing* form?
3 Which verb is followed by an object + *to* + infinitive?

Check your answers on page 150 and do Exercises 1–2.

6 Choose the correct verb form to complete the texts about communication.

Text 1

I need ¹ *to use / using* social media, because all my friends do, but I don't enjoy ² *to use / using* it. I find that a lot of my friends often post messages without thinking: they say things that they don't mean ³ *to say / saying*. And then they spend a lot of time ⁴ *to apologize / apologizing* for what they said. So I often write a draft message first and then come back to it a few hours later to see if I really want ⁵ *to send / sending* it.

Text 2

When people send you a message electronically, they expect you ¹ *to answer / answering* immediately and often you can't. I'm quite slow at replying to messages. Sometimes people send me a second message before I can finish ² *to write / writing* a reply to the first one. They think that I'm avoiding ³ *to write / writing* back to them when in fact, I'm just slow. I wouldn't consider ⁴ *to do / doing* that myself. I think it's rude.

7 Complete these sentences with the correct verb forms so they are true for you. Then compare your answers with a partner.

1 Phone calls: I always try to avoid …
2 Emails: I spend a lot of time …
3 Letters: I need …
4 Presentations: I hate …
5 Social media: I enjoy …

GRAMMAR Infinitive and *-ing* clauses

8 Read the sentences in the Grammar box. Answer the questions (1–2).

INFINITIVE AND *-ING* CLAUSES

It's cheaper to speak to someone directly.
Speaking to someone directly is cheaper.

1 Which sentence uses *to* + infinitive and which sentence uses the *-ing* form of the verb?
2 Is there a difference in meaning between the two sentences?

Check your answers on page 150 and do Exercises 3–5.

9 Rewrite the sentences using the alternative *to* + infinitive or *-ing* form.

1 Speaking in public is stressful.
   It's stressful to speak in public.
2 It was a bad idea to call him late at night.
3 Writing clearly is very important.
4 It's tiring to look at a computer all day.
5 It is always useful to hear different points of view.
6 Knowing the right means of communication to use is sometimes difficult.
7 Texting rather than phoning is lazy.
8 Writing a good letter is hard.

SPEAKING Means of communication

10 **21st CENTURY OUTCOMES**

Work in pairs. What means of communication can you use to communicate the following messages (1–4)? What is the right thing to say or write?

1 Two friends in Canada are getting married. You would like to wish them a happy wedding day.
2 You need to apologize to a customer for sending them the wrong information.
3 You have to tell an employee that they are going to lose their job because the office is closing.
4 You want to tell all your friends about a fantastic new song that you heard on the radio.

   1 *We decided to send them a card. It says 'Congratulations on your wonderful news! I hope you have a fantastic day.'*

6.3 Good communication

READING Why we don't listen any more

1 Work in pairs. Think of two people (colleagues, public figures, people on TV) that:

a you like listening to.
b you don't like listening to.

Discuss with a partner why you like / don't like listening to these people.

2 Read the article. Why does the writer say we have stopped listening to our leaders? Do you agree with these reasons? Why? / Why not?

3 Read the article again. Choose the correct option (a–c) to answer the questions.

1 What kind of growth does the speaker promise?
 a strong growth
 b long-term growth
 c slow growth

2 What kind of transport does he promise?
 a cheap and green
 b cheap and public
 c efficient and fast

3 What kind of society does he promise?
 a a rich society
 b a different society
 c an equal society

4 How did the writer feel after hearing the speech?
 a inspired
 b no different
 c surprised

5 What do people like their politicians to have?
 a a gift for speaking
 b opinions which they really believe
 c similar political opinions

6 Why do business people use jargon?
 a to have respect
 b to express ideas clearly
 c to make progress in their career

7 What do business people mean when they say 'issues'?
 a ideas
 b problems
 c arguments

8 What, according to the writer, is the key to effective communication?
 a to do what you can
 b to do what you know
 c to do what you say

4 Complete the sentences with words or expressions from the article.

1 Everyone wants a _____ transport system.
2 A good speaker can _____ their arguments.
3 We want our politicians to speak from _____.
4 Your actions must always _____ your words.
5 If you don't keep your promises, people will lose _____ in you.

5 Work in pairs. Discuss the two most important lessons from the article. Use the list in Exercise 4.

VOCABULARY Communication collocations

6 Work in pairs. Match the verbs in box A with the nouns in box B to make verb + noun communication collocations. There is sometimes more than one possibility.

A

have   give   make   post   send   write

B

a comment	a presentation
an email	a report
a letter	a speech
a meeting	a text message
a phone call	

7 Complete the sentences with the collocations from Exercise 6. You sometimes need to change the form.

1 Will you excuse me? I need to _____. I promised Jess I'd speak to her before twelve.
2 I get really nervous before I _____, but when I start speaking, my nerves go away.
3 I loved R.J. Palacio's book *Wonder*. I _____ on her blog last week to tell her how much I liked it.
4 I _____ him _____ an hour ago, but I didn't get a reply.
5 I can't meet for lunch, I'm afraid. I _____ with the other people in my department from 10 a.m. to 3 p.m. today.
6 I didn't _____ the _____ myself. I just _____ a few _____ on it when Karen showed it to me.
7 I couldn't contact her on the phone, so I am going to _____ her _____ instead. Do you know her address?

8 Work in pairs. Tell each other which of the things in Exercise 6 you did in the last week. What was the subject of each one?

I posted a comment on a news blog about people driving too fast in my area.

WHY we don't listen any more

Read this speech and then think for a moment about how it makes you feel.

'Our vision is that, ten years from now, our economy will be very different from the economy of today. We will build growth that lasts. We will have reliable transport so people can get to work without it damaging their pockets or damaging the Earth. We will have a fair society where every child, rich or poor, has opportunities; where each home, community and office looks after its environment. I know what I believe. I believe the country wants something different. Only our party can offer a difference and hope for the future.'

I wonder if you felt the same as me. It's a well-constructed speech (*I know what I believe. I believe …*). It's an eloquent speech (*transport that doesn't damage your pockets or damage the Earth*). It promises good things (*growth that lasts*). But in the end I feel nothing. I don't even know which party this leader belongs to. Why is that? Why is it that when many politicians and corporate leaders speak, we simply switch off? They speak well; their arguments are well-constructed; they can defend these arguments. But they have failed to understand two basic lessons of communication.

The first is that eloquence is not the important thing. People enjoy hearing a good speaker, but they don't want to hear an actor. They want to hear someone real. They respect politicians who speak from the heart. Many corporate leaders make the same mistake. They believe using jargon will make them sound more business-like and authoritative. 'Clearly there are some *issues around* schedules and budgets, but *going forward* we are confident of *delivering* a great product'. We would respect them more if they simply said, 'The product is a bit late and over-budget, but it will be a good product'.

The second reason is that their actions don't match their words. Your behaviour is your most important tool in communication. So, if you say one thing and do another, people stop listening. They lose trust in you. An example of this is a government which promises to listen to people and then ignores what people tell them. The rule is: if you can't do it, don't say you can.

---

eloquent (adj) good at talking or expressing yourself
genuine (adj) real
switch off (v) stop listening or paying attention

SPEAKING Communication skills

9 `21st CENTURY OUTCOMES`

The article talks about leaders' communication skills. Work in small groups. Discuss which communication skills (1–5) are most important to the people (a–f) in their work and why.

1 listening skills
2 speaking skills
3 writing skills
4 reading skills
5 none of these

a teachers
b doctors
c electricians
d scientists
e researchers
f customer advisors at a call centre

10 Talk about your job (or another job) or the subject you are studying and say which communication skills are important for it.

6.4 Is it your first time here?

VOCABULARY Small talk phrases

1 Imagine two strangers on their lunch break. Which scenario in the photos (A–B) is more probable where you live?

2 Work in pairs. Where is it normal to speak to strangers: on a train, in a doctor's waiting room, at a bus stop, at a hotel? Discuss.

3 Read the explanation of small talk. Then decide which opening sentences (1–8) are good examples of small talk.

> Small talk is light conversation with someone you don't know well. It involves talking with another person about things you have in common and having a conversation which is light, friendly and fun.

1 Do you come from Spain?
2 Is it your first time in Vienna?
3 Can you believe this weather we're having?
4 I love the food in this hotel.
5 I like your jacket. It's a really nice colour.
6 Oh, you're reading *Wonder*. I really enjoyed that book.
7 I find these kinds of conferences really boring.
8 Do you know anything about the political situation here?

4 Match the answers (a–h) with the opening sentences (1–8) in Exercise 3.

a Yes, it's great.
b Yes, I do. How did you know?
c Yes, it is. I really like it.
d Oh – I'm sorry to hear that.
e I know, it's amazing. A bit hot for work, though.
f Thanks. I just bought it yesterday, actually.
g Um, no. I'm afraid I don't.
h Yes, I've only just started it, but I can't put it down.

LISTENING Follow-up questions

5 🎧 34 Work in pairs. Think of a natural follow-up question or comment to continue the conversations (1–6) from Exercises 3 and 4. Then listen to the conversations and compare your answers.

A: Do you come from Spain?
B: Yes, I do. How did you know?
A: It was your accent. Whereabouts in Spain are you from?
B: From Madrid. Do you know it?

Pronunciation Sentence stress

6a Complete the answers with these words.

actually   do   great   really   so

1 A: Are you here on business?
  B: No, we're on holiday, _____.
2 A: Are you enjoying the party?
  B: Yes, it's _____.
3 A: I'd really like to visit the city centre.
  B: Yes, _____ would I.
4 A: Do you speak Portuguese?
  B: No, not _____. Just a few words.
5 A: Don't you love the food here?
  B: Yes, I _____. It's fantastic.

6b 🎧 35 Listen to the conversations in Exercise 6a and check your answers. Underline the words that are stressed in each answer.

6c Practise saying the conversations with your partner.

SPEAKING Small talk

7 Work in pairs. Imagine you are at a conference. It is lunchtime and you sit down next to someone you don't know. Have a short conversation. Use the expressions in the Useful language box to help you. Then change partner and act out another conversation.

SMALL TALK

Openers

Are you enjoying the conference?
Oh, I see you work for GE. I have a friend who works for them.
I like your jacket.
Is it your first time here?
I can't believe all this rain. It doesn't stop.

Follow-up questions

Whereabouts in Spain are you from?
What's the weather like in France at the moment?
Have you visited …?
Where did you get it?

Short answers

Yes, it's great.
No, I'm on holiday, actually.
Yes, so are we.
Yes, I do.
I know, it's amazing.

WRITING Short emails

8 Look at the short emails (A–E). Match the emails with the subjects (1–5).

1 thanks
2 confirmation of booking
3 sorry
4 web link
5 room hire

Writing skill Reasons for writing

9a Find the elements (1–4) in the emails. Then say which emails are formal and which are less formal.

1 greeting
2 reason for writing
3 action wanted
4 ending

9b Complete the sentences giving the reason for writing with these words.

about   for   for   if   that

1 I apologize _____ our mistake.
2 I'm enquiring _____ the price of delivery.
3 Thank you _____ your letter.
4 I'm writing to ask _____ you can help me.
5 I can confirm _____ we received your order.

10 **21st CENTURY OUTCOMES**

Work in pairs. Look at the situations below. Write a short email, starting with the reason for writing.

Student A: You want to stay in a hotel for two nights next month. Send an email to the hotel asking about availability.

Student B: You forgot to send a friend a reply to their email of two weeks ago asking about jobs at your company. Send an email to say sorry and say that there are no positions available at the moment.

11 Exchange emails with your partner. Check that your partner has:
- included the reason for writing
- started and ended the email in an appropriate way

12 Write another short email replying to your partner's email.

A

TO: *Click here to add recipients*   CC:
SUBJECT:

Hi Julia

It was good to meet you at the conference. I'm just writing to ask if you could send me the link to the furniture website that you mentioned.

Thanks and best wishes

Jim

B

TO: *Click here to add recipients*   CC:
SUBJECT:

Hi Federica

Just a quick note to say thank you for showing me around the town last Saturday. We really enjoyed it.

Kevin

C

TO: *Click here to add recipients*   CC:
SUBJECT:

Dear Ramón

I apologize for not coming to your talk. I had to leave early to catch my train. I hope it went well.

Kind regards

Stephanie

D

TO: *Click here to add recipients*   CC:
SUBJECT:

Dear Mr Hamley

This is to confirm that we have reserved a double room for you for the night of 20 July.

We look forward to seeing you then.

Yours sincerely

Sarah Morgan (Reservations)

E

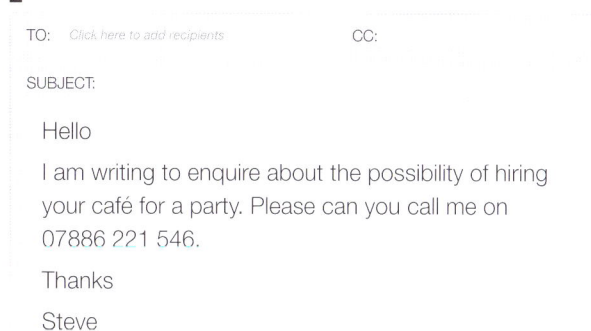

TO: *Click here to add recipients*   CC:
SUBJECT:

Hello

I am writing to enquire about the possibility of hiring your café for a party. Please can you call me on 07886 221 546.

Thanks

Steve

EFFECTIVE COMMUNICATION Explaining your purpose

Review 3 | UNITS 5 AND 6

READING

1 Work in pairs. Before you read the article, discuss what you think the organization called Morally Marketed does. Then read the article and compare your answers.

2 Read the article again. Are the sentences true (T) or false (F), according to the article?

1 Advertisements don't really affect the way we think.
2 Often advertisements don't tell the truth.
3 Morally Marketed is only concerned with advertisements which give the wrong message.
4 Marketers have a responsibility to show people how to act in a positive way.
5 The Thai anti-smoking film shows nine-year-old children smoking.

GRAMMAR

3 Complete the summary with a comparative or superlative form of the adjectives. Use two words to complete each space.

Morally Marketed wants companies to be
¹ _____ (honest) and open about their products. This can be difficult for companies, because they want to present their products in ² _____ (good) way possible. But they realize that people are
³ _____ (careful) about the things they buy than they were in the past. It's not ⁴ _____ (easy) as it was to mislead customers. Also, with social media, if companies do something wrong, news about this travels ⁵ _____ (fast) it did in the past.

4 Complete the comments by people who watched the Thai anti-smoking advert. Use the correct form of the verbs (*to* + infinitive or *-ing*).

1 'I didn't enjoy _____ (watch) it, but I thought it was very good.'
2 'I found it very interesting. The adults seemed _____ (be) very surprised that the children wanted _____ (smoke).'
3 'When the children gave them the piece of paper, none of the adults continued _____ (smoke). They put their cigarettes out.'
4 'I wonder how many of the adults considered _____ (stop) smoking there and then. It certainly persuaded me _____ (stop).'
5 'I think the message was very true. We spend a lot of time _____ (think) about what other people are doing wrong, but we don't look at ourselves.'

Morally Marketed

Morally Marketed is a website that promotes honesty and openness in marketing. It was founded in 2012 by marketer Stuart Ralph. We imagine that no one really takes advertisements too seriously, but Ralph believes marketing has more influence on us than we think. He worries that, in their advertisements, companies often communicate messages that are misleading.

Morally Marketed encourages an open conversation about what is good and bad practice in marketing. Its aims are to get marketers to promote positive values in society and to stop marketers advertising things which are bad for our physical or mental well-being.

An example of the right kind of advertisement, they believe, is the 2012 public information film by the Thai Health Promotion Foundation. Many people think this is the best anti-smoking advertisement ever. The film shows two children (aged around nine) approaching various adult smokers in the street and asking them for a light. The adults refuse to give the children a light, telling them that smoking is dangerous and bad for their health. The children then hand the adults a piece of paper and walk away. The paper says, 'You worry about me. But why not about yourself? Call 1600 to quit smoking.'

VOCABULARY

5 Complete the text about honesty in advertising with these words.

developed	did	had	listened	promote
posted	run	send	wrote	launched

A few years ago the comedian David Mitchell ¹_____ an interesting article about honesty in advertising. He suggested that companies should be open with their customers. He gave the example of a new breakfast cereal. The company ²_____ market research, ³_____ to what their customers wanted and decided to make a chocolate cereal. Their scientists then ⁴_____ the new cereal. It was delicious. Before they ⁵_____ the product, they ⁶_____ a meeting to discuss how to ⁷_____ the cereal. But at the meeting someone noticed a problem with the product. 'When you add milk, the milk turns brown.' The head of marketing realized that they could turn this into a positive if they were truthful. 'Let's ⁸_____ a campaign,' he said, 'with the slogan "So chocolatey, it turns the milk brown."' A lot of people read the article and several people ⁹_____ comments online about what other companies could say to be more truthful about their products. For example, 'I'm a PC. I can do the jobs you need to do, like ¹⁰_____ emails, but I break down a lot.'

DISCUSSION

6 Work in pairs. Think of two advertisements and describe them to each other. How open and honest are the advertisements?

1 an advertisement that promotes something that is good for us
2 an advertisement that promotes something that is fun (but probably not so good for us)

7 Think of two other products or services you know (e.g. a car, a bank). Write 'truthful' slogans for these, like the examples in the text in Exercise 5.

SPEAKING

8 Read the conversations about advertisements. Then complete the conversations using the prompts.

1 A: ¹ *you / know / anything / advertising on the Internet?*
   _____
   B: ² *It / depend / what you mean by advertising.*
   _____
   A: Well, I just want more people to find our website.
   B: Oh, I see. ³ *Well, / my experience / it / be / good idea* to get an expert to advise you on that.
   _____

2 A: ⁴ *What / you / think / the new Marks and Spencer advertisement?*
   _____
   B: ⁵ *I / not / tell you.* I haven't seen it.
   _____

3 A: ⁶ *you know / Lowe Alpine / make good winter jackets?*
   _____
   B: ⁷ *Yes, they / be / great.* I've got one myself. ⁸ *I / recommend / them.*
   _____
   _____

9 Work in pairs. Look at the small talk opening lines (1–4). Take turns to act out small talk conversations. Ask a follow-up question after each response.

1 Where are you from?
2 I like your jacket.
3 Is it your first time here?
4 I can't believe this hot weather we're having.

10 🎧 36 Listen to four small talk conversations (1–4). Compare the conversations you hear with the conversations you had in Exercise 9. Did you use the same follow-up questions and responses?

A: Where are you from?
B: I'm from Italy.
A: Whereabouts in Italy?
B: Milan. Do you know it?

WRITING

11 Read the online review of a pair of walking shoes. Then complete the review in your own words.

CUSTOMER REVIEWS
★ ★ ★ **Nice shoes**

I saw the advertisement for these shoes on the TV and went straight online to buy them. At $95 they are not cheap, but ¹_____. They are extremely comfortable and the best thing is that they are waterproof. Someone says in another comment that they got wet when he wore them in heavy rain. However, ²_____. The only thing I don't like about them is that they are quite heavy. Having said that, ³_____. Overall, I think these shoes are great and good value for money. Would recommend.

12 Work in pairs. Exchange reviews and compare your ideas. Did you use similar ideas to complete your reviews?

7 Experience

A girl flies a kite as the sun sets, Bnaider, Kuwait

TEDTALKS

FAITH JEGEDE is a writer, poet, word lover and a truth seeker. She blogs words and moments she finds inspiring, often for causes she believes in, like autism* awareness. Faith Jegede also works as a presenter and producer of a radio show. In this talk, Faith Jegede discusses her experience of growing up with two autistic brothers and how this has changed her view of what is 'normal'.

Faith Jegede's idea worth spreading is that just because someone is different and not 'normal', it doesn't mean they are wrong – being different can be a way of standing out and being extraordinary.

People with autism are less able to interact with the world than other people. They often find the following things difficult: verbal and non-verbal communication, social awareness, imaginative play.

BACKGROUND

1 You are going to watch a TED Talk by Faith Jegede called *What I've learned from my autistic brothers*. Read the text about the speaker and the talk. Then work in pairs and discuss the questions.

What do you imagine it feels like to be the brother or sister of someone with a disability? Which of the following things do you think children in this situation are likely to feel? Give reasons for your answers.

- embarrassed about their brother or sister?
- jealous of the attention that parents and others give their brother or sister?
- stressed from looking after their brother or sister?
- more sensitive and understanding of people who are different?
- something else?

KEY WORDS

2 Read the sentences (1–6). The words in bold are used in the TED Talk. First guess the meaning of the words. Then match the words with their definitions (a–f).

1 **Hyperactive** children find it difficult to sit still and concentrate.
2 My parents always taught me to be honest and never **tell a lie**.
3 She had a **tantrum** in the supermarket when her mother refused to buy her some sweets.
4 On the family holiday, he was **greedy** and asked for a third piece of cake.
5 No two people are the same. Each person is **unique**.
6 My brother was born with a bone disease that has no **cure**.

a say something that is not true
b wanting more than you need
c a solution to a disease or illness
d extremely active, always doing things
e the only one of its kind
f a fit of anger and frustration (often in young children)

AUTHENTIC LISTENING SKILLS Weak forms

Weak forms are words which are not stressed. They are grammatical or functional words which hold the content or information words together. The most common weak forms are prepositions (*to, of, from*); auxiliary verbs (*are, was*); conjunctions (*and, but*); and articles (*a, the*). Most of these weak forms are pronounced using the schwa sound /ə/.

3a 🎧 37 Look at the Authentic listening skills box. Then listen to the first two sentences from the TED Talk. Underline the weak forms.

1 Now, I'd like to introduce you to my brothers.
2 Remi is 22, tall and very handsome.

3b 🎧 38 Work in pairs. Underline the weak forms in the third and fourth sentences from the talk. Then listen and check.

3 He's speechless, but he communicates joy in a way that some of the best orators cannot.
4 He remembers the year of release for every song on my iPod.

3c 🎧 39 Listen to the four sentences again. Practise saying the sentences.

7.1 What I've learned from my autistic brothers

TEDTALKS

1 ▶ **7.1** Watch the TED Talk and answer the questions.

1 What's the opposite of *ordinary*? Who does Faith Jegede describe in this way?
2 What are some examples of the way her brothers act and behave?

2 ▶ **7.1** Watch the first part (0.00–1.52) of the talk again. Complete the notes about Faith Jegede's brothers.

	Remi	Samuel
Age	22	5 _____
Appearance	1 _____ , 2 _____	6 _____ , 7 _____
Qualities	Shows a lot of 3 _____ for others. Has never told a 4 _____	Has an incredible 8 _____

3 ▶ **7.1** Watch the second part (1.52–3.51) of the talk again. Choose the correct option to complete the sentences.

1 Faith Jegede says autism affects everyone in a *similar / different* way.
2 According to Faith Jegede, autism is becoming more and more *common / difficult to find*. There is no cure.
3 Faith Jegede was very *worried / excited* when Remi was born.
4 Remi spent much of his time in his own *world / bedroom*.
5 He often had tantrums and was hyperactive, but he also had a *pure and innocent / kind and gentle* nature.

▶ chocolate bar **BR ENG**
▶ candy bar **N AM ENG**

▶ washing machine **BR ENG**
▶ (clothes) washer **N AM ENG**

4 ▶ 7.1 Complete Faith Jegede's ideas (1–5) with these words. Then watch the third part (3.51 to the end) of the talk again and check your answers.

beauty   different   extraordinary
normal   progress   wrong

1 'Normality overlooks the _____ that differences give us.'
2 'The fact that we are different doesn't mean that one of us is _____. It just means that there's a _____ kind of right.'
3 'You don't have to be normal. You can be _____.'
4 'The chance for greatness, for _____ and for change dies the moment we try to be like someone else.'
5 'Please – don't tell me I'm _____.'

5 Work in pairs. Is it always a bad thing to try to be like someone else? Is there someone you try to be like? Discuss your answers.

VOCABULARY IN CONTEXT

6 ▶ 7.2 Watch the clips from the TED Talk. Choose the correct meaning of the words.

7 Complete the sentences in your own words. Then compare your sentences with a partner.

1 I recall very well the day that I …
2 I am not familiar with …
3 I find … a very challenging subject.
4 My greatest wish is to have a never-ending supply of …

CRITICAL THINKING A speaker's authority

8 It's important to know what a speaker's experience is when you are evaluating the strength of their argument. What experience does Faith Jegede have that gives her the authority to talk about people 'who don't fit into society's version of normal'?

a first-hand experience – as one of these people herself
b first-hand experience – as someone in close contact with one of these people
c second-hand experience – as someone who has heard about these people

9 Read this comment* about the TED Talk. How does the viewer's experience and outlook compare with Faith Jegede's?

Viewers' comments

C Caroline – I appreciate Faith's positive thinking. I have an autistic brother and it is not easy to live with him day to day and to stay positive. It takes a lot of patience and understanding. But when you see things from their point of view, you can enjoy their world.

*The comment was created for this activity.

10 Work in pairs. What is 'positive' about Faith's experience? Are there any parts of her experience that she describes in a negative way?

PRESENTATION SKILLS Being concise

11 Work in pairs. Look at the Presentation tips box. Why do you think being concise when you give a presentation is a good quality?

> **TIPS**
> TED Talks are a maximum of eighteen minutes and many are shorter. Speakers are able to convey a powerful idea in a short space of time. To do this they must be concise. Being concise means that you:
> - focus on the one big idea or message you want to share.
> - get to the point – be clear about what you want your audience to take away.
> - express ideas briefly and simply.
> - leave out unnecessary details and complicated jargon.
> - work out the right length for the talk.

12 ▶ 7.3 Watch the clips from the TED Talk. Which of the techniques did Faith Jegede follow?

13 Work in pairs.
Student A: Turn to page 171.
Student B: Turn to page 172.
Read the information. Make the information as concise as possible (three short sentences). Then present it to your partner.

▶ telly / tv BR ENG
▶ tv N AM ENG

7.2 What have you learned?

Statistics about THE UK

① ___% of people have **NEVER HAD A JOB**

② ___% of people working in London have **BEEN TO UNIVERSITY**

③ ___% of the population have **NEVER USED THE INTERNET**

④ ___% of Britons have **TRAVELLED ABROAD** at some time in their lives

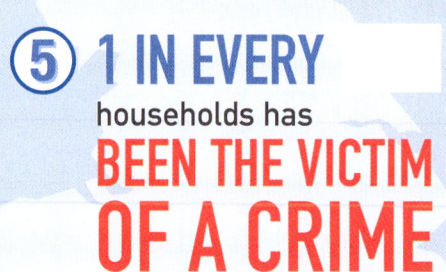

⑤ 1 IN EVERY ___ households has **BEEN THE VICTIM OF A CRIME**

⑥ ___% of people say the partner they have chosen is their **COMPLETE OPPOSITE**

GRAMMAR Present perfect simple

1 🎧 **40** Look at the infographic showing some interesting UK statistics. Guess the missing numbers. Then listen to a report about these statistics and check your answers.

2 Work in pairs. Answer the questions.

1 Did any of the statistics surprise you? Which ones?
2 Did you expect the figures to be higher or lower? Why?
3 Do you think the figures are similar in your country?

3 Read the sentences in the Grammar box. Choose the correct option (a–c) to answer the question.

PRESENT PERFECT SIMPLE

*Eighty per cent of Britons **have travelled** abroad at some time in their lives.*
*Some of the population **have never used** the Internet.*
*One in every six households **has been** the victim of a crime.*

Do the verbs in bold refer to:

a a specific time in the present?
b a specific time in the past?
c a time in the past that is not specified?

Check your answers on page 152 and do Exercises 1–2.

4 Complete the comments with the correct form of the present perfect. Then say which statistic in the infographic they refer to.

1 I _____ (never / like) going out much in the evenings. But my girlfriend doesn't like staying in.
2 My mum _____ (have) several jobs in her life, but she _____ (also / be) a full-time mother.
3 All of my colleagues _____ (study) journalism. But I haven't. I trained while I was working as a journalist.
4 My grandmother _____ (never / use) a computer, but my grandfather loves computers.
5 He _____ (be) abroad many times, but he _____ (never / live) abroad.
6 Burglars _____ (break) into their house three times before. One burglar broke in last week.

Pronunciation Weak forms: *have*, *has* and *been*

5a 🎧 41 Listen to the underlined weak forms in sentences 1 and 2.

1 Six per cent of people in the UK <u>have</u> never had a job.
2 One in every six households <u>has been</u> the victim of a crime.

5b 🎧 42 Look at sentences 3 and 4 and underline the weak forms in the verbs. Then listen and check your answers.

3 Eleven per cent of the population have never used the Internet.
4 Sixty per cent of people working in London have been to university.

5c 🎧 43 Listen to all four sentences again. Practise saying the sentences (1-4) with your partner.

GRAMMAR Present perfect simple and past simple

6 Read the sentences in the Grammar box. Answer the questions (1–2).

PRESENT PERFECT SIMPLE AND PAST SIMPLE

*Burglars **have broken** into their house three times before. One burglar **broke** in last week.*

1 Which verb in bold describes an event at a specific time in the past?
2 Which verb in bold describes an event at a time in the past that is not specified?

Check your answers on page 152 and do Exercises 3–6.

7 Choose the correct options to complete the conversations.

1 A: *Have you travelled / Did you travel* much for your work?
   B: Yes, I *have / did*.
   A: What was the most interesting place you *have visited / visited*?
   B: I *have really liked / really liked* Hong Kong. I *have gone / went* there again last year for a holiday.

2 A: How many jobs *have you had / did you have* in your life?
   B: Oh, probably four or five.
   A: What *has been / was* your first job?
   B: When I *have been / was* sixteen, I *have worked / worked* part-time in a greengrocer's selling fruit and vegetables.

3 A: *Have you ever won / Did you ever win* a competition?
   B: No, I *haven't / didn't*. But I *have come / came* second in a story competition when I was at school.
   A: *Has the school published / Did the school publish* your story?
   B: Yes, they *have put / put* it in the school magazine.

4 A: *Have you ever been / Were you ever* the victim of cyber-crime?
   B: Yes. A couple of years ago, someone *has hacked / hacked* my email account.
   A: *Have they stolen / Did they steal* money from you?
   B: No, they *haven't / didn't*. But I *have had / had* to change all my passwords.

8 Work in pairs. Talk about your own experiences. Use the four opening questions from Exercise 7.

SPEAKING Life experiences

9 21st CENTURY OUTCOMES

Work in pairs. Look at the list of life experiences. Ask and answer questions about your own life experiences. Make notes if you need to.

Life experiences

- learn any useful skills
- experience a different culture or lifestyle
- be a fan / supporter of something
- speak to a large group of people
- be in a dangerous situation
- fail to get something you really wanted
- do a job you didn't like
- succeed with a physical challenge

A: What useful skills have you learned in your life?
B: I learned to drive when I was eighteen.

10 Discuss which of the experiences you discussed in Exercise 9 have helped you most in your life. Why?

7.3 Encouraging diversity

READING France's new CV law

1 Look at the list of items (a–l). In your country, which of these items is it necessary to include on a CV? What does a CV not tell you about a person?

a Name
b Age / Date of birth
c Address
d Email address
e Marital status
f Nationality
g Ethnic origin
h Sex
i Work experience
j Education
k Other skills
l Hobbies / Interests

2 *Anonymous* means 'not named or identified'. For example an anonymous letter is one where the writer is not known. What is the point of an 'anonymous CV'? Discuss with a partner. Then read the article and check your answer.

3 Read the article again. Are the sentences true (T) or false (F)?

1 Companies in France are not using the new law yet.
2 The purpose of the law is to increase the number of young people in the workplace.
3 A lot of companies think that the law will not work.
4 In France you can always tell someone's sex from their job title.
5 Interviews can also be anonymous.
6 There is a little more diversity in French companies than there was eight years ago.
7 Some companies require a certain percentage of employees to be women.
8 The writer is certain that the law will fail.

4 Look at the definitions (1–4). Find words in the first two paragraphs that match the definitions.

1 someone who applies for a job: an _____
2 someone who is employed to do a job: an _____
3 a person or organization that employs people: an _____
4 all the people employed by a company: the _____

5 Complete the sentences with words from the article. The first letter is given for you. You may have to change the form of the word.

1 I like your idea of having more young people in our team, but I don't think it will be easy to i _____ . (para 1)
2 If you favour young people, you will d _____ against older people. (para 2)
3 Can you t _____ how old she is? She's older than you imagine. (para 3)
4 Employers often get f _____ with new laws because it's usually expensive to implement them. (para 4)
5 We all want to see d _____ in the workforce because it makes work more interesting. (para 5)

6 Work in small groups. Can you think of solutions to the problems of anonymous CVs that the employers in the article mentioned?

- knowing the person's age from the dates on their CV
- the interview
- not being able to discriminate positively

VOCABULARY Personal qualities

7 Look at these words for talking about personal qualities. Which words describe you: very well (✓✓), well (✓) or not very well (✗)?

ambitious	caring	easy-going	enthusiastic
hard-working	independent	organized	reliable
sociable	a team-player		

8 Work in pairs. Which qualities in Exercise 7 would you not include in a CV? Give reasons.

SPEAKING Diversity at work

9 **21st CENTURY OUTCOMES**

Imagine you work at a science and engineering college. Currently only seven per cent of the students are female and you want to encourage more women to apply for engineering courses. Work in small groups. Look at the ideas and think of other ideas if you can.

- use role models of successful women already working in engineering
- encourage schools to get girls interested in engineering at a younger age
- set a quota of thirty per cent women on all engineering courses
- encourage companies to offer special benefits to women applying for engineering jobs

10 Discuss the ideas from Exercise 9. Say what the advantages and disadvantages of each idea are.

France's new CV law

A French court has said that the government must implement a law which was passed eight years ago that requires job applicants to write anonymous CVs. The Council of State says that the government has had a 'reasonable' period of time and that companies with more than fifty employees now have six months to implement the new rules.

The purpose of the law is to stop employers discriminating against candidates on the basis of their age, sex or ethnic origin. In principle, an employer will no longer be able to see from someone's CV if that person is old or young, male or female, or black or white. This should, in theory, increase diversity among the workforce.

The reason that the law has taken so long to implement is that many companies think it is not practical. According to Jessica Ip, an employment expert, it is too easy to tell these differences from other details on a CV. You can guess someone's age from the date of a person's university degree or from the number of years work experience they have. In the case of a French CV, it is easy to see someone's sex, since job titles often have a masculine and a feminine form, like 'assistant' for a man and 'assistante' for a woman. Someone's ethnic origin is often obvious from the languages they speak.

Then there is the interview. 'Even though you get an idea of the candidate from their skills and experience, the employer still has to meet them before offering the job,' says Ip. Others agree. 'What will the next law be?' said one frustrated French employer, Gerard Lemoine. 'That applicants have to come to the interview with a bag on their heads?'

In the years since the law was passed, French companies have taken steps to encourage more diversity in the workplace (although some people argue that progress has been slow). Some have used positive discrimination, setting quotas for the number of women or people from different ethnic backgrounds. This progress, employers believe, could now be in danger. 'How can you discriminate positively, if you are not allowed to know if you are employing a man or a woman, for example?' says Lemoine. It seems that the law will not, perhaps, have the results that its supporters hoped for.

---

discriminate against (v) treat someone differently because they are different in some way
diversity (n) having a range of different people or things
frustrated (adj) angry because you cannot do what you want
implement (v) to make something (e.g. a law) start or happen
quota (n) a fixed percentage or amount

21st CENTURY OUTCOMES CREATIVE THINKING Being open to diversity and responding to different ideas

7.4 I love a challenge

LISTENING A job interview

1 Work in pairs. Write four questions that you would expect to be asked at a job interview. Then work with another pair and compare your questions. What is the most difficult question to answer? Give reasons.

2 Look at the description of the organization, RSQ. What jobs do people in the company do?

> RSQ is a UK-based organization which helps to protect endangered animals all over the world. We work with governments and other charity organizations to save species which are in danger. We organize media campaigns from the UK and also send workers into the field to help with animal protection work. The money for this work is raised by RSQ volunteers and employees in the UK.

3 🎧 **44** Harry is a recent economics graduate. He is interested in working for RSQ as a field worker. Listen to his interview with the company's founder. What are his answers to these questions?

1 What attracted you to this job?
2 What are your long-term ambitions?
3 What can you do, practically?
4 What other experience do you have that's relevant to this position?

4 🎧 **44** Work in pairs. Complete the sentences from the interview. Then listen again and check your answers.

1 I'm very interested _____ in the field, in countries where animals are in danger.
2 I'm keen _____ something practical and more useful, I guess.
3 I'd like _____ the environment.
4 I've travelled a lot and I'm very willing _____ .
5 I'm good _____ people.
6 I really love _____ challenge and I'm not afraid _____ risks.

5 Do you think Harry will get the job he wants? Why? / Why not?

Pronunciation Linking words

6 🎧 **45** Listen to the sentences and connect the sounds that are linked. Then work in pairs and practise saying the sentences.

1 I'm interested in learning new skills.
   I'm‿interested‿in learning new skills.
2 I'm keen on working abroad.
3 I'm good at working with my hands.
4 I love a difficult challenge.
5 I'm not afraid of working hard.

SPEAKING Describing skills and interests

7 Work in pairs. Look at the jobs (a–c) which are available at RSQ. Decide which job you want to apply for. Think about how your own experience will help.

a a field worker helping to protect animals in danger
b a media campaigner helping to write literature and prepare campaigns
c a fundraiser for RSQ

Take turns to play the roles of job interviewer and interviewee. Act out the interview. Use the expressions in the Useful language box to help you. Would you give your partner the job?

DESCRIBING SKILLS AND INTERESTS

I'm interested in working …
I'm keen on developing my skills.
I'd like to work in the voluntary sector.
I love a challenge.
I'm willing to work hard.
I'm not afraid of working hard.
I'm good at persuading people.

WRITING A CV

8 Read the sentences about CVs. Are they true (T) or false (F)?

1 Use as many pages as you need, but lay them out clearly.
2 Include this basic information: education and qualifications; work history / experience; skills relevant to the job; interests / achievements.
3 Change the CV to fit each new job you apply for.
4 Emphasize both your individual talents and your interests.
5 Describe your experience in neutral not positive language.

9 Look at this extract from a CV. Which of the points in Exercise 8 can you identify?

Jessica Redfern
22 Addison Drive, Abingdon
01235 657000   j2redfern@gme.com

Personal profile and key skills

A hard-working and caring individual, keen to use my knowledge to help society. My key skills are an understanding of economic issues and a willingness to learn. Recent achievements include creating a successful fundraising campaign.

Employment History

Fundraiser, RSQ *(August 2015–Present)*
Responsibilities:
- Maintaining a database of donors and keeping in regular contact with them
- Thinking of new fundraising ideas and running fundraising campaigns

Achievements:
- Increased the number of donors by 6%
- Increased donations by 10% in twelve months

Education

University of London *(September 2011–June 2015)*
BA in Economics (specialized in Labour Economics and Economic Geography)

Hobbies & Interests

Reading, Mountain biking, Acting (played the lead role in Shakespeare's *Romeo and Juliet*)

Writing skill Verb forms

10 Look at the headings (a–e). Which verb forms (1–3) are used in these sections of the CV?

a Personal profile and key skills
b Responsibilities
c Achievements
d Education
e Hobbies and interests

1 past tense
2 *-ing* form
3 present tense or no verb

11 Rewrite these sections so that they are in the same style as the CV above.

Personal profile

I am an organized and hard-working IT engineer. The key skills I have are a knowledge of Microsoft products and of security software.

Responsibilities

I had to visit clients and install new software. I also helped them to solve their IT problems.

Achievements

I achieved a customer satisfaction rating of 96% and I won a prize for best customer service.

12 **21st CENTURY OUTCOMES**

Imagine you are applying for a job as a field worker at RSQ. Write your own CV. Use the CV in Exercise 9 as a model.

13 Work in pairs. Exchange CVs. Check that your partner has:

- used the correct verb forms in each section
- described their experience using positive language
- adapted the CV to this particular job
- written a persuasive CV

8 Seeing the future

BACKGROUND

1 You are going to watch a TED Talk by Sanjay Dastoor called *A skateboard, with a boost*. Read the text about the speaker and the talk. Then work in pairs and discuss the questions.

1 What quick and eco-friendly forms of transport can you think of?
2 How do you get to work or college?
3 Do you enjoy your daily commute to work or your place of study? Why? / Why not?

TEDTALKS

SANJAY DASTOOR is the co-founder of Boosted Boards, a company based in San José, California, which aims to make the world's lightest electric vehicles.

Sanjay Dastoor's idea worth spreading is that with a bit of creativity, you can turn an everyday object like a skateboard into a quick and eco-friendly way to get around the city. In this talk he presents his amazing electric skateboard that he hopes will change how we commute to work.

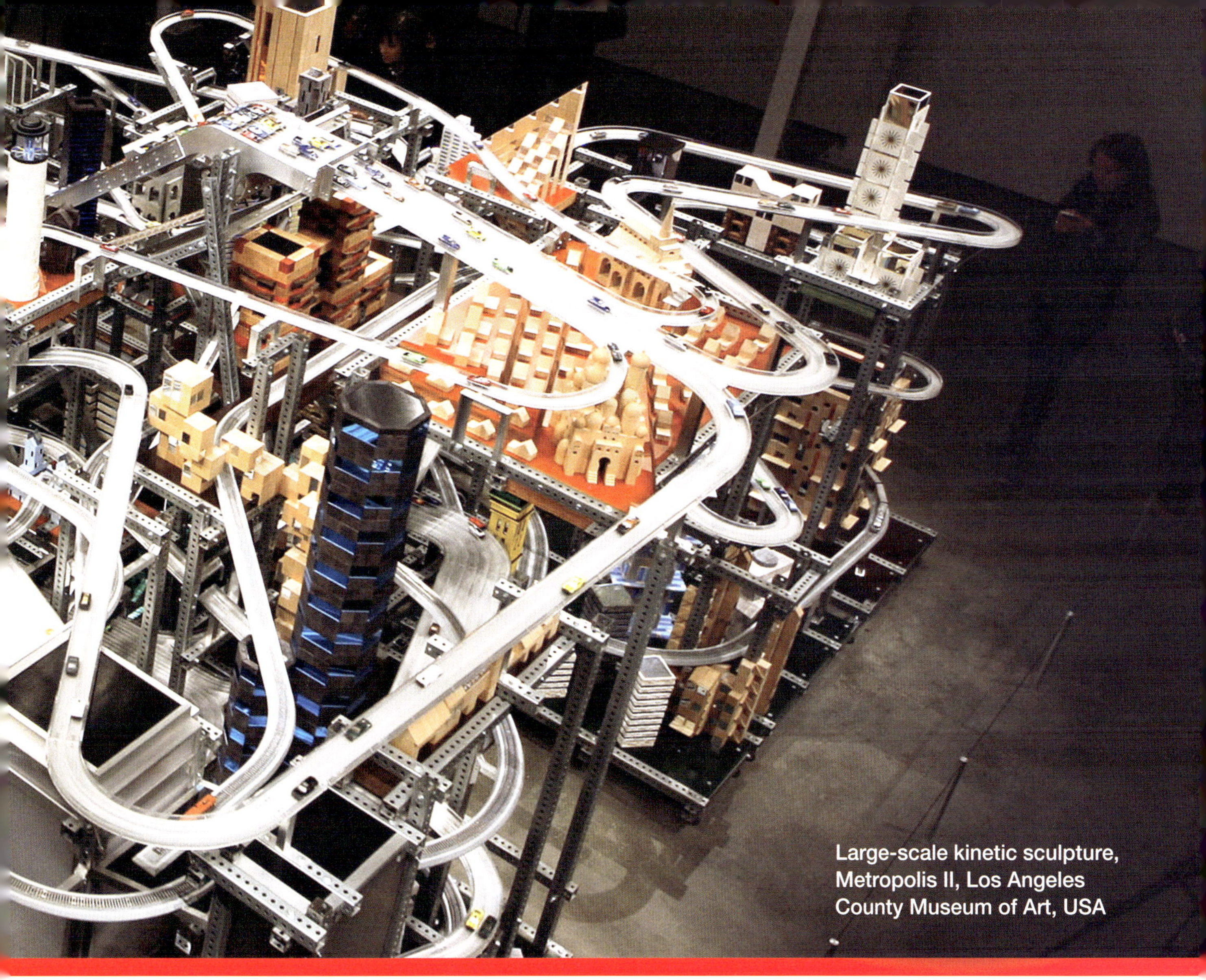

Large-scale kinetic sculpture, Metropolis II, Los Angeles County Museum of Art, USA

KEY WORDS

2 Read the description of a remote controlled car. The words in bold (1–8) are used in the TED Talk. First guess the meaning of the words. Then match the words with their definitions (a–h).

This children's toy car weighs 1 kg (which makes it very ¹ **portable**) and has a ² **range** of 200 m. You can use the ³ **remote control** to make the car ⁴ **accelerate** (up to 20 kph) or ⁵ **brake**, and go forwards or ⁶ **reverse**. It runs on batteries which you can ⁷ **charge** with ⁸ **sustainable** solar energy.

a go faster
b go more slowly or stop
c fill with electricity
d possible to carry
e the distance something can travel
f go backwards
g not using up natural resources
h device for operating something (e.g. a TV) from a distance

AUTHENTIC LISTENING SKILLS Prediction

Often you will have an idea of what a speaker is going to talk about. You can use this knowledge to help you predict what the speaker will say. But you must be careful. Don't stop listening because you think you know what the speaker is going to say. Make your predictions and then listen carefully to see if these predictions are correct. Always listen for the content words (nouns and verbs that are stressed) that give you the key information.

3a 🎧 **46** Look at the Authentic listening skills box. Discuss what you think Sanjay Dastoor is going to talk about. Then listen to the first sentence from the TED Talk and complete the first part of the sentence with the content words.

'Today I'm going to ¹ _____ you an ² _____ ³ _____ that weighs ⁴ _____ than a ⁵ _____ …'

3b 🎧 **47** Work in pairs. Predict what type of things Sanjay Dastoor might say next about the vehicle. Then listen and compare your answers with what he actually says. Listen carefully for the content words.

85

8.1 A skateboard, with a boost

TEDTALKS

1. ▶ 8.1 Watch the TED Talk. Discuss with a partner how this electric skateboard works (in simple terms) and what its main benefit is.

2. ▶ 8.1 Watch the first part (0.00–1.16) of the talk again. Complete the facts about the electric skateboard.

   1. Weight: _____ a bicycle
   2. Charge time: _____ minutes
   3. Cost per 1,000 kms: _____ dollar(s)
   4. Top speed: _____ kilometres per hour
   5. Battery range: _____ kilometres
   6. Number of US car trips possible with board: _____ of all trips

3. Work in pairs. What does Sanjay Dastoor say most people think of when they hear the word 'vehicle'?

4. ▶ 8.1 Watch the second part (1.16–1.44) of the talk again. What does Sanjay Dastoor emphasize about the following things:

   1. where the components in the skateboard come from
   2. the experience of using the skateboard

5. ▶ 8.1 Watch the third part (1.44–2.51) of the talk again. What images accompany each of the four subtitles? Discuss with your partner what you saw and what each subtitle means.

   1. 6 Mile Range
   2. Top Speed Near 20 mph
   3. Uphill Climbing
   4. Regenerative Braking

▶ wall outlet **N AM ENG**
▶ wall socket **BR ENG**

▶ a store **N AM ENG**
▶ a shop **BR ENG**

6 ▶ **8.1** Watch the fourth part (2.51 to the end) of the talk again. Complete the sentences with these words.

carry   cheap   footprint   remote control   twenty   new

1 It's very easy to control acceleration and braking with the _____.
2 The board is very easy to _____.
3 The boards use _____ times less energy than a car.
4 The boards are really _____ to build.
5 As a transport solution, it reduces your energy _____.
6 It's important that all of us think in _____ ways, when we think about vehicles.

VOCABULARY IN CONTEXT

7 ▶ **8.2** Watch the clips from the TED Talk. Choose the correct meaning of the words.

8 Work in pairs. Think of examples for these ideas.

1 the best way to get around your city
2 a novel way to get to work
3 a machine with many different components

CRITICAL THINKING Evaluating claims

9 When you hear or read a particular argument, think about the claims that the speaker makes to support this argument. Work in pairs. List all the advantages of Sanjay Dastoor's electric skateboard (compared to other forms of transport). Then think of any possible disadvantages.

10 Read these comments* about the TED Talk and compare them with your ideas from Exercise 9. Do you think these are good comments?

Viewers' comments

D **Dirk** – I just can't see this as anything more than a fun toy. He makes a lot of comparisons to cars, but I don't think car drivers are going to choose between this and their car for commuting. They might buy one to have fun at the weekend.

P **Polly** – Running and cycling use less than a dollar of electricity too and they're much better for you.

Z **Zac** – I like this idea and it's probably great in sunny California. But what happens when it's raining? Also, how comfortable is it over six kilometres? I don't have good knees!

* The comments were created for this activity.

11 What, in summary, are the most important arguments for and against the electric skateboard? Discuss.

PRESENTATION SKILLS Signposting

12 What are road signposts for? What do you think signposts are in a talk or presentation? Discuss with a partner.

13 Look at the Presentation tips box and compare them with your answers. Who are the signposts useful for?

> **TIPS**
>
> 'Signposting' means giving your audience directions about what you are going to say. You can do this 1) at the beginning of a presentation; 2) when you move on to a new part of the presentation; 3) when you go back to an earlier point; or 4) when you want to signal the conclusion of your talk. Examples of signposting language include:
>
> **Starting**
> Today I'd like to talk about …
> Today we're going to look at …
>
> **Moving on**
> So now I'm going to show you …
> So now let's look at / let's move on to …
>
> **Going back**
> Let's go back to the example of …
> Remember what we said about …
>
> **Concluding**
> So, I'd like to finish by reminding you …
> So, to sum up / in conclusion, …

14 ▶ **8.3** Watch the clips from the TED Talk. What signposting phrases does Sanjay Dastoor use at these stages?

1 Starting   3 The demonstration
2 Moving on   4 Concluding

15 Work in pairs. You are going to give a short presentation about the best form of transport in your country or area (trains, cars, buses, etc.). Discuss your ideas. Then prepare the opening paragraph and plan/structure of your presentation. Use signposting language to describe what your presentation is going to focus on.

16 Work with a new partner. Introduce your presentation. Did your partner use signposting language effectively? Did you have similar ideas?

▶ has gotten **N AM ENG**
▶ has got **BR ENG**

▶ kilometer **N AM ENG**
▶ kilometre **BR ENG**

8.2 The future of transport

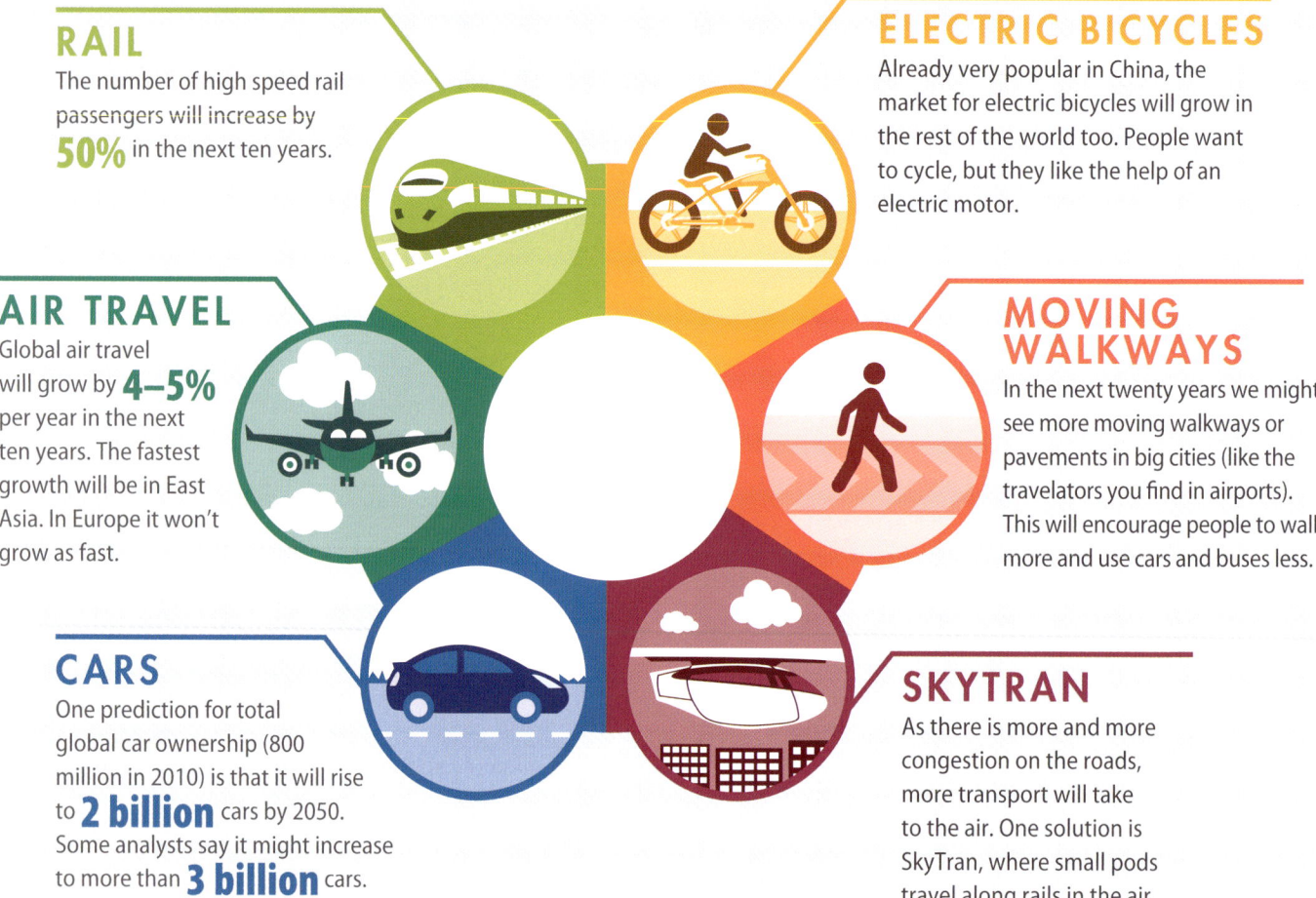

THE FUTURE OF TRANSPORT

RAIL
The number of high speed rail passengers will increase by **50%** in the next ten years.

ELECTRIC BICYCLES
Already very popular in China, the market for electric bicycles will grow in the rest of the world too. People want to cycle, but they like the help of an electric motor.

AIR TRAVEL
Global air travel will grow by **4–5%** per year in the next ten years. The fastest growth will be in East Asia. In Europe it won't grow as fast.

MOVING WALKWAYS
In the next twenty years we might see more moving walkways or pavements in big cities (like the travelators you find in airports). This will encourage people to walk more and use cars and buses less.

CARS
One prediction for total global car ownership (800 million in 2010) is that it will rise to **2 billion** cars by 2050. Some analysts say it might increase to more than **3 billion** cars.

SKYTRAN
As there is more and more congestion on the roads, more transport will take to the air. One solution is SkyTran, where small pods travel along rails in the air.

GRAMMAR Predictions with *will* and *might*

1 What are the main problems with modern transport systems – cars, buses, trains, underground trains, bicycles, air travel? Tick (✓) the items below. Then compare and discuss your answers with a partner.

- a traffic congestion
- b delays
- c high cost
- d lack of comfort
- e poor connections
- f safety

2 Work in pairs. Do you think the problems in Exercise 1 will get better or worse in the future?

3 Look at the infographic and answer the questions.
1 Which standard form of transport will grow the most?
2 What kind of trains will we see more of?
3 Where can you find moving walkways now?
4 What problem does SkyTran solve?

4 Read the sentences in the Grammar box. Answer the questions (1–3).

PREDICTIONS WITH *WILL* AND *MIGHT*

*Total global car ownership **will rise** to two billion cars by 2050. Some analysts say it **might increase** to more than three billion cars.*
*In Europe air travel **won't grow** as fast.*

1 What time is referred to in each sentence: the present or the future?
2 Which verb form gives a less certain prediction: *will* or *might*?
3 What is the contracted form of *will not*?

Check your answers on page 154 and do Exercises 1–2.

5 Work in pairs. Find one more example of *will* and *might* in the infographic. Which prediction is less sure?

6 Complete the predictions using *will* and *might*. Sometimes both forms are possible.

1 There _____ (certainly / be) an increase in the number of electric vehicles in the next ten years.
2 As people buy more cars, there _____ (be) more congestion on the roads.
3 Environmentalists hope that people _____ (use) their cars less in future.
4 It's not certain, but the development of high speed rail _____ (encourage) passengers to use the train instead of flying or driving.
5 Air travel _____ (grow) faster in developing countries than in developed countries.
6 SkyTran is still a new technology. We _____ (not / see) it in cities in the near future.
7 Having electric bicycles _____ (mean) that many more old people start riding bicycles.
8 Moving walkways _____ (not / be) cheap to install.

Pronunciation *want* /wɒnt/ and *won't* /wəʊnt/

7 🎧 **48** Listen to the sentences. Underline the form you hear.

1 I won't help. / <u>I want to help</u>.
2 <u>They won't wait</u>. / They want to wait.
3 They won't go / They want to go by car.
4 I won't know / I want to know the answer before Tuesday.
5 I won't tell / I want to tell him.
6 They won't leave / They want to leave here before eleven o'clock.
7 She won't come. / She wants to come.
8 They won't do / They want to do business with us.

8 Work in small groups. What other ideas might be the future of transport? Discuss. Use *will*, *won't* and *might*.

GRAMMAR Decisions with *going to*

9 🎧 **49** Listen to a city councillor talking about her ideas for solving the city's traffic problems. Complete the names of the different plans she mentions.

1 a City _____ scheme
2 Park and _____ car parks
3 smart _____ meters

10 🎧 **49** Listen to the city councillor again. Complete the descriptions of how the ideas will work. Then discuss what you think of these ideas with a partner.

1 People will be able to _____ at different locations.
2 People will be able to park their cars and then _____ .
3 People will be able to pay for parking _____ , but it will be _____ .

11 Read the sentences in the Grammar box. Answer the questions (1–2).

DECISIONS WITH *GOING TO*

How **are you going to do** that?
We**'re going to introduce** a City Bicycle scheme.
We**'re going to create** special Park and Ride car parks around the city.
We**'re going to make** parking in the city easier, but much more expensive.

1 Are the sentences referring to present or future actions?
2 Is the speaker making the decision now (at the moment of speaking) or have they already decided?

Check your answers on page 154 and do Exercise 3.

12 Complete the texts with the correct form of *will* (for predictions) or *going to* (for decisions).

Text 1

We were chatting at work the other day about driving to work. Out of seventeen people, twelve of us drive alone to work! So this is what we decided. We ¹_____ (have) a car share scheme. So firstly, people who live near each other ²_____ (take) turns to drive to work. In addition, we ³_____ (also / ask) people in the office without cars if they would like a lift. If so, they can pay something for the petrol. It's a great idea. It ⁴_____ (save) money and it ⁵_____ (be) good for the environment.

Text 2

I've decided that I ⁶_____ (start) cycling more. I think it ⁷_____ (help) me to get fit and it ⁸_____ (probably / save) me time. I spend about thirty minutes in traffic every morning in the car. But I ⁹_____ (get) a new bicycle first. My bike is really old.

SPEAKING Transport options

13 **21st CENTURY OUTCOMES**

You would like to show the different transport options in your city or a city you know well. Work in pairs. Work out a route from one side of the city to the other using at least four different kinds of transport. Consider the time, cost and environmental impact.

So, we can begin by walking to the station at Shepherd's Bush. From there can we take the underground train to ...

14 Work with a new partner and describe your plans. Explain your route. Then discuss the good and bad things about transport in this city.

We're going to begin by walking to the station at Shepherd's Bush. Then we're going to ...

21st CENTURY OUTCOMES   SYSTEMS THINKING Analysing complex systems

Unit 8 Seeing the future

8.3 This might be the answer

READING Our pick – new gadgets

1 Work in pairs. Discuss the questions
  1 Do you like gadgets and new technology? Why? / Why not?
  2 What is your favourite and most useful tool or gadget?
  3 Can you think of an everyday task that there isn't a gadget for?

2 Read the article recommending three new gadgets. Complete the table according to what *you* think of each one. Then compare your answers with a partner.

	Fun	Useful	Good value
1 Netatmo Bracelet			
2 Goji Smart lock			
3 Panono Camera			

3 Read the article again. Then read the sentences (1–8). Write **N** (Netatmo Bracelet), **G** (Goji Smart Lock) or **P** (Panono Camera) if the sentence is true for that gadget. Sometimes more than one answer is possible.

  1 You use this device with your smartphone.
  2 You can carry this device around with you.
  3 This device has a camera in it.
  4 This device uses batteries.
  5 This device is attractive to look at.
  6 The article claims this device is not the same as similar devices you can buy.
  7 This device is easy to install according to the makers.
  8 The article doesn't say what material this device is made of.

4 Find these words in the article. Then choose the word with the same meaning (a–b).

  1 **monitoring** (line 2)
    a checking   b improving
  2 **specifically** (line 3)
    a particularly b only
  3 **a tap** (line 11)
    a a light hit   b a hard push
  4 **claim** (line 16)
    a say   b hope
  5 **shaped like** (line 20)
    a in the form of b feeling like
  6 **detects** (line 24)
    a gives a signal b notices

5 Work in small groups. Discuss the questions.
  1 Which of these gadgets do you think is the most useful? And the least? Why?
  2 Which of the gadgets do you think will be the most successful?

VOCABULARY Describing devices

6 Look at the article again. Complete the phrases about the devices. Use verbs from the text.

  1 The function: **It** _allows_ **you to** open your front door.
  2 The material: **It's** _____ **of** strong plastic.
  3 The weight: **It** _____ 300 grams.
  4 The size: **It** _____ 11 centimetres in diameter.
  5 The price: **It** _____ $99.
  6 The energy source: **It** _____ **on** four AA batteries.
  7 The capacity: **It can** _____ any number of digital keys.
  8 The advantage: **It doesn't** _____ any batteries.
  9 The appearance: **It** _____ great.
  10 The different options: **It** _____ in three colours.

7 Look at the ways of describing size. Complete the sentences with these words.

across   deep   high   length   width

  1 The camera measures 11 centimetres **in diameter**.
    = It is 11 centimetres _across_.
  2 The garden measures 20 metres in _____.
    = It is 20 metres **long**.
  3 The building measures 104 metres **in height**.
    = It is 104 metres _____.
  4 The room measures 4.5 metres in _____.
    = It is 4.5 metres **wide**.
  5 The swimming pool measures 3 metres **in depth**.
    = It is 3 metres _____.

8 Work in pairs. Look at the photos (A–B).

Student A: Turn to page 171.

Student B: Turn to page 172.

Read the information. Then present the gadget and its benefits.

90

SPEAKING Can I live without it?

9 **21st CENTURY OUTCOMES**

Work in groups. Look at the machines and gadgets (1–8) in the home. You are allowed to keep only four of them. Discuss the advantages of each machine and what they allow you to do. Then vote on the four to keep.

10 Work with another group. Compare your answers. Did you choose to keep the same items?

1 microwave oven   2 telephone (landline)   3 dishwasher   4 vacuum cleaner   5 wi-fi router   6 radio / music player   7 games console   8 kettle

OUR PICK – NEW GADGETS

Looking for an unusual gift? Or just someone who loves gadgets? Here are three novel pieces of technology that you might like.

NETATMO'S JUNE BRACELET There are quite a few bracelets on the market for monitoring your health or level of activity. The Netatmo's June bracelet is different because it is designed specifically for people who are worried about getting too much sun. The gemstone bracelet costs $99 USD and comes in three colours – gold, silver or gunmetal. The bracelet measures the strength of the sun and then sends the information to an app on your phone, telling you if you need to wear a hat, sunglasses or to put on some sun cream. It doesn't need any batteries, it looks great and it could also save your skin from sunburn.

GOJI SMART LOCK The Goji Smart Lock allows you to open your front door with a simple tap on your phone screen. But it does more than that. Using an in-built camera, it can take pictures of people at your door and send a photo message to your phone. So if your child has forgotten their key, you can see that they're there and send a digital key to their phone. (It can store any number of digital keys.) It runs on four AA batteries and (the manufacturers claim) is very simple to fit to your front door. Another advantage is that the Goji Smart Lock sends you a text message when all the doors are safely locked. It costs $278 US.

PANONO PANORAMIC CAMERA Did you think all cameras were more or less the same? Think again. The Panono is a camera shaped like a football and has 36 image sensors on it. It weighs 300 grams and measures 11 centimetres in diameter. When you hold it, you want to throw it up in the air. And that's exactly what you are supposed to do. An accelerometer detects when the Panono has stopped going up and at that point the camera uses all 36 sensors to take a single 360 degree photo, which you can view on your phone or computer with a special app. Like most cameras, it has a rechargeable battery. It's made of strong plastic, so it won't break easily. But don't throw it too hard! Price approx. $500

21st CENTURY OUTCOMES **COLLABORATION** Reaching agreement in a team

8.4 Speak after the tone

LISTENING Phrases in telephoning

1 Read the recorded message on someone's voicemail. Complete the sentences with these words.

available   call   message   tone   voicemail

This is the ¹_____ of John Waterfield. I'm sorry I'm not ²_____ to take your ³_____. Please leave a ⁴_____. Speak after the ⁵_____.

2 What information do you need to give when you leave a voicemail message?

3 🎧 50 Listen to four messages on John's voicemail. You will hear each message twice. Complete the table.

	Work (W) or personal (P)	Name of caller	Subject (1–3 words)	Next step
1				
2				
3				
4				

4 Work in pairs. Compare your answers in Exercise 3. Who do you think the third call is from?

5 🎧 50 Answer the questions about the language the callers used. Then listen again and check your answers.

1 How do you say who you are when you leave a message?
2 How do you say why you are calling?
3 How do you ask a person to return your call?
4 How do you say it's not necessary to return a call?
5 How do you apologize for troubling someone when they are busy?
6 How do you say that you will keep the person updated?
7 How do you apologize for not answering a call?

Pronunciation Contraction '*ll*

6a 🎧 51 Listen to the two sentences. Notice the pronunciation of '*ll*. Repeat the sentences.

1 I'll let you know what happens.
2 I'll send you all the information in an email.

6b Work in pairs. Practise saying these sentences.

1 Sorry, I can't speak now. I'll call you back.
2 One moment. I'll see if she's here.
3 I'll try to call you again later.
4 I'll wait to hear from you.

SPEAKING Leaving messages

7 Work in pairs. Put your chairs back to back. Take turns to receive and leave messages on someone's voicemail. Use the expressions in the Useful language box to help you.

Student A: Turn to page 171.

Student B: Turn to page 172.

When you receive the message, note down the details.

LEAVING MESSAGES

Hello. This is … / It's … here. / It's … from …
I'm (just) calling about …
Sorry to bother you.
Sorry I missed your call.
Please call me back. / Can you call me back?
No need to call back.
I'll try to call you again later.
I'll be in the office this afternoon.
I'll send you an email.
I'll let you know what happens.

See page 154 for more information about the use of will *for spontaneous offers, and do Exercises 4–5.*

WRITING Short emails

8 Read the emails (A–D). Then match the emails with the responses (1–4).

A

Hi Francis

I spoke to Bill and he said that next Thursday was no good for him. He has a dentist appointment that afternoon. Can you suggest another day?

Pete

B

Dear Tara

Sorry to trouble you. Do you remember – I asked if you could look at my report. I'd really appreciate your opinion.

Best wishes

Paul

C

Hello

I ordered this chair from you last Monday. Your website said that it would take two working days, but it hasn't arrived. Can you let me know what's happening?

Yours sincerely

Zak Lehman

D

Dear Ms Decker

I came for an interview last week, but I haven't heard anything from you. I told you that I had had another job offer and that I needed to give the other company an answer. Can you tell me if you are still considering me for this position?

Yours sincerely

Hannah Brown

1 I am sorry to hear about this delay. <u>I'll look into it</u> and respond within the next 24 hours.
2 Thank you for your email. Owing to the large number of applications, the interview process has taken longer than expected. <u>We'll let you know</u> in the next two days.
3 OK. I'll check my diary and <u>I'll get back to you</u> later today.
4 Sorry, I've been really busy. <u>I'll have a look</u> at the report today and send you my comments.

9 Look at the four underlined phrases which promise action in the responses (1–4) in Exercise 8. Match each phrase with the correct meaning (a–d).

a contact you again
b investigate something
c look at something
d tell you

Writing skill Reported speech

10a Look at the reported statements from the emails. Rewrite the statements using direct speech.

1 He said that next Thursday was no good for him.
   'Thursday is no good for me.'
2 I asked if you could look at my report.
3 Your website said that it would take two working days.
4 I told you that I had had another job offer.
5 I told you that I needed to give the other company an answer.

See page 154 for more information about reported speech, and do Exercise 6.

10b Rewrite the sentences using reported speech.

1 'Friday is the best day for me.'
   She said that Friday _____.
2 'They have postponed the meeting.'
   She said that they _____.
3 'Can you let me know by the end of the week?'
   I asked if you _____.
4 'I will pick you up from the airport.'
   He told me that he _____.
5 'We do not accept returns.'
   In your email you said that you _____.
6 'I will read it when I have a moment.'
   You kindly said that you _____.
7 'Are you happy with the changes?'
   You asked if I _____.
8 'I left the parcel at reception.'
   You told me that you _____.

11 Look at the full reply to email B in Exercise 8. Find and underline these elements in the email.

1 the subject   2 the explanation   3 the next steps

Dear Paul

I'm sorry for not getting back to you about your report. I know I said that I would look at it as soon as I could, but I've been really busy. I'll have a look later today and send you my comments.

Best wishes

Tara

12 `21st` **CENTURY OUTCOMES**

Write a reply to email C above. Apologize and explain that the chair is from a new supplier who promised delivery in 3–5 days. Include the elements (1–3) listed in Exercise 11.

13 Exchange emails with your partner. Check that your partner's email:

- introduces the subject
- explains the problem
- tells you what action they are going to take
- uses reported speech correctly

`21st` **CENTURY OUTCOMES** LIFE AND CAREER SKILLS Using email to communicate a message effectively

Review 4 | UNITS 7 AND 8

LISTENING

1 Look at the photo. Then read the article about One World Play Project. Answer the questions.

1 What message does One World Play Project want to send the world?
2 How is it supporting this message practically?

ONE WORLD PLAY PROJECT

It started with a ball and the idea that everyone likes to play. Now One World Play Project is an established company that donates footballs and cricket balls to disadvantaged communities all over the world. One World Play Project believes that through play we become stronger individuals and can build better communities.

2 🎧 52 Read the notes. Then listen to a journalist talking about One World Play Project. Complete the notes.

The idea: Came from Tim Jahnigen. In ¹ _____, he saw boys in Sudan playing football on a TV ² _____. They had a ball made of ³ _____.

The product: A ball made of ⁴ _____. It's very ⁵ _____ and never ⁶ _____.

The success: One World Play Project has delivered over ⁷ _____ footballs.

The funding: Some money comes from ⁸ _____ who have their ⁹ _____ on the ball. They started sponsoring the project at the 2010 ¹⁰ _____. Also each time One World Play Project ¹¹ _____ a ball, they ¹² _____ a ball to a poor community.

GRAMMAR

3 Complete the text about Tim Jahnigen's background. Use the past simple and present perfect form of the verbs.

Tim Jahnigen is an inventor who lives in San Francisco. He ¹ _____ (enjoyed) playing sports all his life, but he ² _____ (never / play) soccer. As a boy he ³ _____ (swim) and ⁴ _____ (play) American football. Jahnigen ⁵ _____ (also / travel) a lot, so when he ⁶ _____ (see) the news programme about Darfur in 2006, he ⁷ _____ (already / know) that soccer was the world's most popular sport. Immediately, he ⁸ _____ (start) trying to design a football that ⁹ _____ (suit) their situation better.

4 Choose the correct options to complete the description of the future for One World Play Project.

One World Play Project has delivered over one million footballs and hopes that this number ¹ *will soon be / is soon going to be* 1.5 million. Jahnigen thinks that the footballs ² *will encourage / are going to encourage* communities to play together. He also hopes that through play, people ³ *will become / are going to become* more confident and ⁴ *might feel / are going to feel* more positive about the future. The project has been so successful that Jahnigen ⁵ *might continue / is going to continue* his work. One World Play Project also makes a cricket ball and they ⁶ *will look / are going to look* at other products that encourage play.

VOCABULARY

5 Complete the description of One World Play Project football with the correct verbs. The first letter has been given.

1 **Size:** It m_____ 21 centimetres in diameter (standard size 5).
2 **Material:** It's m_____ of strong plastic.
3 **Weight:** It w_____ the same as a regular football.
4 **The price:** It c_____ $39 to buy one and give one free.
5 **Options:** It c_____ in two colours – orange and blue.
6 **Appearance:** It l_____ nice and it has the Chevrolet brand name on it.
7 **Advantages:** It never breaks and it doesn't n_____ a pump.

94

6 Complete the text about playing team sports with these words. There is one extra word.

ambitious	easy-going	enthusiastic	organized
reliable	sociable	a team player	

A lot of people are ¹_____ about playing sport, but they don't have an opportunity to play with other people. Playing a team sport like football or cricket can teach you important life skills. It teaches you to co-operate with others and be ²_____. Teams have to work together and be ³_____ to be successful – each person can't just do their own thing. So you have to learn the importance of fitting into a system and being ⁴_____, because other players depend on you to do a particular job. Team sports also help you to become more ⁵_____ and to interact with people in other areas of your life. Lastly, competitive sport can make you more ⁶_____ – you set higher goals for yourself for the future.

DISCUSSION

7 Work in pairs. Discuss the questions.

1. What sports or team activities have you done in your life?
2. How have they benefitted you?
3. What do you think of One World Play Project? Who are the winners?

SPEAKING

8 Read the telephone answer messages. Then complete the messages using the prompts.

1. A: This is the voicemail of Sarah Farmer. ¹ *Please leave / message / and / I / call / you / back as soon / possible.*
   B: Oh, hi, Sarah. ² *It / be / Kate here.* ³ *I / just / call / about the dinner on Friday.* ⁴ *I / like / come, if that's possible.*

2. A: Kyle Blackmore is not available. Please speak after the tone.
   B: Hi, Kyle. ⁵ *Sorry / I / miss / call.* Call me back. ⁶ *I / be / in / office / afternoon.*

3. A: You have reached the offices of One World Play Project. We are sorry there is no one here to take your call. Please leave a message and we will try to call you back as soon as possible.
   B: Oh, hello. ⁷ *My name / be / Jake Edwards.* ⁸ *I / be / interested / the job you advertised in the paper.* ⁹ *I / be / keen / learn / more about it.* My number is 07966 396635. ¹⁰ *I / try / call / you / again later.*

4. A: Syreeta Khan is not available. Please leave a message after the tone.
   B: Hi, Syreeta. It's me. ¹¹ *Sorry / bother / you.* ¹² *I just wanted to let / know that* I can help at the fundraising event on Saturday. ¹³ *I / be / good / get / people to donate money!* ¹⁴ *No need / call back.* See you there.

WRITING

9 Look at the email exchange below. Read the first email. Then complete the reply, promising action. Use one word in each space.

1
TO: *Click here to add recipients*   CC:
SUBJECT:

Dear Customer Services

I booked some tickets for an Elton John concert in December. The concert is not until June but it is now May and I have not received them yet. I am getting a bit worried. Please can you let me know when I can expect them.

Nuhla Ramen

2
TO: *Click here to add recipients*   CC:
SUBJECT:

¹_____ Nuhla

Please ²_____ not worry. This is normal. We ³_____ send the tickets out to you ⁴_____ the next two weeks. So you ⁵_____ receive them in good time for the concert ⁶_____ 17th June. If you need any further help, please ⁷_____ me know.

⁸_____ sincerely

Tom Hardy
Customer Services

10 Read the email. Write a short reply to the email promising action.

TO: *Click here to add recipients*   CC:
SUBJECT:

Dear Ms Geavons

I am writing because I have not had further news about my application. Four weeks ago I sent an application for a job at your company. You replied saying you were interested in my application and would like to meet me for an interview. That was the last communication I had. Can you let me know if you are going to take my application any further? Thank you.

Yours sincerely

Sasha Michaels

11 Work in pairs. Exchange emails and compare your replies. Did you offer a similar solution?

95

9 Being effective

Street seller, Hanoi, Vietnam

TEDTALKS

TERRY MOORE is the director of the Radius Foundation, a forum for exploring and gaining insight from different cultures and worldviews. He believes that we can all learn from each other, even in the simplest tasks.

Terry Moore's idea worth spreading is that sometimes doing things differently, even for a small or common task like tying your shoes, can be better than your current method.

BACKGROUND

1 You are going to watch a TED Talk by Terry Moore called *How to tie your shoes*. Read the text about the speaker and the talk. Then work in pairs and discuss the questions.

1 Who does Terry Moore believe that we should learn from?
2 What ideas have you picked up from other places or cultures (e.g. ways to dress, ways to cook food, working habits, etc.)?

KEY WORDS

2 Look at these words which are used in the TED Talk. Match the words with their definitions (1–6). Then match four of these words to the pictures (A–D).

bow (n)	knot (n)	loop (n)
shoe laces	tie (v)	to come untied

1 the cords that hold the shoe tight around your foot
2 to attach or fasten with a string or cord
3 a join made by tying two pieces of string or cord together
4 a curved shape that comes round and crosses itself
5 a knot tied with two loops and two loose ends
6 when a knot fails and unties itself

AUTHENTIC LISTENING SKILLS Word boundaries

Certain combinations of words in English appear very frequently. In these cases often the words merge and are difficult to hear separately. It's very important to be able to recognize these combinations.
What do you think? /ˈwdʒəˈθɪŋk/

3a 🎧 **53** Look at the Authentic listening skills box. Listen to these sentences from the TED Talk said at two speeds – slow and then fast. Notice how the word boundaries merge.

1 I'm used to thinking of the TED audience …
2 some of the most effective …
3 As it turns out, …
4 We are going to do this one more time.

3b 🎧 **53** Listen to the four extracts again. Practise saying them at the fast speed.

3c 🎧 **54** Work in pairs. Say these phrases with merged word boundaries. Then listen and compare your pronunciation.

1 First of all, …
2 What do you think?
3 Of course I can.
4 Could you give me a minute?

A

B

C

D

9.1 How to tie your shoes

TEDTALKS

1 ▶ 9.1 Work in pairs. Watch the TED Talk. Then show your partner Terry Moore's method of tying your shoes.

2 ▶ 9.1 Watch the first part (0.00–0.31) of the talk again. Answer the questions.
   1 How does Terry Moore describe his TED audience?
   2 What piece of bad news does he give them?

3 ▶ 9.1 Watch the second part (0.31–1.12) of the talk again. Complete the summary below.

   Terry Moore bought some ¹ *exercise / expensive* shoes. But they came with ² *round / flat* laces and he couldn't keep them ³ *tied / tight*. So he took them ⁴ *off / back*. He said to the salesman, 'I love the ⁵ *style / shoes*, but I hate the laces.' And the salesman said, ⁶ *'You're tying them wrong.' / 'They're too long.'* Moore was surprised because he thought by the age of ⁷ *40 / 50*, he had learned how to tie shoes.

4 ▶ 9.1 Watch the third part (1.12–2.09) of the talk again. Answer the questions.
   1 What does Terry Moore demonstrate first?
   2 What does his second demonstration show?
   3 What are the advantages of the second method he describes? Complete the notes.
      It's a ¹_____ knot. It will come ²_____ less often. It will let you ³_____ less. And it ⁴_____ better.

5 ▶ 9.1 Watch the fourth part (2.09 to the end) of the talk again. According to Terry Moore, what does this way of tying your shoes teach us? Complete the sentence.

   'A ¹_____ advantage someplace in ²_____ can yield ³_____ results someplace ⁴_____.'

▶ a store **N AM ENG**
▶ a shop **BR ENG**

▶ start over **N AM ENG**
▶ start again **BR ENG**

VOCABULARY IN CONTEXT

6 ▶ 9.2 Watch the clips from the TED Talk. Choose the correct meaning of the words.

7 Work in pairs. Think of examples of the following.

1. a rule in your college or workplace that you think is ludicrous
2. a computing technique that you have really nailed
3. a time when a person (friend, colleague) or a machine (car, computer) let you down

CRITICAL THINKING Understanding the main argument

8 Usually a talk will contain one main argument, but it is not always easy to identify what this is. Work in pairs. Discuss what you think Terry Moore's main argument is.

9 Read these comments* about the TED Talk. Discuss the questions.

1. Have any of the viewers identified the same main argument as you?
2. Which of the arguments do you think Terry Moore wanted to make?

Viewers' comments

P **Pavel** – In my opinion, the speaker is trying to show us the importance of doing the basic things right before we try to do more complicated things.

C **Cherry** – He is telling us that it is never too late to learn from other people if we are open-minded. He was 50 when he learned this!

W **Werner** – The message is simple: there is no single correct way to do a task.

* The comments were created for this activity.

10 Work in pairs. Choose two comments from Exercise 9 and think of an example to illustrate each argument.

'There is no single correct way to do a task.'

Some people use a paper diary to remember things, others use an electronic diary.

PRESENTATION SKILLS Demonstration

11 Work in pairs. What are three important things to remember when giving a demonstration of how something works?

12 Look at the Presentation tips box. Compare your answers from Exercise 11 with the tips for speakers.

TIPS

When you want to explain how something works, it is very useful for your audience to see a demonstration. But only if the demonstration works! Here are a few tips for giving demonstrations.

- Practise the demonstration until it feels easy. Film yourself giving the demonstration or practise in front of a mirror.
- Practise it in front of people who know the subject well, and outsiders too.
- Avoid technical terms. If you have to use them, explain them to your audience.
- Describe your own personal experience of learning this thing.
- If you need to reinforce your message, give the demonstration twice.

13 ▶ 9.3 Watch the clip from the TED Talk. Which of the techniques from the Presentation tips box did Terry Moore follow?

14 Work in pairs. Do you know an alternative way of doing a simple, everyday task, e.g. tying a tie, making a plait in your hair, sending a text message, taking a photo of yourself? Prepare a demonstration. Use the techniques from the Presentation tips box.

15 Work with a new partner. Give your demonstration. Did you use similar techniques?

▶ someplace **N AM ENG**
▶ somewhere **BR ENG**

9.2 You'll find it useful

BENEFITS OF LEARNING A LANGUAGE

TRAVEL

The number of international students is increasing every year by **12%**

97% of people say learning another language helps when travelling

BENEFITS OF SPEAKING THE LANGUAGE IN A FOREIGN COUNTRY

- FEEL SAFE
- ORDER FOOD
- GET A JOB
- MAKE FRIENDS

INTELLIGENCE

- BENEFITS TO THE BRAIN
- BETTER MEMORY
- CAN MULTI-TASK
- LONGER ATTENTION SPAN

WORK

Over 30% of companies want people with good language skills

Multilingual employees with foreign languages **earn 2–4% more** than monolingual employees

LOVE

270 British dating agencies say **PEOPLE WHO SPEAK A FOREIGN LANGUAGE ARE MORE ATTRACTIVE**

Students who **study languages for at least four years do better at school** than their classmates

GRAMMAR Zero and first conditional

1 Work in pairs. Discuss the questions. Then look at the infographic and compare your list of benefits.

1. How has speaking English (or another foreign language) been useful to you in your life?
2. What are the benefits of speaking another language? Make a list of these benefits, e.g. for travel.

2 Look at the infographic again. Complete the sentences.

1. _____ of people believe that if they learn another language, it will help them when travelling.
2. Unless you speak the native language, you will find it difficult to get a _____ in a foreign country.
3. When you learn foreign languages, it improves your ability to do many _____ at the same time.
4. If your child learns another language, they will earn _____ more in their working life.
5. If people speak a foreign language, they are more _____ to a potential boyfriend or girlfriend.

3 Read the sentences (1–4) in the Grammar box. Answer the questions (a–d).

ZERO AND FIRST CONDITIONAL

Zero conditional

1. *If people speak the local language, they make friends more easily.*
2. *When you learn a language, it helps your brain.*

First conditional

3. *If I learn to speak English, I'll be able to travel around America more easily.*
4. *Unless you speak English, you will find it difficult to get a job with a multinational company.*

a Which sentences (1–2 or 3–4) refer to something that is generally true?
b What tense is used in the *if* or *when*-clause?
c What tense is used in the main clause in sentences 1–2? And in sentences 3–4?
d What word means *if … not*? Can you rewrite this sentence with *if*?

Check your answers on page 156 and do Exercises 1–3.

4 Choose the correct options to complete the text about learning a language.

There are three things you need to learn a language: motivation, time and the right method of learning. It's a fact that it ¹ *is / will be* very difficult to make progress when any one of these things ² *is / will be* missing. Motivation can come from inside. For example, if you really ³ *love / will love* France and its culture, you ⁴ *find / will find* it easier to learn French. But motivation can also come from outside. So, for example, if tomorrow your employer ⁵ *offers / will offer* you a fantastic job abroad (and you need to speak the language), then you ⁶ *have / will have* a clear motive to learn that country's language. Secondly, you must invest time in learning. People don't learn if they ⁷ *don't / won't* practise. Lastly, choose the right method of learning. For example, if you ⁸ *want / will want* to focus on speaking, you ⁹ *make / will make* faster progress by taking conversation classes.

5 Look at the advertisement for e-learning courses. Discuss the benefits of e-learning compared with traditional classroom learning. What are the disadvantages?

Hoping to move on in your career?
Be ready when the chance comes!

With **Septon e-learning** courses, you can
- build your work skills
- choose from over 60 courses
- learn when you want
- be part of a large learning community

• 20% discount before 1 May •
free tutorial when you start • money back if not satisfied

6 Put the words in order to write sentences describing the advertiser's promises. Add punctuation if necessary.

1 will / you / a large community / you / be part of / if / the e-learning course / join /
2 a 20% discount / they / people / before 1 May / enrol / get / if /
3 start / give / they / people / they / a free tutorial / when
4 you / your money back / if / aren't / give / will / you / satisfied / they

7 Work in pairs. Use the information in the infographic (or your own ideas from Exercise 1) to make three more sentences with *when / if / unless* about the benefits of learning foreign languages. Use the zero and first conditional.

GRAMMAR Imperatives in conditionals

8 Read the sentences in the Grammar box. Answer the questions (1–3).

IMPERATIVES IN CONDITIONALS

Ask if you need anything.
Be ready when the chance comes.

1 What kind of verb forms are *ask* and *be*?
   a imperative (order)
   b interrogative (question)
   c conditional (*if*)
2 What word replaces *if* in the second sentence?
3 What tense are the verbs in the *if/when*-clause?

Check your answers on page 156 and do Exercises 4–6.

9 Complete the sentences using the verbs in the correct form.

1 Let me know if you _____ (have) any problems.
2 Don't turn off the computer until it _____ (finish) installing the update.
3 Take advantage of the 20% discount before the offer _____ (end).
4 _____ (tell) me if you think it's a good course.
5 Call me when you _____ (be) ready to go.

10 Work in pairs. Complete these commands in your own words.

1 Have a break if …
2 Please wait until …
3 Don't worry if …

SPEAKING Practical solutions

11 21st CENTURY OUTCOMES

Work in pairs. Look at the everyday problems (1–5). Think of solutions and then write sentences using the first conditional or an imperative with *if*, *when*, *before* and *after*.

1 People often forget their passwords.
2 People often feel stressed at work and become unproductive.
3 People are often short of spending money at the end of the month.
4 Employees often feel they have to stay late at work to show they are working hard.
5 People often feel they don't have enough time to do sport or exercise.

   1 It is important to change your password regularly. But people worry that if they change their password they will forget it. One answer is to …

12 Exchange ideas with another pair. Which solutions did you find the most useful?

9.3 Small details matter

READING Getting the basics right

1 Work in pairs. Look at the title of the article. What are the 'basics' you have to get right in these tasks (1–3)?

1. writing a letter of application for a job
2. training a new member of staff
3. ordering a product online

2 Read the article quickly. There are two messages in the article. Choose the two correct messages from the four options (a–d).

a. No company can get all the details right.
b. Some companies find it difficult to get the simple things right.
c. Customers don't want to be disappointed.
d. Customers want a great experience.

3 Read the article again and answer the questions.

1. Why did the kitchen tools company hire a consultant?
2. What two basic things did the company fail to do?
3. Who or what does the author think is responsible for this failure?
4. How can consistency of customer experience benefit a company?
5. Why is consistency of experience important to Starbucks' customers?
6. How does a company achieve consistency of customer experience?

4 Find the words in bold in the article. Then answer the questions.

1. Are **competitive** prices 'cheap' or 'expensive' prices compared to other companies? (para 1)
2. What does it mean if you **hire** a consultant? Do you employ them for a long time or a short time? (para 1)
3. What's the opposite of **in stock**? (para 2)
4. What's the opposite of **detached**? (para 3)
5. Do you think **disciplined** means 'strict' or 'flexible' in the way companies work? (para 5)
6. Does **empower** mean give the power to someone or take it away? (para 5)

5 Work in small groups. Think of a company that offers a consistently good experience. Discuss the reasons why the company 'gets things right'.

VOCABULARY Being effective

6 Work in pairs. Complete the sentences in your own words.

1. The most effective way to learn a new language is to …
2. A washing machine is only effective if it …
3. The most effective way to keep a house warm is to …

7 Match the verbs (1–5) with the phrases (a–e) to complete the expressions.

1. he **gets**
2. it **is**
3. we try to **keep**
4. it **saves** / **wastes**
5. it **works**

a. things simple / costs down
b. well / for us
c. results / the job done / the details right
d. economical / quick
e. time / money

8 Complete the sentences using these words.

down	economical	gets	quick
save	simple	wasted	worked

1. In the old days, we had to input all the data manually – it took ages. Now it's all done automatically, so it's _____ and easy.
2. When I wanted to change job, I registered with a recruitment agency. It _____ for me.
3. One way to keep your travel costs _____ is to buy a season ticket for the train; you'll _____ a lot of money that way.
4. The restaurant is successful because they keep things _____, serving a limited number of dishes that they know people like.
5. We _____ a lot of money in the past advertising in the wrong places. Now we do internet advertising focussed on the right groups of people. It's more _____ and it _____ results.

SPEAKING Offering a good service

9 **21st CENTURY OUTCOMES**

Look at the categories. Choose an organization you know in each of these categories. Then answer the questions (1–2).

Categories
- a fast food chain
- a hotel chain
- a supermarket
- a mobile phone operator

1. On a scale of 1–10, how good is the quality of the company's services or products? Give reasons.
2. What are the basic things that the company needs to do to offer a good service?

10 Work in small groups. Discuss your ideas from Exercise 9.

GETTING the BASICS RIGHT

You sell a range of simple kitchen tools: lemon squeezers, potato peelers, salad spinners. The designs are attractive, the tools are different enough to get people's interest and the prices are very competitive. But they're not selling and you want to know why. So you hire a consultant. Two weeks later she comes back to you with some shocking news.

She went online to buy a lemon squeezer. It said 'item in stock', so she put it in her basket. But when she got to the checkout it said 'item out of stock'. She telephoned customer services. They said the item was in stock and they would fix the problem immediately. 'Great,' she said, 'and could you send me a catalogue in the post, please?' 'Sure' was the answer. A week later she tried to buy the lemon squeezer online again. Same problem. And the catalogue? It still hadn't arrived.

Does this story sound familiar? I think we have all had experiences like this: where a company can't seem to get even the most basic things right. Why does this happen? Too often in companies, the brain of the business (the management who create the strategy) has become detached from the body (the employees who implement the strategy). A business plan or strategy doesn't need to be complicated, but it needs to be implemented. In the case described above, it's clear that the management is ineffective; it is not making sure that the employees are implementing the basic actions that make the business work.

These days it's difficult to offer the customer something different: there's a lot of competition out there. So getting the details right is very important. Because what customers want above all is a consistent experience. They don't want to be let down.

Recent research by management consultancy firm Oliver Wyman, in the USA, found that if you improve the consistency of the customer experience, the result will be an increase in sales of ten per cent or more.

Companies like Starbucks understand this very well. A busy commuter who decides to stop at Starbucks on their way to work does not want to risk having a bad experience. So Starbucks train their staff very carefully in the values and practices of the company before they put them to work. Companies have to be very disciplined if they want to get the details right. They need to have clear and simple goals and they need to empower front-line managers to make sure that these are achieved.

---

catalogue (n) a list of the products or services that a company offers
consistent (adj) done in the same way each time
implement (v) put into practice

Unit 9 Being effective

21st CENTURY OUTCOMES   BUSINESS LITERACY   Demonstrating an understanding of business

9.4 Here's a trick that works

VOCABULARY Practical solutions (adverbial phrases)

1 Look at the photo. What's the problem?

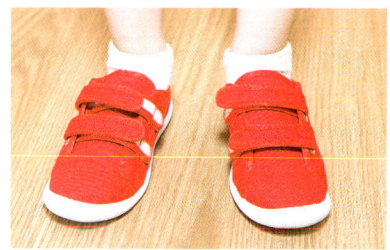

2 Complete the sentences with these phrases.

back to front	inside out
the wrong way round	upside down

1 I think you've got your shoes on _____.
2 I think your T-shirt is on _____. I can see the label.
3 If you turn the bottle _____, then the shampoo will run to the top.
4 He always wears his baseball cap _____.

Pronunciation Word stress

3a 🎧 55 Listen to the sentences in Exercise 2 and check your answers. Mark where the stress falls in each adverbial phrase.

3b Work in pairs. Practise saying these sentences
1 Turn the bag inside out and shake it.
2 You've written her first name and surname the wrong way round.
3 My whole world was turned upside down.
4 He can ride a bicycle sitting back to front.

4 Write four sentences of your own using the phrases from Exercise 2.

LISTENING Practical instructions

5 Work in pairs. Look at these phrases and answer the questions (1–2).

fold your shirt
pack your clothes (into a suitcase)
roll the towel

1 Can you explain or demonstrate to your partner what the verbs in bold mean?
2 The opposites of these verbs all have the same prefix. What is it?

6 🎧 56 Listen to some practical instructions. Answer the questions.
1 Who is the advice for?
2 What problem does it solve?

7 🎧 56 Listen again. Number the instructions (a–e) in the order you hear them.

a By doing this, you'll make sure that there are no lines or creases in the jacket when you unroll it.

b Just to be sure, hang your jacket in the bathroom when you arrive at your hotel.

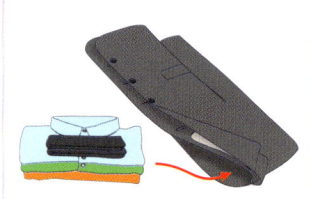

c But before you do that, put some other clothes inside the shoulder of the jacket.

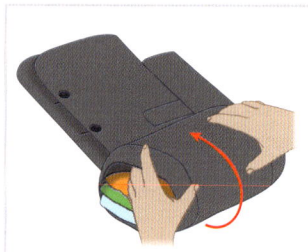

d Now roll the jacket, like you would do with a towel.

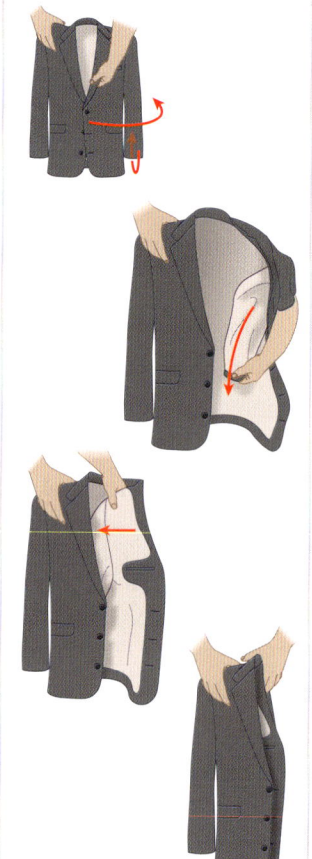

e Turn one half of the jacket inside out. Then fold the jacket in half.

SPEAKING Giving instructions

8 Work in pairs. Cover Exercise 7. Then repeat the instructions for packing a jacket to your partner. Use the expressions in the Useful language box to help you.

GIVING INSTRUCTIONS

Firstly, fold / turn / put …
Then fold / turn / put …
But before you do that, …
When / After you've done that, …
By doing this / that, you will …
Make sure that …
Just to be sure, …

9 Work in pairs.

Student A: Turn to page 171.
Student B: Turn to page 172.

Look at your instructions and memorize them. Then give each other your instructions. Use the phrases in the Useful language box to help you.

WRITING An email to a visitor

10 Read the email to a visitor and answer the questions.

1 Why is the visitor coming to Brugg?
2 What two destinations does the writer give directions to?

TO: Click here to add recipients   CC:
SUBJECT:

Dear Annie

Thank you for your email. We are looking forward to seeing you in Brugg in September. You asked about directions to the conference centre. I'm attaching a map, but this is how to get there from the station.

When you arrive at the station, go down the steps to the underpass and turn right. Look out for signs to the Hochschule. You'll come into a large square. Just cross the square and you will see the Hochschule opposite you. The conference centre is along the same street on your left.

I don't know what your exact plans are, but if you arrive the day before, you will be very welcome to join us for dinner at the *Grotto* with some other delegates. It's a Portuguese restaurant on Hummelstrasse, also near the train station, but on the other side of the railway lines. We will be there from eight o'clock. If you let me know, I will add your name to the list (about ten other delegates have also said they will attend).

I look forward to hearing from you.

With kind regards

Stephanie Huber (Conference Organizer)

---

11 Work in pairs. Identify the parts of the email in Exercise 10 which do the following.

1 State the purpose of the email.
2 Make a positive comment.
3 Give directions.
4 Make an invitation.
5 Tell the reader what to do next.

Writing skill Giving directions

12a Look at the directions in the email. Then complete the summary with the correct prepositions.

Go ¹ _____ the steps and turn right; come ² _____ a large square. Cross the square – Hochschule is ³ _____ you. The conference centre is ⁴ _____ your left.

12b Match (1–6) with (a–f) to make sentences giving directions.

1 Go out of
2 At the traffic lights,
3 Carry on walking
4 Cross
5 Walk along
6 You will see our building

a until you come to a large white building on your right.
b directly opposite you.
c turn right.
d the river for about 400 m.
e the hotel and turn left.
f the main road and go over the bridge.

13 **21st CENTURY OUTCOMES**

Write an email for someone who is coming to visit your college or place of work. Tell them how to get there from the nearest station or bus stop and invite them to join you for lunch.

14 Work in pairs. Exchange emails. Read the email and check that your partner's email includes these points:

- a greeting and positive comment
- the purpose of the email
- directions using correct prepositions
- an invitation
- what they want the reader to do next

Unit 9 Being effective

21st CENTURY OUTCOMES   **LIFE AND CAREER SKILLS** Writing clear instructions

10 The environment

A chef at a Vancouver hotel harvests apples, British Columbia, Canada

TEDTALKS

PAM WARHURST is the Chair of the Forestry Commission in the UK. She also co-founded Incredible Edible Todmorden, a local food-growing partnership.

Pam Warhurst's idea worth spreading is to create public gardens on plots of land that are unused. In this way communities can come together and have a closer relationship with the food they eat.

BACKGROUND

1 You are going to watch an edited version of a TED Talk by Pam Warhurst called *How we can eat our landscapes*. Read the text about the speaker and the talk. Then work in pairs and discuss the questions.

1 What word in the text means 'you can eat it'?
2 Do many people in your town grow their own food? Where do they do this? What do they grow?
3 What are some good reasons to grow your own food?

KEY WORDS

2 Read the sentences (1–7). The words in bold are used in the TED Talk. First guess the meaning of the words. Then match the words with their definitions (a–g).

1 I always use fresh **herbs** in my cooking.
2 We are a small charity organization and we don't have the **resources** to help everyone.
3 We encourage young people to **engage in** community life and decisions about their local area.
4 If people **share** things, it means that we all have to buy fewer things.
5 We don't have a garden, but we have a small **bed** on our terrace where we grow flowers.
6 It looks like a **prickly plant**, but it's quite soft to touch.
7 They're not animal farmers: they grow wheat and **corn**.

a take part in, become involved in
b divide something (equally) between two or more people
c a plant with sharp points on it, e.g. a cactus
d plants that are used to flavour food
e a kind of cereal with yellow grains
f an area, often in a garden, where plants or flowers are grown
g the things you need to do something, e.g. money

3 Which words in bold in Exercise 2 do the pictures (A–D) illustrate?

AUTHENTIC LISTENING SKILLS
Understanding fast speech

Some people speak very fast – often because they are enthusiastic about what they are saying. How can you deal with this?

- Try to get the main idea and then relate the other details you hear to this.
- Look for visual clues to help you understand.
- Ask for clarification – this could be from the speaker themselves, or from someone else who is listening, or even from a transcript, if you are listening to a recording.
- Accept that you are not going to understand every word – celebrate what you do understand!

4a 🎧 **57** Look at the Authentic listening skills box. Listen to the introduction to the talk. What is the main point Pam Warhurst makes about her town, Todmorden? Choose the correct option (a–b).

a It's a traditional, small gardening town.
b It's a small town that has been transformed by gardening.

4b 🎧 **57** Work in pairs. What kind of plants do they grow in the town? Listen again and check.

4c 🎧 **58** Listen to the next point Pam Warhurst makes about what has happened in her town. Describe it to your partner.

 A
 B
 C
 D

10.1 How we can eat our landscapes

TEDTALKS

1 ▶ 10.1 Watch the edited version of the TED Talk. Write one or two examples of each of the following (1–3).

1 places in Todmorden where people grow food
2 types of food they grow or produce locally
3 people and groups involved in the project

2 ▶ 10.1 Watch the first part (0.00–1.58) of the talk again. Choose the correct option to complete the sentences.

1 Todmorden is a normal town in England of *15,000 / 50,000* people.
2 They grow fruit and vegetables and herbs everywhere, even in front of the *fire / police* station.
3 The town now attracts a lot of *local / vegetable* tourists.
4 Pam Warhurst is encouraging the growing of food locally because she wants to start a *local shop / revolution*.
5 Pam Warhurst believes that through food people can find a new way of *living / doing business*.

3 ▶ 10.1 Watch the second part (1.58–3.08) of the talk again. Complete the sentences with these words. There are two extra words.

| businesses | kitchen | letter | plan |
| public | school | story | university |

1 The idea came when some residents were sitting around the _____ table.
2 They didn't write a _____; they just put the idea to a _____ meeting.
3 The idea was to involve three groups or 'plates': the community, children at _____ and local _____.
4 In every town where Pam Warhurst explains her idea, people respond positively to the _____ of food.

▶ centre **BR ENG** ▶ neighbour **BR ENG**
▶ center **N AM ENG** ▶ neighbor **N AM ENG**

4 ▶ 10.1 Watch the third part (3.08–4.39) of the talk again. Match the first half of each sentence (1–5) with the second half (a–e).

1 They transformed an area of land that was a dog toilet into
2 In a corner of the station car park, they made
3 At the health centre, they replaced prickly plants with
4 At the police station, they planted
5 At the high school, they made an area with

a fruit trees and bushes and herbs and vegetables.
b fish and vegetables.
c corn.
d a herb garden.
e vegetable beds.

5 ▶ 10.1 Read the summary below. Then watch the fourth part (4.39 to the end) of the talk again. Choose the correct words to complete the summary.

The third 'plate' of the strategy was to get people to support local food ¹ *producers / shops* and buy their food. So the group got some blackboards and local traders wrote what they were selling on them. And ² *prices / sales* went up. Then Pam Warhurst's group talked to farmers about the idea, but the farmers didn't think they were ³ *serious / honest*. So the group made a map for people of where to buy fresh local ⁴ *vegetables / eggs* in Todmorden. And sales went up. The farmers saw this and started selling other kinds of food locally, like meat and cheese. These are ⁵ *difficult / small* steps, but they change the way people think. Forty-nine per cent of food traders said their profits had increased. And this is why the project is successful: because it is a project for ⁶ *everyone / business too*.

VOCABULARY IN CONTEXT

6 ▶ 10.2 Watch the clips from the TED Talk. Choose the correct meaning of the words.

7 Work in pairs. Complete the following questions in your own words. Then ask and answer the questions with your partner.

1 Do you think people will come up with any ideas to solve the problem of … ?
2 Do you think that food producers are more interested in their profits than in … ?
3 Do you think people respond well to the idea of eating … ?

CRITICAL THINKING Recognizing tone

8 A speaker or writer's tone or way of speaking has an effect on how you feel about their argument. How could you describe Pam Warhurst's tone? Choose two adjectives.

| angry | direct | down-to-earth | emotional |
| factual | funny | quiet | warm |

9 Did the way Pam Warhurst speaks help her argument or not? How? Discuss with a partner.

10 Read these comments* about the TED Talk. Identify the following:

a what the viewers say about Pam Warhurst's tone
b the effect the talk had on each viewer

Viewers' comments

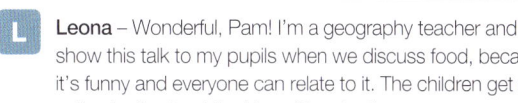

Leona – Wonderful, Pam! I'm a geography teacher and I show this talk to my pupils when we discuss food, because it's funny and everyone can relate to it. The children get really enthusiastic about the idea of local action.

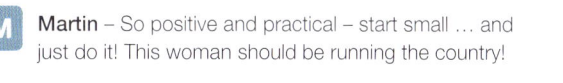

Martin – So positive and practical – start small … and just do it! This woman should be running the country!

*The comments were created for this activity.

11 Work in pairs. What tone(s) could you use to deliver the following messages?

- An argument against cutting down forests to make space for new houses
- A presentation of a new electric vehicle

PRESENTATION SKILLS Being straightforward

12 Work in pairs. How can speakers help their audience relate to them and their ideas? Discuss with your partner.

13 Read the Presentation tips box. Compare your answers from Exercise 12 with the tips in the box.

> **TIPS**
>
> If you want people to relate to what you are saying, it's important to:
> - keep your ideas and language simple and straightforward
> - avoid exaggerating your claims
> - give plenty of concrete examples
> - be personal

14 ▶ 10.3 Watch the clips from the TED Talk. Which of the techniques from the Presentation tips box did Pam Warhurst follow?

15 Work in pairs. You are going to present a practical idea to help your community. Choose one of the ideas below or use your own idea. Prepare a brief description of your idea.

1 A community playgroup for young children run by local parents.
2 A local swap shop where you can exchange things you no longer want for other things.

16 Work with a new partner. Give your presentation. Did you follow the points in the Presentation tips box to make it easy for the listener to relate to you and your message?

▶ railway station BR ENG
▶ train station N AM ENG
▶ car park BR ENG
▶ parking lot N AM ENG

10.2 A big sum of small actions

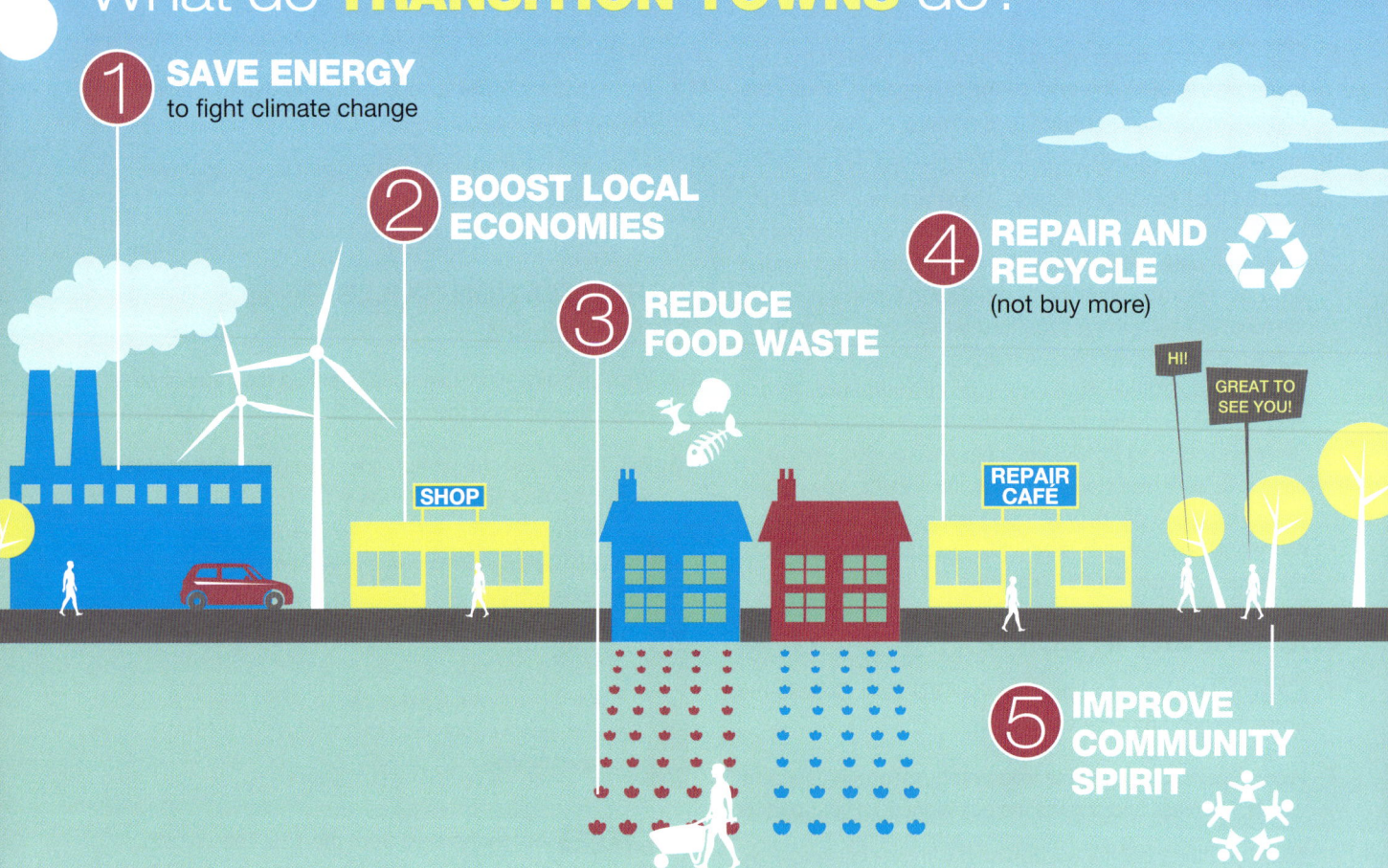

GRAMMAR The passive

1 Work in pairs. What three things would make your town a better, happier place to live in? Discuss with your partner.

2 Look at the infographic. Answer the questions.

   1 A *transition* is when something changes from one system to another. What change is the Transition town movement trying to make?

   2 Which of these things can their actions help to save?
      a money
      b energy
      c time

   3 What can their actions improve?

3 🎧 59 Listen to examples of Transition town projects. What is the aim of each project? Match the projects (a–d) with the aims (1–5) in the infographic. There is one extra aim.

   a Brixton
   b Deventer
   c Oxford
   d Many Transition towns

4 Work in pairs. Which idea do you like most? Why? Are there any similar projects in your community?

5 Read the sentences (1–5) in the Grammar box on page 111. Answer the questions (a–e).

THE PASSIVE

1 *In Transition towns, different ideas **are tried**.*
2 *In Brixton, electricity **is produced** by solar panels on top of people's houses.*
3 *In the past, broken things **were** often **thrown** away.*
4 *Volunteers collect unwanted food. Before, this food **was put** in the rubbish by the supermarkets.*
5 *Now the food **is taken** by volunteers to poorer members of the community.*

a What time does each verb in bold refer to: the present or the past?
b How do we form the passive? The verb _____ + _____
c What is the subject of each sentence?
d Who does or did each action (the agent) in sentences 2, 4 and 5?
e What word introduces the agent in sentences 2, 4 and 5?

Check your answers on page 158 and do Exercises 1–5.

6 Read the text and find two more passive verbs. Who is the agent of the first action?

In many Transition towns, street parties and festivals are organized by local residents. These are occasions when communities can get to know each other better. In the past, events like these weren't organized unless it was a special national holiday.

Pronunciation Stress in passive forms

7 🎧 60 Listen to the sentences. Which part of the verb is stressed: *be* or the past participle? Practise saying the sentences with a partner.

1 Different ideas **are tried**.
2 If they work, they **are put** into action.
3 Volunteers collect food that **isn't wanted**.
4 Broken things **were** often **thrown** away.
5 Before, this food **was put** in the rubbish.

8 Look at the Transition town ideas. Rewrite the verbs in bold so they are passive verbs.

1 In Tooting in London, people **held** a carnival called the 'Trashcatcher's Carnival'.
    In Tooting in London, a carnival called the 'Trashcatcher's Carnival' _____.
2 People **made** all the things for the carnival – costumes, musical instruments, etc. – from old bits of rubbish.
    All the things for the carnival – costumes, musical instruments, etc. _____ from old bits of rubbish.
3 Transition town leaders **see** the carnival as one of the most successful examples of community-spirit building.
    The carnival _____ by Transition town leaders as one of the most successful examples of community-spirit building.
4 Volunteers at 'Cycletastic' in Kilburn in north London **run** cycle repair workshops.
    Cycle repair workshops _____ by volunteers at 'Cycletastic' in Kilburn in north London.
5 People bring their broken bicycles to the workshop and the volunteers **teach** them how to repair them.
    People bring their broken bicycles to the workshop and _____ how to repair them.
6 'Cycletastic' **doesn't throw** away old bicycles. It sells them cheap to local residents.
    Old bicycles _____. Cycletastic sells them cheap to local residents.

9 Write sentences about the food industry. Use the present or past passive. Use *by* + agent where necessary.

1 Vegetables / grow / at home / an increasing number of people.
    Vegetables are grown at home by an increasing number of people.
2 In 2012, almost half of the food eaten in Britain / import / from other countries.
3 More bananas (1 million tons) / eat / British people than any other imported food.
4 Thirty years ago, nearly 100% of Chinese food / produce / in China.
5 Now a lot of Chinese food not / grow there but is imported.
6 In the USA 80% of all consumed water / use / the food industry.
7 15,000 litres of water / need / to produce 1 kilo of beef.
8 In 2012, 40% of the food produced in the USA / not / eat.
9 In the UK 60% of tomatoes / throw away / consumers every year.
10 30% of the world's land / use / animal farmers.

SPEAKING Survey: How 'local' are you?

10 Look at the questions (1–4) about how much time and money you spend in your local area. Think of two more questions of your own.

1 What are the main local businesses in your area?
2 Did you go to a local school?
3 Do you buy food from local shops?
4 Do you belong to any local organizations or groups?

11 Ask three other people in the class the questions in Exercise 10. Write down their answers.

12 **21st CENTURY OUTCOMES**

Work in pairs. Compare your findings from Exercise 11. Write the results in four or five sentences, using both active and passive verbs. Do you think it's important to be involved in your local area?

Most people don't know about the different businesses in their local area.

Local schools are well-supported.

10.3 Running out of time

READING Big rise in greenhouse gas emissions

1 Work in pairs. Look at the phrases about the environment. Discuss what you think they mean.

1 global warming
2 climate change
3 CO_2 emissions
4 greenhouse gases

2 How much attention do people pay to environmental problems in your country? Discuss and give examples to support your view.

3 Read the article (not the comments yet). Are the facts (1–5) true (T), false (F) or possibly true (P)?

1 The level of CO_2 in the atmosphere increased by more than a third between 1990 and 2013.
2 The Earth's temperature will rise by at least five degrees Celsius by the end of this century.
3 The world's oceans normally absorb greenhouse gases.
4 When the oceans cannot absorb CO_2, they become more acidic.
5 According to the report, it is too late to stop climate change.

4 Read the comments on page 113. Then write the correct name(s) next to each question (1–6). If the answer is 'no one', write *N*.

Who:
1 doesn't believe the report? _____
2 feels pessimistic about the future? _____
3 feels optimistic about the future? _____
4 thinks people can solve the problem? _____
5 thinks governments can solve the problem? _____
6 thinks business can solve the problem? _____

5 Find these phrases in the comments. Then choose the correct meaning.

1 **I doubt** (comment 1)
  a I disagree
  b I think it is improbable

2 **It's up to us** (comment 2)
  a it's our responsibility
  b it's the right time

3 **avoid** (comment 3)
  a keep away from
  b not know about

4 **blame** (comment 4)
  a change the behaviour of
  b say it's someone's fault

5 **demanded** (comment 5)
  a asked for strongly
  b suggested

VOCABULARY Phrasal verbs

6 Look at the two phrasal verbs in bold from the article. Discuss with your partner what you think each one means.

> 1 The report concludes that we are '**running out of** time' to tackle climate change.
> 2 We can't **carry on** eating steak every day and driving big cars.

See page 158 for more information about phrasal verbs, and do Exercise 6.

7 Look at the sentences (1–6). Match the phrasal verbs in bold with the expressions (a–f).

1 He left the company in June and **set up** his own environmental consultancy business.
2 He wasn't angry about the mess in the garden. He just **got on with** the job of cleaning it up.
3 She's a very nice person. I'm sure you'll **get along**.
4 There are not many green spaces left, so it's important to **look after** the few that we have.
5 It wasn't a very successful meeting. Only three people **turned up**.
6 Some people say that ten per cent of the world's plastic rubbish **ends up** in the ocean.

a have a good relationship with someone
b take care of
c concentrate on and make progress with
d finally do something or be somewhere
e appear
f establish / organize

8 Complete the sentences using the phrasal verbs from Exercises 6 and 7.

1 We need to _____ a meeting with all the different heads of department.
2 Frances will _____ you in your first week here. Just ask her if you have any questions.
3 Sorry. We got lost driving into the city and _____ at the airport!
4 Sheena is great. She never complains. She just _____ the job.
5 The project was never completed because we _____ money.
6 We haven't found anyone for the job yet, but we're going to _____ looking.

9 Complete the sentences in your own words. Then work with a partner and compare your sentences.

1 Global temperatures will keep increasing if we carry on …
2 Unless we do something about global warming, … will end up …
3 People are worried that we will run out of …
4 We need to look after …
5 One solution to the problem is to set up …

SPEAKING AND WRITING Expressing an opinion

10 Look at the comments below the *Big rise in greenhouse gas emissions* article again. Choose one to add a comment to. Decide if you agree or disagree and write your own comment.

11 21st CENTURY OUTCOMES

Work in small groups. Read each other's comments. Did you respond to the same comment in the article? Did you agree or disagree with the comments?

BIG RISE
IN GREENHOUSE GAS EMISSIONS

According to the World Meteorological Organization (WMO), record amounts of carbon dioxide entered the atmosphere in 2013. Between 1990 and 2013, global warming due to greenhouse gases, such as CO_2, rose by 34%. The Earth's temperature is now predicted to increase by two to five degrees Celsius by 2100. The WMO report also says the world's ecosystems – its oceans and forests – are no longer able to absorb all these greenhouse gases. As a result, the world's seas are becoming more acidic. This is happening faster than at any time in the last 300 million years. The report concludes that we are 'running out of time' to tackle climate change.

COMMENTS

1 Phoenixman
I live in Arizona where the temperature can change from 35 degrees to 23 degrees after a storm. Even if the report is right, which I doubt, I'm not going to worry about a change of two degrees.

2 HarryB
The problem is that we all consume too much. We can't carry on eating steak every day and driving big cars and flying to Thailand for our holidays and expect the problem to go away. It's up to each of us to change our lifestyles.

3 Davina Walker
Why can't governments around the world agree on a global energy policy? We've reduced the amount of CO_2 we produce in Europe, but in other parts of the world, people are burning more coal and gas. I don't see how we can avoid environmental disaster now.

4 Kitesurfer
You can't blame governments. They want their citizens to be rich. The only real answer is to find a technological solution to these problems – cleaner fuels, more recycled goods, new ways of making electricity, etc. Big industry created these problems so industry can find the answers. Governments will listen to big business.

5 Greenjo
Business will only do something when it affects their bottom line – in other words, when change is demanded by their customers. HarryB is right. They won't stop making plastic bags and petrol-fuelled cars until we stop buying them.

absorb (v) take in
acidic (adj) containing acid (a liquid below pH7)

21st CENTURY OUTCOMES   INFORMATION LITERACY Evaluating information critically

10.4 Can you explain?

VOCABULARY Food adjectives

1 Work in pairs. Look at the pictures of different foods (a–f). Match the foods with these adjectives.

filling   light   rich   salty   spicy   sweet

a chillies

b bread

c party snacks

d roast duck

e lemonade

f salad

2 Use each adjective from Exercise 1 to describe another kind of food you sometimes eat.

LISTENING In a restaurant

3 🎧 61 You will hear two conversations. The first conversation is between two friends and the second conversation is between a waiter and a customer. Listen and complete the table.

Dish discussed	Adjective used to describe the dish
1	
2	

4 🎧 61 Listen to the conversations again. Choose the correct options to complete the description of each dish.

1 Bigos is a kind of ¹ *soup / stew*. It is a ² *local / traditional* Polish dish and it is made with ³ *chicken / meat* and sauerkraut. The friend recommends it if you are
⁴ *hungry / in a hurry*.

2 The pepper steak comes with French fries and
¹ *vegetables / salad*. The customer would like her steak
² *medium / well-done* and she would like to drink some
³ *juice / water* with it.

Pronunciation Intonation in questions

5a 🎧 62 Look at the questions (1–7). Does the intonation rise (↗) or fall (↘) at the end of each question? Listen and check.

1 So what are you going to have?
2 What's this?
3 Sauer what?
4 Is it a local dish?
5 Do you recommend it?
6 How hungry are you?
7 Do any vegetables come with it?

5b Work in pairs. Ask and answer the questions in Exercise 5a. Use the correct intonation.

SPEAKING Explaining what's on a menu

6 Work in pairs. Each write a short menu of four or five dishes. Then exchange menus and take turns to play different roles in these situations (1–2). Use the expressions in the Useful language box to help you.

1 A conversation in a local restaurant between you and a guest from another country.
2 A conversation between you and a waiter in a restaurant.

EXPLAINING WHAT'S ON A MENU

Questions

What's this (on the menu)? / Can you explain?
Is it very spicy / sweet / salty / rich / filling?
Is it a local dish?
Does it come with vegetables/ bread / salad?
Do you recommend it?

Answers

It's a kind of stew / soup / pastry / dessert.
It's made with meat / potatoes / chicken.

Waiter says

Are you ready to order?
How would you like your steak?
Can I get you anything to drink?

WRITING A description of a system

7 Work in pairs. Look at the email. Discuss possible ideas for making Eileen's office more environmentally friendly.

TO: Click here to add recipients   CC:
SUBJECT:

Hi Lana

I hope everything is OK with you. I'd like to ask a favour. We were having a discussion at work today about making our offices more environmentally friendly. I know that your company has some good ideas in this area. Can you explain some of them to me so that I can share them with the others here?

Many thanks and all the best

Eileen

8 Read the reply and compare your answers. Were any of your ideas the same? Which of Lana's ideas (1–3) do you like the most?

TO: This reply will be sent to the sender only.   CC:
SUBJECT:

Hi Eileen

Thanks for your email. It's great that your company wants to go in this direction. You are very welcome to visit us here some time and see what we do. But, in the meantime, here are three of the easiest and cheapest ideas.

1) We put small waste bins in people's offices. Bigger recycling bins are put in the corridor. In this way, people are encouraged to recycle more of their waste – for example, paper, cans or food. The small bins are only used for items such as paper tissues. Also, this makes the cleaners' job easier.

2) If you use those big water dispensers with plastic cups, remove the plastic cups and ask people to use the same cups or mugs for water that are used for coffee and tea. By doing this, plastic waste is reduced.

3) When you print documents, always print on two sides. Like that, you only use half the amount of paper. I know it seems obvious, but it's amazing how many people print long documents like reports on one side.

I hope this helps and, as I said, please visit us some time if you want to get more ideas.

All the best

Lana

9 Read the email in Exercise 8 again. What was the result of each action (1–3) that Lana suggests?

Action	Result
1 giving people small waste bins in their offices	a _____ b _makes the cleaners' job easier_
2 asking people to use cups or mugs not plastic cups	_____
3 printing on two sides	_____

Writing skill Explaining results

10a Look at the actions and results in Exercise 9. Underline the phrases in the email which are used to introduce each result.

10b Match the action (1–3) with the result (a–c). Then link the action with the result using a phrase to introduce the result. Use a different phrase in each sentence.

1 Put a lot of plants in your offices.
2 The heating is set at a maximum of 18 degrees.
3 Employees are encouraged to use the stairs not the lifts.

a They get more exercise and we use less electricity.
b You will create better air for people to breathe.
c We save on our energy bills.

11 **21st CENTURY OUTCOMES**

Look at the ideas (1–3). Think how each idea helps the environment (the result). Then write an email to Eileen using these ideas and one of your own.

1 Employees read documents on the computer and don't print them out.
2 Fit automatic lights which switch off when no one is in the room.
3 Put food waste in special bins. Use the waste to make compost for office plants.

12 Work in pairs. Exchange emails. Read your partner's email and check that it includes these points:

- a greeting and the reason for writing
- a list of possible actions and the results of these actions
- some examples
- correct use of active and passive verbs

INFORMATION LITERACY Using information to address the issue at hand

Review 5 | UNITS 9 AND 10

READING

1 What 'clean' ways of making electricity can you think of, i.e. without burning fossil fuels (gas, coal or oil)? Discuss with your partner.

2 Read the article about a company called Pavegen. Where does Pavegen's clean electricity come from?

Pavegen

Pavegen are a 'clean tech' company based in London, UK. The company was founded by Laurence Kemball-Cook in 2009 to develop technologies that can change people's attitudes to energy. Kemball-Cook believes that if we don't always want to rely on oil and other fossil fuels, we will have to think in new and imaginative ways.

Pavegen leads the world in 'footfall energy'. The company makes flooring that converts the energy from people's footsteps into electricity. The flooring can be used in office buildings, shopping malls, railway stations or in the street – anywhere in fact where there is heavy pedestrian traffic. The energy is then used to power lighting, such as street lighting, or is stored in batteries for later use.

The flooring comes in large squares or tiles and it is made mainly from recycled materials, including 100 per cent recycled rubber. It can be fitted onto an existing floor or installed as part of a new development. At the moment, it is still relatively expensive, but Kemball-Cook believes that if enough people use it in future, then the cost will come down. Kemball-Cook was given the prize for Businessman of the Year at the 2013 People, Environment and Achievement (PEA) Awards.

3 Read the article again. Which of the sentences (a–c) is not true?

1 Kemball-Cook's goal is to:
   a make people think differently about energy.
   b use fossil fuels more imaginatively.
   c get people to think more creatively.

2 Pavegen flooring can be used:
   a outside.
   b in workplaces.
   c in people's homes.

3 Pavegen flooring is:
   a environmentally friendly.
   b cheap to buy.
   c an award-winning idea.

GRAMMAR

4 Complete the description about how Pavegen flooring works. Use the passive and active (present simple and past simple) form of the verbs.

The idea for Pavegen flooring [1] _____ (develop) by Laurence Kemball-Cook when he was studying at Loughborough University. He [2] _____ (start) the company in 2009. No one knows exactly how the technology works because it [3] _____ (keep) a secret by Pavegen. But the basic principle is this: When someone [4] _____ (step) on a Pavegen floor tile, the tile [5] _____ (bend) a little. When the floor tile bends, it releases kinetic energy. The energy [6] _____ (store) in a battery under the tile or it [7] _____ (convert) directly into electricity. In some tiles there is a small light in the centre. This lights up when someone walks on the tile. Pavegen tiles [8] _____ (use) very successfully in this way on a dance floor at the Bestival music festival in 2011.

5 Complete the sentences about the lessons to learn from the Pavegen story. Use the zero and first conditional.

Lessons to learn from the Pavegen story

1 If we _____ (continue) to use fossil fuels, they _____ (run) out.
2 If you _____ (invent) a product that helps the environment, people _____ (pay) attention.
3 If you _____ (want) your idea to become a reality, you _____ (need) to believe in it passionately.
4 Ideas _____ (be) more successful when they _____ (involve) ordinary people.
5 If you _____ (discuss) your latest idea on social media, people _____ (find out) about your product.
6 You _____ (be) more successful if the media (newspapers, TV, etc.) _____ (be) on your side.

VOCABULARY

6 Complete the notes about other People, Environment and Achievement Award winners. Use these words and phrases.

end up	get	look after	keep	run out of
saves	set up	turned up	waste	works

Arts, fashion and music award: *Creative Common*
Creative Common turned an area in Bristol, in the UK, into a centre for culture – film, theatre, music and art. In the nine months it was active, over 100,000 people [1] _____ to see the events.

Best documentary film: *Chasing Ice*
This documentary shows how the world's glaciers are disappearing. It encourages people to act before we [2] _____ time to save them.

Community award: *Conserve me Foundation*
Conserve me is a charity that helps teach children how we can [3] _____ our environment and wildlife. The charity doesn't get much funding, so they have to [4] _____ costs down. But they [5] _____ fantastic results.

Entrepreneur of the year: *Shruti Barton* for *Flower Pozzy*
Shruti Barton noticed that bought flowers use a lot of plastic wrapping. Also you usually [6] _____ damaging the flowers by the time you get home. So she designed a flower carrier. It [7] _____ well and [8] _____ packaging.

Responsible travel award: *Jamie Andrews* for *Loco 2*
You can [9] _____ a lot of time trying to find ways to travel responsibly. Jamie and his sister Kate [10] _____ a website where people can book trains as easily as planes.

DISCUSSION

7 Work in pairs. Discuss the questions.

1 Do you like the Pavegen idea? Why? / Why not?
2 Can you think of any more places where Pavegen flooring could be used?
3 Can you think of any other kinds of 'wasted' energy that could be turned into electricity? Think about physical movement, heat, etc.

SPEAKING

8 Linda is in Turkey on business. Sadar, her colleague, has invited her to a restaurant. Read the conversation. Then complete the conversation using the prompts.

Sadar: So, [1] *what / you / have* for your main course?
Linda: I'll have a kofte kebab. [2] *it / come / vegetables or salad?*
Sadar: It comes with salad and bread.
Linda: [3] *you / recommend?*
Sadar: Yes, it's good.
Linda: Great. And what's this on the table?
Sadar: It's called Ezme. [4] *It / be / kind / salad or dip.* Try some.
Linda: Mm. It's delicious. What's in it?
Sadar: [5] *It / make / tomatoes and onion and spices.*
Linda: Is it easy to make?
Sadar: Very easy. You just crush the onion with the spices. [6] *After you / do / that,* you add the tomato.
Linda: Is that it?
Sadar: Yes, but [7] *make / sure / you / leave / for two to three hours* before you eat it. [8] *By / do / that,* you give time for the flavour to come through.

WRITING

9 Complete the email to a visitor giving directions. Use up to three words in each space.

Dear Xavier

Thank [1] _____ email. We [2] _____ forward to welcoming you to the National Science Institute in June. I [3] _____ map to this email, but maybe it's easier if I explain how [4] _____ the Institute from the station, because it is very near.

When you come [5] _____ the station, turn left and walk about 100 m to the end of the road. You [6] _____ to a large square. [7] _____ the square and look [8] _____ for signs to Harman Street. Walk [9] _____ Harman Street for about 200 m and you [10] _____ a large glass building [11] _____ left. This is the Science Institute.

If you arrive before 1.00 p.m., you will be very welcome [12] _____ us for lunch in the canteen.

Please let [13] _____ you need any more information and I look forward [14] _____ you in June.

Best [15] _____,

Marjorie

10 Work in pairs. Exchange emails and compare your answers. Did you use the same words to complete your emails?

11 Leaders and thinkers

BACKGROUND

1 You are going to watch an edited version of a TED Talk by Richard Branson called *Life at 30,000 feet*. Read the text about the speaker and the talk. Then work in pairs and discuss the questions.

1 What do Richard Branson's companies have in common?
2 Apart from business, what are some of Richard Branson's other interests?
3 Has his career in business been easy or not? Why do you say this?

TEDTALKS

RICHARD BRANSON is the CEO (Chief Executive Officer) of *Virgin*, a group of more than 250 companies, from gyms to banks to airlines, all carrying the *Virgin* brand name. He's passionate about many humanitarian issues, such as climate change. In this interview with TED's Chris Anderson, he describes the ups and downs of his career and his motivations in business.

Richard Branson's idea worth spreading is that succeeding in business means a lifetime of taking risks, failing and picking yourself up again.

Maasai leaders gather to discuss the building of a village school, Tanzania

KEY WORDS

2 Read the sentences (1–6). The words in bold are used in the TED Talk. First guess the meaning of the words. Then match the words with their definitions (a–f).

1 No company can succeed without financial **backing**.
2 The two brothers are going to **launch** their new business next year.
3 Every now and then a new company with a new idea comes along and **shakes up** an industry.
4 The company's decision to donate ten per cent of its profits was a **PR** success.
5 People say you need to be **ruthless** to be successful in business, but it is possible to be kind and caring and still be successful.
6 They say it takes years to build a good **reputation** and only days to destroy one.

a set something going, start it, e.g. a rocket, a business
b support (often financial, i.e. investment)
c public relations, trying to have a good relationship with the public
d trying to reach your goal without any thought for other people's feelings or interests
e the opinion (good or bad) that other people have about you
f tries to reorganize or change something that has been the same for a long time

AUTHENTIC LISTENING SKILLS Fillers in conversation

People use 'fillers' in conversation to give them time to think before they speak. These fillers can be sounds, such as *um* or *er,* or they can be phrases like *you know* or *well*.

Many speakers have favourite fillers and use them often. We also use fillers to pause before starting a new sentence. When this happens, the first sentence isn't properly finished.

These are some of the most common fillers: *actually, basically, I mean, like, right, so, well, you know, you see.*

3a 🎧 **63** Look at the Authentic listening skills box. Listen to the extract from Richard Branson's talk. Answer the questions.

1 Which fillers does Richard Branson use?
2 What is his favourite filler?

3b 🎧 **64** Listen and complete the sentence. At what point does Richard Branson restart his sentence?

'And if I see – [1]_____, if I fly,[2]_____, if I fly on somebody else's airline and find the experience is not a pleasant one, which it wasn't, 21 years ago, then I'd think, [3]_____, [4]_____, maybe I can create the kind of airline that I'd like to fly on.'

119

11.1 Life at 30,000 feet

TEDTALKS

1 ▶ **11.1** Watch the edited version of the TED Talk. Tick (✓) the sentences that describe Richard Branson's business philosophy. Then compare your answers with a partner. Which of Richard Branson's ideas do you like?

1 You can run any business if you have good people around you.
2 You need to have a lot of money behind you in case things go wrong.
3 It's important to have fun and enjoy what you do.
4 You mustn't take too many risks.
5 You have to be ruthless in business – if not, other people will destroy you.

2 ▶ **11.1** Watch the first part (0.00–1.40) of the talk again. Answer the questions.

1 Is it difficult to run lots of different companies, according to Richard Branson? Why? / Why not?
2 According to Richard Branson, what is the key to running a successful company?
3 Why did he decide to start an airline?

3 ▶ **11.1** Watch the second part (1.40–3.40) of the talk again. Are the sentences true (T) or false (F)?

1 When Richard Branson sold Virgin Records and invested heavily in Virgin Atlantic, people thought it was a good business decision.
2 British Airways helped Richard Branson's new airline, Virgin Atlantic.
3 Richard Branson wanted to save people's jobs at Virgin Records and Virgin Atlantic.
4 For Richard Branson, the Virgin brand represents good quality.
5 Virgin is a company that likes to do things in a fun and different way.

▶ jewellery **BR ENG**
▶ jewelry **N AM ENG**

4 ▶ 11.1 Watch the third part (3.40–5.11) of the talk again. Choose the correct option (a–b) to answer the questions.

1 Richard Branson has done many expeditions in boats and balloons. What does he say about them?
   a They weren't dangerous.
   b He is lucky to be alive.
2 Why do some people say he does these expeditions?
   a for marketing reasons
   b to improve his own reputation
3 What joke does he make about the expeditions and his businesses?
   a They are not a good advertisement for an airline.
   b He went in a balloon because he couldn't get a plane ticket.

5 ▶ 11.1 Look at the interviewer's last question. Then watch the fourth part (5.11 to the end) of the talk again. Complete Richard Branson's reply using these words.

| come | fairly | reputation | run |
| small | successful | top | well |

Question: You've been accused of being ruthless. Is any of it true?

Branson: I don't actually think that the stereotype of a business person treading all over people to get to the ¹_____, generally speaking, works. I think if you treat people ²_____, people will ³_____ back for more. And I think all you have in life is your ⁴_____ and it's a very ⁵_____ world. And I actually think that the best way of becoming a ⁶_____ business leader is dealing with people ⁷_____ and well, and I like to think that's how we ⁸_____ Virgin.

VOCABULARY IN CONTEXT

6 ▶ 11.2 Watch the clips from the TED Talk. Choose the correct meaning of the words.

7 Work in pairs. Discuss the questions with your partner.
1 Can you think of a new activity that you were worried about doing, but in the end decided to 'give it a go'?
2 What does the Apple brand stand for, do you think?
3 Can you think of a company in your country that went out of business? Why did this happen?

CRITICAL THINKING Fact or opinion

8 Work in pairs. Are the following sentences fact (F) or opinion (O)?
1 Richard Branson is a successful businessman.
2 He likes to take risks.
3 He has changed people's approach to business.
4 He does adventurous things to get publicity.
5 He can be ruthless.

9 For the 'opinion' sentences in Exercise 8, whose opinion was this: Richard Branson's, the interviewer's or someone else's?

10 Read this comment* about the TED Talk. Do you agree with it? What facts and what opinions about Richard Branson does the viewer refer to?

Viewers' comments

 Ulla – I really like that Richard Branson does not just do business to make money – that he wants to change things. I also admire that he has achieved so much, but isn't proud. It is very inspiring for any young person who wants to start a business.

*The comment was created for this activity.

PRESENTATION SKILLS Dealing with questions

11 Work in pairs. At the end of a talk, how can you:
1 deal with a question when you don't know the answer?
2 deal with someone who disagrees with you strongly?

12 Look at the Presentation tips box. Which suggestions answer the questions in Exercise 11? Were your answers the same?

TIPS

Here are some suggestions for answering questions:
- Check that you understand the question. (*If I understood you correctly, you're asking if …?*)
- Thank the questioner for their question. (*I'm glad you asked that.* OR *That's an interesting question.*)
- If you don't know the answer, say so. (*I'm afraid I can't answer that. Can anyone else comment?*)
- If you disagree, don't argue – just move on. (*Well, I understand that. All I'm saying is …*)
- Relate the question to your argument. Bring the conversation back to the point that you want to make.

13 ▶ 11.3 Watch the clip from the TED Talk. Answer the questions.
1 What is Richard Branson's answer to the question about what his brand stands for?
2 Why doesn't the interviewer like his answer?
3 How does Richard Branson deal with this? Which of the points from the Presentation tips box is he following?

14 Work in pairs. At the end of a presentation, you are asked these questions. Discuss how to answer them.
1 You said in your talk that the main reason for doing business is to make money. But what about social reasons, like creating jobs?
2 You said that you have to pay your employees well to do a good job. Is that really their only motivation?

15 Work with a new partner. Practise asking and dealing with the questions.

121

11.2 Who are the CEOs?

Who are the top 500 CEOs?

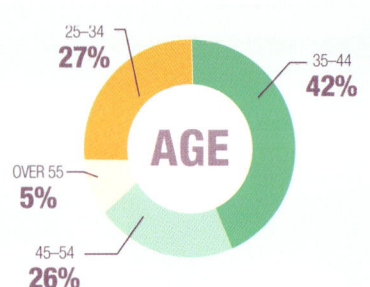

AGE
- 25–34: 27%
- 35–44: 42%
- 45–54: 26%
- OVER 55: 5%

MANAGEMENT IS IN THEIR BLOOD.

49% had a parent who was an entrepreneur

Which parent was the entrepreneur?

- Father 59%
- Mother 11%
- Both 30%

Average number of days holiday CEOs take each year: **10**

8% NEVER take a day off

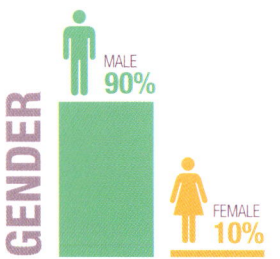

GENDER
- MALE 90%
- FEMALE 10%

The average age when CEOs started their first companies: **27**

Number of **nights per month** married CEOs **eat dinner** with their families:
- 1 TO 4: 15%
- 5 TO 9: 22%
- 10 TO 15: 20%
- 16+: 39%
- NONE: 4%

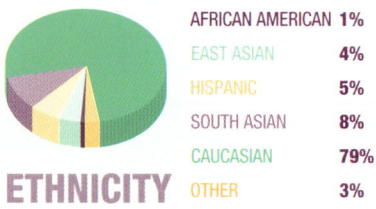

ETHNICITY
- AFRICAN AMERICAN: 1%
- EAST ASIAN: 4%
- HISPANIC: 5%
- SOUTH ASIAN: 8%
- CAUCASIAN: 79%
- OTHER: 3%

We asked CEOs which entrepreneur they most admired. They said Richard Branson.

Some of them have a home life.

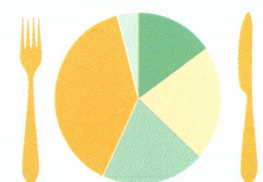
- 70% are married
- 14% are single
- 7% are divorced

GRAMMAR Modal verbs (1)

1 Look at the infographic. Answer the questions.

1. What is the biggest age group among the CEOs?
2. On average, how old were the CEOs when they started their first companies?
3. How many of the CEOs eat dinner with their families less than once a week?

2 🎧 **65** Listen to a journalist talking about the statistics in the infographic. Complete the conclusions he makes.

1. There are too few _____ CEOs.
2. If there is no diversity at the _____ of the company, there will be no diversity in other parts.
3. It's _____ that 27% of CEOs are under 35.
4. CEOs _____ too much.
5. It helps to have a _____ who was an entrepreneur.

3 Read the sentences (1–7) in the Grammar box. Answer the question.

MODAL VERBS (1): *must, mustn't, have to, don't have to, need to, don't need to, can*

1. We **must** get more women running companies.
2. In Germany company boards **have to** be at least 30% female.
3. We also **need to** have more ethnic diversity.
4. You **mustn't** discriminate against older people..
5. You **don't have to** work all the time to be efficient.
6. You **don't need to** be male to be a CEO, but 90% are.
7. You **can** run a business if your parents weren't entrepreneurs, but it certainly helps if they were.

Which sentences mean:

a it's possible or permitted? _____
b it's necessary? _____, _____, _____
c it's not permitted? _____
d it's not necessary? _____, _____

Check your answers on page 160 and do Exercises 1–2.

4 Look at the frequently-asked questions (FAQs) by new employees in a company. Choose the correct options to complete the answers.

▸ **What kind of clothes do I have to wear to work?**

Clothing ¹ *must / mustn't* be appropriate. For example, you ² *mustn't / don't need to* wear jeans or shorts. You ³ *mustn't / don't have to* wear formal clothes, like a suit, unless you are meeting a customer.

▸ **Can I use the computer for my own personal emails?**

If there is some emergency, for example if you ⁴ *can / have to* arrange a doctor's appointment, then you ⁵ *can / have to* use the company computers for this purpose. But you ⁶ *mustn't / don't have to* do personal business in company time. This includes things like chatting to friends or doing online shopping.

▸ **What happens if I am late?**

You ⁷ *need to / can* be on time for work each day. If you are going to be late, you ⁸ *have to / don't have to* call and check that your manager is informed.

▸ **Do I have to stay late if I haven't finished my work?**

You ⁹ *must / can* take responsibility for your own work. You ¹⁰ *mustn't / don't have to* stay late, after your regular hours of work to finish your work, but you always ¹¹ *need to / can* tell your manager if you have not finished.

5 Work in pairs. Compare your answers from Exercise 4. Then answer the questions.

1 Are the rules fair or not?
2 How do these rules compare to rules in the workplace(s) that you know?

6 Look at three more FAQs by new employees. Discuss possible answers. Then write the answers for the company's webpage. Use at least two modal verbs in each answer.

1 Can I use the company car park free of charge?
2 Can I take a part-time job with another company?
3 Do I get paid if I am sick?

GRAMMAR Modal verbs (2)

7 Work in pairs. Would you like to be your own boss / run your own business? Why? / Why not?

8 🎧 **66** Listen to a short conversation between two friends about starting a business. Answer the questions.

1 What is Jane's reason for wanting to start her own business?
2 What two things does her friend say she needs to start a business?

9 Read the sentences in the Grammar box. Answer the question.

MODAL VERBS (2): *should* and *shouldn't*

You **should find** a financial backer – maybe go and see the bank.
You **shouldn't start** a business just because you don't like the company that you're working for.

Do we use *should* and *shouldn't* to say something is necessary or to give a recommendation/advice?
Check your answers on page 160 and do Exercises 3–5.

10 Rewrite the sentences giving advice. Use *should* and *shouldn't*.

1 It's a good idea to get advice before you start a business.
You *should get advice before you start a business*.

2 It's important to employ people who have skills you don't have.
You _____ .

3 Is it a good idea to keep my current job while I'm planning my new business?
_____ ?

4 It's important not to expand your business too fast.
You _____ .

5 It's a bad idea to choose a business partner that you don't know well.
You _____ .

6 If you know other people who have their own company, speak to them.
You _____ .

SPEAKING Dilemmas

11 **21st CENTURY OUTCOMES**

Work in small groups. Read the situation and decide what the right thing for Harry to do is. Use modal verbs to discuss your answer and conclusion.

Harry works for a company called KPC. It gives IT support to four or five big companies. He likes the company and is well paid for his work. But it is a small company and there are very few opportunities to progress in his career. One day a colleague at KPC comes to Harry and says he is setting up his own IT company. He has spoken to two of KPC's main customers who say they will work with him. He wants Harry to join him in his new company. He says the pay will be better and there will be good opportunities to learn new things. What should Harry do?

21st CENTURY OUTCOMES CRITICAL THINKING Solving problems

11.3 Famous quotes

READING Words of wisdom

1 Work in pairs. Discuss the questions.

1 Do you like reading quotations by famous people? Do you think they can be useful? Why? / Why not?
2 Do you have a favourite quotation about work or life in general?

2 Read the quotations by various CEOs, thinkers and leaders. Match the topics (1–5) with the person or people who talk about it.

1 having new and different ideas
2 looking after the environment
3 getting the best from employees
4 cutting costs
5 making money

3 Which quotation do you like the most? Why?

4 Work in pairs. Read the quotations again and answer the questions.

1 Who does Anita Roddick say should be different?
2 Why does Richard Branson put his staff first?
3 How does Richard Branson want to feel about his business?
4 What kind of products does Richard Branson like to sell?
5 What does Prince Charles think business should invest in?
6 What does Henry Ford mean by 'poor'?
7 What lesson must companies learn from Charles Darwin if they want to survive?
8 Who does Mary Kay Ash mean when she says 'our people'?
9 Who do you think Thomas Edison was talking to?
10 What does Gordon Bethune think of making a pizza without cheese?

5 Find words or phrases in the quotations that mean the following.

1 the people who invest in or own a part of the business (para B)
2 employees (para B)
3 put something onto the market for the first time (para C)
4 a thing which we own that has a positive value (para E)
5 kings and queens (para H)

6 Work in pairs. Discuss the questions about the quotations.

1 Who do you think most companies put first: employees, customers or shareholders? Why is this?
2 What do you think are the world's natural 'assets' which we need to look after?
3 Can you think of a successful company with very low costs and prices?

VOCABULARY make and do

7 Look at the sentences with *make* and *do* from the quotations. Choose the basic meaning (a–b) of each verb.

1 They're not going to **do** things with a smile.
  a create   b perform

2 You can **make** a pizza so cheap, nobody will eat it.
  a create   b perform

8 Complete the sentences with phrases from the two boxes.

A	B
make a suggestion	do my best
make decisions	do my food shopping
make a lot of progress	do business
make a difference	do me a favour
make a lot of money	do something

1 Don't just sit there. _____!
2 I'm not sure I can help you, but I'll _____.
3 Having the right tools can really _____ when you are doing a job.
4 Can you _____ and carry this bag for me?
5 You can _____ as a lawyer, but it's hard work.
6 I usually _____ on Thursdays.
7 Can I _____? Try turning off the computer and then switching it on again.
8 That was a good meeting. I think we managed to _____.
9 Thank you. It was a pleasure to _____ with you.
10 He doesn't find it easy to _____.

SPEAKING Life advice

9 **21st CENTURY OUTCOMES**

Work in pairs. Choose three of the items (1–6) below and write a piece of advice – something that you have learned from your experience – to guide and help others.

You shouldn't be afraid of choosing the more difficult way. If you always choose the easy way, you won't make progress.

1 making progress
2 making decisions
3 making money
4 doing favours for other people
5 doing business
6 doing your best

10 Work with a new partner. Tell each other your advice. What do you think of your partner's advice?

WORDS of WISDOM

A '"Whatever you do, be different" – that was the advice my mother gave me, and I can't think of better advice for an entrepreneur.'

Anita Roddick, Body Shop

B 'If the person who's working for your company is … not looked after, is not appreciated, they're not going to do things with a smile, and therefore the customer will be treated in a way in which they don't want to come back for more. So my philosophy has always been, if you can put your staff first, your customers second, and your shareholders third, effectively in the end the shareholders do well, the customers do better, and your staff are happy.'

C 'Above all, you should work on building a business you're proud of. I have never gone into any business purely to make money. If money is your only motive, then I believe you shouldn't launch the business at all.'

D 'People have to think: What's not being done well by other people? How can I create something that's really going to make a difference in people's lives?'

Richard Branson, Virgin

E 'You would think … that protecting the ultimate … asset upon which all future income depends – in other words this fragile planet – was worth investing in, seriously and urgently.'

Charles, Prince of Wales

F 'A business that makes nothing but money is a poor kind of business.'

Henry Ford, Ford Motor Company

G 'It is not the strongest … that survive, nor the most intelligent, but the ones who are most responsive to change.'

Charles Darwin, Naturalist

H 'We treat our people like royalty. If you honour and serve the people who work for you, they will honour and serve you.'

Mary Kay Ash, Mary Kay Inc

I 'There's a way to do it better – find it!'

Thomas Edison, Inventor

J 'You can make a pizza so cheap, nobody will eat it. You can make an airline so cheap, nobody will fly it. … Let's say that you would reduce the cost of pizza by doing something smart like taking the cheese off? How many pizzas are you going to sell?'

Gordon Bethune, Continental Airlines

Unit 11 Leaders and thinkers

21st CENTURY OUTCOMES — LEADERSHIP Guiding and inspiring others

11.4 How did it happen?

LISTENING Problem solving

1 Put the verbs in order to complete the problem-solving process.

analyse   identify   solve   ~~tackle~~

1. _____ the problem
2. _____ the problem
3. _tackle_ the problem
4. _____ the problem

2 🎧 **67** Read the tip about how to solve a problem. Then listen to two people in a university administration office who are discussing a problem and answer the questions.

> The way to solve a problem is to identify its root cause (how the problem started). To do this, keep asking why and how events happened until you arrive at the root cause.

1. What is the problem?
2. What is the root cause of this problem?
3. What are the possible solutions?

3 🎧 **67** Read the problems (1–4) and complete the replies. Then listen to the conversation again and check your answers.

1. I didn't send it to him.
   Really? Why _____?
2. It isn't finished.
   Why _____ it finished?
3. I didn't feel confident about my English.
   Why _____ you get some English lessons?
4. Well, I want to, but it's too expensive.
   You _____ ask the university to pay.

Pronunciation Positive and negative questions

4a 🎧 **68** Listen to the questions. Underline the words you hear.

1. Why *did / didn't* you ask me for some help?
2. Why *were / weren't* the books sent here?
3. *Did / Didn't* you get the train tickets?
4. Why *was / wasn't* the talk cancelled?

4b Work in pairs. Read the sentences in Exercise 4a as a positive or a negative question. Ask your partner to answer the question. Check which type of question they heard.

SPEAKING Analysing problems and suggesting solutions

5 Work in pairs. You are going to discuss two problems.

Problem 1   An office computer was destroyed.
Problem 2   The rubbish in bins outside people's houses smells very bad.

Student A: Turn to page 171.
Student B: Turn to page 172.

Use the expressions in the Useful language box to help you. At the end, suggest possible solutions.

ANALYSING PROBLEMS AND SUGGESTING SOLUTIONS

Analysing problems

How did that happen?
Why did they complain …?
Why didn't you report it?
Why isn't it finished?
Why not?

Suggesting solutions

Why don't you get some lessons?
You should ask the company to pay.
Another solution is to ask someone else to check it.
You could …

6 Think of a problem you have faced recently. Explain the problem to your partner and then analyse it in the same way.

126

WRITING Posting advice on a forum

7 Do you ever go online to look for advice? What do you look for advice about?

1. travelling
2. something you want to buy
3. technical questions
4. personal health
5. work or study
6. places to stay, visit or eat

8 Read the questions (A–D) which have been posted on forums. Match the questions with the categories (1–6) in Exercise 7.

A

I wanted to take my son to see the England–Brazil football match at the weekend, but the tickets are sold out. Any ideas? He's really keen to go.

Comment

B

Our plane arrives at Stansted airport at 11.30 p.m. The last bus into the centre of London is at 11.50 p.m. We'll never make it. I know taxis are really expensive. Does anyone have any other suggestions?

Comment

C

We will be in New York City for one night. We don't need an expensive hotel but the cheap ones look really horrible. Any suggestions?

Comment

D

Does anyone know how to connect a computer to a data projector? I don't have the right port on my computer. I need it for a presentation I am giving next week.

Comment

9 Read the suggestions (1–4). Then match the suggestions with the questions (A–D) in Exercise 8. What do you think of the advice?

1

You need to buy a USB to HDMI adaptor. They're about $25. Alternatively, you could borrow someone else's laptop.

2

Sorry, I don't think you have a choice – you need to get a taxi. But why don't you book one in advance? You'll get a much better price.

3

I suggest you just go there on the day. There are always people selling tickets outside the stadium. You should probably decide before how much you are happy to pay, though.

4

How about AirBnB? It's where people rent you a room for the night in their own homes. The places are often nice and you also meet someone local who can tell you where things are.

10 Look at the suggestions in Exercise 9 again. Which of the following elements do they include?

a a greeting
b the reason for writing
c an answer to the question
d a suggestion
e an explanation of why this is a good suggestion

Writing skill Features of online posts

11 Work in pairs. Look at the posts in Exercises 8 and 9 again. Choose the correct option to complete the sentences.

1. They use *long / short* sentences.
2. The tone is *formal / conversational*.
3. Language is *direct / indirect*.
4. They *use / don't use* greetings and signing off expressions.

12 21st CENTURY OUTCOMES

Work in pairs. Each write a request for advice about something you'd like help with. Then exchange requests and write a reply to your partner's request.

13 Read your partner's reply. Was it good advice? Check that your partner has included the following points:

- an answer to the question
- appropriate language for making suggestions
- an explanation of why this is a good suggestion

21st CENTURY OUTCOMES   COLLABORATION   Using written communication to instruct and advise

Unit 11 Leaders and thinkers

12 Well-being

Morning exercise and 'tai chi', Forbidden City, Beijing, China

TEDTALKS

ARIANNA HUFFINGTON is the co-founder and editor-in-chief of the online news site *The Huffington Post*. She's also a columnist, the author of thirteen books, and co-host of *Left, Right & Center*, a political roundtable radio programme.

Arianna Huffington's idea worth spreading is that a good night's sleep can lead to increased productivity and happiness – and smarter decision-making.

BACKGROUND

1 You are going to watch an edited version of a TED Talk by Arianna Huffington called *How to succeed? Get more sleep*. Read the text about the speaker and the talk. Then work in pairs and discuss the questions.

1 What do you think Arianna Huffington's main interests are? What do you think her working life is like?
2 How do you think 'a good night's sleep' can help us?
3 How many hours' sleep do you normally get?

KEY WORDS

2 Read the sentences (1–6). The words in bold are used in the TED Talk. First guess the meaning of the words. Then match the words with their definitions (a–f).

1 It is difficult to function properly if you are **deprived** of sleep.
2 It was so hot in the room that two people actually **fainted**.
3 As CEO, he likes to be in touch **24/7** about what is happening in the company.
4 When his colleague said he had worked until midnight, John told him he had worked until 3 a.m. just for **one-upmanship**.
5 The *Titanic* sank when it hit an **iceberg** in the North Atlantic.
6 Today's young generation is **hyperconnected** and they are always on their phones.

a competing with others always to be one level better than them
b being connected with others through many different digital media
c all the time
d a large floating piece of ice in the sea
e lose consciousness for a short time
f being without something that you need or want

AUTHENTIC LISTENING SKILLS
Discourse markers

When you listen to a speaker, the discourse markers they use (e.g. *surprisingly, in particular*) tell you what kind of information is going to come next. For example, if you hear the phrase 'a few years ago', you can be fairly sure that you are going to hear a story or example to illustrate a point. If you hear 'fortunately' you know that the person is going to tell you a positive fact.

3a Look at the Authentic listening skills box. Match the discourse marker (1–5) with its function (a–e).

1 two and a half years ago
2 in fact
3 unfortunately
4 so
5 especially

a introduces a sad or negative fact
b introduces a conclusion
c introduces a strong example
d introduces a story from the past
e introduces the real truth of a situation

3b 🎧 **69** Listen to three sentences from the talk. Complete the sentences with the discourse markers that you hear.

1 There is now a kind of sleep deprivation one-upmanship – *unfortunately / especially* here in Washington …
2 … we, at the moment, have had brilliant leaders in business, in finance, in politics, making terrible decisions. *So / Two and a half years ago* a high IQ does not mean that you're a good leader.
3 *Unfortunately, / In fact,* I have a feeling that if Lehman Brothers was Lehman Brothers and Sisters, they might still be around.

3c 🎧 **70** Listen to another sentence from the end of the talk. Complete the conclusion that Arianna Huffington makes.

'So I urge you to ¹_____ and ²_____ _____ that lie inside us, to shut your engines and discover the power of sleep.'

12.1 How to succeed? Get more sleep

TEDTALKS

1 ▶ 12.1 Watch the edited version of the TED Talk. Why is it important to get more sleep, according to Arianna Huffington? Tick (✓) the items she mentions.

    a to be more productive
    b to get ahead in your career
    c to have better relationships
    d to see the big picture

2 ▶ 12.1 Watch the first part (0.00–1.23) of the talk again and complete the sentences.

  1 Arianna Huffington describes the women in the audience as Type _____ women.
  2 She says she learned the value of sleep 'the _____ way'.
  3 Two and a half years ago, Arianna Huffington _____ at her desk.
  4 According to Arianna Huffington, a life with more sleep is a 'more _____, more inspired, more joyful life'.

▶ gotten **AM ENG**
▶ got **BR ENG**

3 ▶ **12.1** Watch the second part (1.23–1.51) of the talk again. Then complete the summary using the words below.

| five | four | interesting |
| revolution | sleep | women |

Arianna Huffington says that the sleep [1] _____ is going to be led by [2] _____. She thinks the problem is that men boast about [3] _____ deprivation. She says she had dinner with a man who said he had only had [4] _____ hours' sleep the night before. She thought, 'Well, this dinner would have been more [5] _____ if he had had [6] _____ hours' sleep.'

4 ▶ **12.1** Watch the third part (1.51 to the end) of the talk again. According to Arianna Huffington, are the sentences true (T) or false (F)?

1 Women are in competition with each other for who can function with the least sleep.
2 We have great leaders, but without sleep they make bad decisions.
3 Lehman Brothers failed because they were too busy trying to make more and more money.
4 Someone with more sleep would have seen the 'iceberg' that Lehman Brothers were going to hit.
5 Sleep isn't just important for individuals; it's important for the world.

VOCABULARY IN CONTEXT

5 ▶ **12.2** Watch the clips from the TED Talk. Choose the correct meaning of the words.

6 Complete the sentences in your own words. Then compare your sentences with a partner.

1 When I was deciding what to study, my parents urged me …
2 I don't like it when people brag about …
3 I don't know the details about … , but the big picture is that …

CRITICAL THINKING Adapting an argument to an audience

7 People sometimes adapt their arguments to suit a specific audience. You need to think how this affects the strength or weakness of their argument. Work in pairs and answer the questions

1 What type of people are in Arianna Huffington's audience?
2 How did she adapt her talk to suit this audience?
3 How did the audience react to her talk? Would it be successful with a different audience?

8 Read these comments* about the TED Talk. How might Arianna Huffington respond to each of them? What do you think of each comment?

Viewers' comments

M **Mikel** – OK, it's a simple message and it's probably true: many of us don't sleep enough. But why is it a man's problem? Perhaps her audience likes hearing that, but it made me want to stop listening.

J **Jill** – I don't think she's attacking men. She is just saying that most business leaders are men and lack of sleep leads them to make bad decisions.

M **Megumi** – I agree with Jill. If there were more women business leaders, this wouldn't be a problem, because women often find a better balance than men between work and other parts of their life.

*The comments were created for this activity.

PRESENTATION SKILLS Using humour

9 Work in pairs. Answer the questions.

1 Do you think using humour in a presentation is a good idea? Why? / Why not?
2 If someone was going to use humour, what tips would you give them? Write two tips.

10 Read the Presentation tips box and compare your answers from Exercise 9.

TIPS

People use humour in presentations as a way of connecting with their audience. You don't have to use it, but if you do use humour, remember these points:

- Its purpose is to relax people. If you feel unnatural or nervous using humour, then don't use it.
- Practise in front of friends or colleagues. If they say the humour isn't working, leave it out.
- Use humour carefully so that you don't offend your audience.
- Make it personal (about your experience) if possible.
- Check that it's illustrating the point you are making and not distracting the audience from your message.
- Depending on the topic of your talk, humour may not be appropriate.

11 ▶ **12.3** Watch the clips from the TED Talk. What jokes did Arianna Huffington make about:

1 a dinner with a man who had had four hours' sleep
2 the collapse of the bank, Lehman Brothers

12 Did Arianna Huffington's humour follow the advice in the Presentation tips box? Give reasons.

13 Think of a funny story about the effects of not having enough sleep. Make some notes about your story.

14 Work in small groups. Present your stories. Were they similar?

12.2 If you walked every day ...

IF YOU WALKED AN EXTRA 30 MINUTES A DAY FOR YOUR WHOLE LIFE, ...

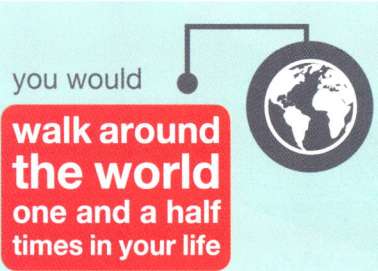 you would **walk around the world one and a half times in your life**

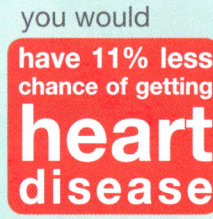 you would **have 11% less chance of getting heart disease**

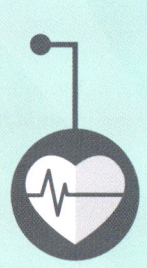

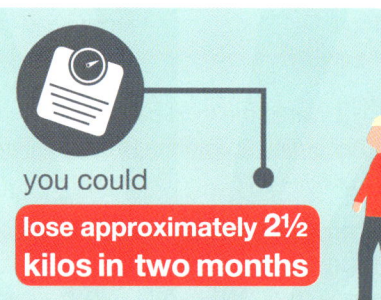 you could **lose approximately 2½ kilos in two months**

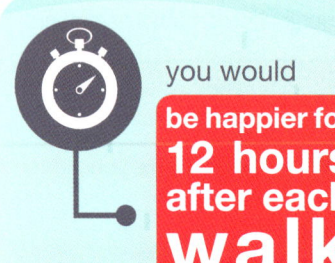 you would **be happier for 12 hours after each walk**

 you would **get fewer colds**

 you would **sleep twice as well**

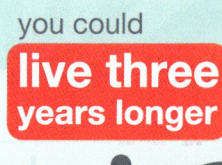 you could **live three years longer**

GRAMMAR Second conditional

1 Look at the list of items (a–f) to do with well-being. Choose the three items that you think are most important for your physical and mental well-being. Then compare your list with your partner. How well do you look after yourself in each of these areas?

   a diet (food and drink)
   b exercise
   c enjoyment of work
   d work-life balance
   e relationships with others
   f sleep

2 Look at the infographic. Answer the questions.

   1 What does the infographic say we should do to improve our well-being?
   2 How far would we walk if we took this advice?
   3 What effects would it have on our physical health? And our mental health?

3 Read the sentences in the Grammar box. Answer the questions (1–4).

SECOND CONDITIONAL

*If you **walked** an extra thirty minutes a day for your whole life, you **would get** fewer colds.*
*If you **walked** an extra thirty minutes a day for your whole life, you **could live** three years longer.*

1 What time are the sentences referring to: the future or the past?
2 Is the idea of walking an extra thirty minutes a day for your whole life a real possibilty or an imaginary situation?
3 What tense is used in the *if*-clause? What modal verbs are used in the main clause?
4 Which word expresses a more certain result: *would* or *could*?

Check your answers on page 162 and do Exercises 1–5.

4 Put the verbs in these sentences into the correct form.

1. If everyone in the USA _____ (run) regularly, Americans _____ (lose) almost one billion kilos in weight.
2. If everyone in the world _____ (become) a vegetarian, CO_2 emissions _____ (fall) by seventeen per cent.
3. If everyone in the UK _____ (eat) a healthy diet, it _____ (save) 33,000 lives a year.
4. If everyone _____ (drink) two litres of water a day, their skin _____ (look) much healthier.
5. If people _____ (sleep) eight hours a night, they _____ (be) more productive during the day.
6. If everyone _____ (understand) the relationship between physical and mental health, we _____ (all / be) happier and healthier.

5 We often use the second conditional to talk about present situations that are not actually the reality. Look at the exchange between Nancy Astor and Winston Churchill. Are they married?

If you were my husband, I'd poison your tea.

Madam, if you were my wife, I'd drink it!

6 Look at the sentences. Underline the verbs. Then describe what the reality of each situation is.

1. If I <u>were</u> you, I <u>wouldn't work</u> so hard.
   The reality is: *I am not you.*
2. If I knew the secret of happiness, I'd write a book about it.
3. If they lived in Europe, we'd see them more often.
4. If he wasn't a professional golfer, he'd be some other kind of sportsman.
5. If she didn't like working here, she wouldn't stay.
6. If I were ten years younger, I could probably beat him at tennis.

Pronunciation Contraction 'd

7a 🎧 **71** Work in pairs. Listen to three sentences from Exercise 6. What word is 'd a contraction of?

7b Work in pairs. Practise saying the sentences in Exercise 6. Pay attention to the contraction 'd.

8 Complete the sentences to make zero, first and second conditional sentences. Then change the second half of the sentences so they are true for you. Compare answers with your partner.

1. If I _____ (can) have any job I wanted, I _____ (be) a professional musician.
2. Generally, if I _____ (not / get) a good night's sleep, I _____ (find) it difficult to concentrate.
3. If I _____ (be) the boss of a big company, I _____ (pay) every employee well.
4. I find that if you _____ (eat) a proper breakfast every morning, it _____ (help) you to concentrate.
5. If I _____ (earn) $1 million dollars a year, I _____ (live) in Florida.
6. I _____ (retire) when I _____ (be) 65.
7. If I _____ (have) more free time, I _____ (spend) it reading.
8. If I _____ (get) any free time this afternoon, I _____ (try) to go to the gym.

SPEAKING Well-being and productivity

9 **21st CENTURY OUTCOMES**

Work in small groups. Read the case study below. Then use the ideas to discuss possible actions the company could take. Think of reasons for and against each action.

> **Workers at a call centre have complained of tiredness, stress and boredom at work.**
>
> They work in front of a computer screen, trying to sell insurance. Customers often refuse to speak to them and are sometimes rude. Workers are paid the minimum wage, but get bonuses for winning new customers. They work eight-hour shifts with two breaks of fifteen minutes and one break of thirty minutes. The call centre has a coffee machine, but no canteen and no recreation facilities.

Possible actions
- allow workers to stand up during calls
- change the break times
- put in some recreational areas (comfortable chairs, games)
- encourage workers to exercise
- offer workers healthy food
- pay workers in a different way

We could pay workers in a different way. For example, if they had a bigger basic salary, they would feel happier.

HEALTH LITERACY Establishing health and well-being goals

12.3 Tell me what's good for me

READING Health and well-being news

1 Work in pairs. Look at these things (1–5). Which do you think are good and which are bad for you?

1. eating salt
2. sleeping in the day
3. jogging in the city
4. being in the sun
5. spending a lot of time on social networks

2 What other things have you been told are good or bad for you? Do you follow the advice?

3 Read the five short news stories (A–E) about well-being. Match the titles (1–5) with each news story.

1. Leave work at work
2. It's what you eat that matters
3. Internet friendly
4. At the end of the day, it's all food
5. It's OK to be caught sleeping

4 Read the stories again. Are the sentences true (T) or false (F) or is the information not given (NG)?

1. People buy superfoods because they think these foods will make them healthier.
2. The British Dietetic Association says that superfoods are not healthy.
3. Superfoods are generally more expensive than other food.
4. On average German workers feel more stressed than they did twelve years ago.
5. If the new law is passed in Germany, employees could not work from home at the weekend.
6. Some Japanese companies recognize that employees need to rest sometimes.
7. Doing exercise makes you feel hungry.
8. The best way to lose weight is to do exercise and eat the right kind of food.
9. Having online friends can help you feel better, emotionally.
10. Users of Facebook have to be careful who they make friends with.

5 Find the words in bold in the text. Then match the words with their definitions (a–b).

1. **banned** (line 4)
   a not allowed b changed
2. **misleading** (line 7)
   a clever b not truthful
3. **combat** (line 13)
   a reduce b fight against
4. **power naps** (line 24–25)
   a short sleeps b rest areas
5. **cancel out** (line 29)
   a add to b undo
6. **close** (line 45)
   a good b interesting

6 Work in small groups. Discuss the conclusions in the news stories. Do you agree with the conclusions?

VOCABULARY Well-being adjectives

7 We often use different words to describe something and to say how it makes us feel. Complete the sentences with the correct adjective.

1. *relaxing / relaxed*
   a Reading is a _____ activity.
   b I feel _____ when I read.
2. *at home / welcoming*
   a People are very _____ to us in the village.
   b We feel _____ in the village.
3. *stressed / stressful*
   a It's a _____ job.
   b I feel _____ by my work.
4. *tiring / tired*
   a It was a _____ journey.
   b I felt _____ after my journey.
5. *valued / appreciative*
   a My boss is _____ of my work.
   b I feel _____ by my boss for my work.
6. *happy / enjoyable*
   a It was _____ watching them play.
   b I felt _____ watching them play.

8 Choose the correct option to complete the questions. Then ask and answer the questions with a partner.

1. Which activity do you find the most *relaxing / relaxed*?
   a gardening c walking
   b cooking d surfing the Internet
2. Which situation makes you feel most *stressful / stressed*?
   a taking an exam c getting ready to go on a trip
   b starting a new job d moving house
3. Which place in your life has been the most *at home / welcoming* place to be?
   a school / college c your neighbourhood
   b your work d another country you have visited
4. Which of these things do you find the most *tiring / tired*?
   a travelling c walking around museums
   b sitting in front of a computer d driving a car
5. Who do you feel most *appreciative / valued* by?
   a your family c your friends
   b your colleagues d your boss
6. What do you find really *enjoyable / happy*?
   a spending time alone c being active
   b shopping d being close to nature

SPEAKING Proposals for well-being

9 **21st CENTURY OUTCOMES**

Work in small groups. Imagine you are in government. Identify the risks to people's well-being in each of the areas (a–e) below. Then discuss what proposals you would make to improve the population's (adults and children) well-being.

a food and a healthy diet
b exercise and physical activity
c work-life balance
d health and medicine (smoking, health checks)
e social support for old people

People often don't know what food is good or bad for them. We could propose a law saying that food manufacturers had to put the nutritional value on the packaging.

HEALTH & WELL-BEING NEWS

A

According to YouGov research, over sixty per cent of people in the UK have bought food because it had the label 'superfood' on it. Now the British Dietetic Association has called for the term 'superfood' to be banned. They say that perhaps products like goji berries, coconut water, quinoa and pomegranate juice are healthy and have good nutritional benefits, but to call them 'superfoods' is misleading. It suggests that they are better than other food and that you should pay more for them. As one professor of nutrition pointed out, 'You don't see apples, oranges and bananas being advertised as superfoods, but they are just as healthy.'

B

In Germany, the government is wondering what it can do to combat a fifty per cent increase in stress and psychological illness in the workplace in the last twelve years. One proposal is to give employees the right not to be 'permanently reachable by modern means of communication'. If such a law was passed, it would mean that companies would not be allowed to contact employees by email or mobile phone outside normal working hours.

C

If the person next to you at work fell asleep at their desk, you would probably be worried that the boss would catch them and get angry. Not in Japan. Some companies are allowing their workers a twenty-minute sleep at their desks or in specially designed lounges. They hope that these 'power naps' will improve performance.

D

Exercise doesn't always help you lose weight. It sounds strange, but recent research in both the UK and the US shows that people often eat more after physical activity and so cancel out the benefits of the exercise. Dr Susan Jebb of the Medical Research Council in the UK says that you have to do a lot of exercise to burn off calories. For example, cycling for two hours burns off 500 calories. But if you then reward yourself with two doughnuts, you put 500 calories back into your system. The key is to make sure you burn more calories than you consume and also to choose your food carefully. A study in Brazil showed that eating apples before meals also contributed to weight loss.

E

Research by Pew, a research centre in the United States, shows that people who use online social networks have a better sense of emotional well-being. Nearly fifty per cent of US adults use at least one social network. Pew found that these people felt it gave them significant emotional support – offering them access to advice, information and friendship. Compared with non-Facebook users, Facebook users said they had more close friendships and trusted other people more. It is important to note, though, that the study did not show that social network users had a better emotional well-being; just that they *believed* they had.

21st CENTURY OUTCOMES   **HEALTH LITERACY** Understanding public health issues

12.4 What are the options?

LISTENING Time wasting

1 Work in small groups. Answer the questions.

  1 How much time do you think you waste each day?
  2 What activities do you consider a waste of time?

2 🎧 72 Listen to two people discussing the question of how to reduce the time people waste at work. Answer the questions.

  1 What is the woman's idea for reducing wasted time?
  2 What alternative idea is suggested by the other speaker?
  3 Why did the woman reject the alternative suggestion?

3 🎧 72 Complete the sentences using the verbs in the correct form. Then listen again and check your answers.

  1 The idea is that if you make them more aware of this, they _____ (become) more productive.
  2 And how would you _____ (do) that?
  3 Well, one way would be _____ (ask) them to keep a record of how they spend their time.
  4 Would that work? I mean, most people _____ (not answer) honestly.
  5 Rather than _____ (tell) them, why don't we just watch them without _____ (tell) them?
  6 We just want people _____ (think) about how they're using their time.

Pronunciation Stress in suggestions

4 🎧 73 Listen and repeat the sentences. Notice which words are stressed. Then practise saying the sentences with your partner.

  1 One way would be to use a different company.
  2 You could try phoning him.
  3 Another alternative would be to eat here.
  4 Rather than taking the bus, why don't you take the train?

SPEAKING Discussing options

5 **21st CENTURY OUTCOMES**

Work in small groups. On average, workers 'waste' two hours a day doing things that are not part of their job. Look at the picture and discuss the questions. Use the expressions in the Useful language box to help you.

  1 Which of the things in the picture are definitely a waste of a company's time?
  2 What other time-wasting activities can you think of?
  3 What could a company do to reduce wasting time at work? Brainstorm ideas.

DISCUSSING OPTIONS

Options

One way would be to ask them to keep a record of how they spend their time.
Another alternative would be to monitor them.
You could give them a kind of time sheet.
If you offered people more money, then they would work harder.
Rather than telling them, why don't we just watch them?

The key point

That's not the point. The point is that …

Questions

How would you do that?
Would that work?

WRITING A reply to an enquiry

6 You want to join a yoga club. A friend has recommended a club, but it does not have a website. You wrote an email asking for more information. Read the reply and answer the questions.

1 What options does the yoga teacher offer?
2 How would you describe the tone of her email?
3 What is the next step?

Dear Rashmi

Thank you for your enquiry about yoga classes. We would love to welcome you to the club. You mentioned that you would like to take two or three classes a week. We have Vinyasa yoga classes every day. For payment, there are three options:

1 Pay on the day: you pay for each individual class ($15 per class)
2 One-month package: ten classes, any time you choose ($120 per month)
3 Six-month package: as many classes as you like ($600)

I attach a schedule of all the classes for you to look at. In future, this schedule will be on our website, which we are redesigning at the moment. What new members often do is come along one day or evening and try a class. If you did that, you could also have a chat with us and some of our other members.

We look forward to seeing you soon.

Kind regards

Rosie Gere

7 Work in pairs. Read the email in Exercise 6 again. Match the elements (a–c) with sentences in the email.

a referring to previous communication
b introducing the options
c suggesting the next step

Writing skill Listing options

8 Look at the three options (1–3) which are listed in the email in Exercise 6. Compare them with the spoken version below. What are the differences?

'One option would be to just come along and pay on the day. That means you just pay for each individual class that you take. That costs $15 per class. Another possibility would be to buy a one-month package for $120. That would give you the possibility of taking ten classes in one month. Or lastly you could buy a six-month package for $600. With that option, you can come as many times as you like each week.'

9 Imagine you work for a gym and fitness centre. Read the email from someone who wants to join the gym. Then write a reply.

Hello

I'm interested in joining your gym. I'd like to use the gym and the swimming pool, but I'm not sure how often I can get there because I work out of town. Also, I might be moving in the next six months, so I don't want a yearly membership. Can you let me know what the options are?

Thanks and look forward to hearing from you.

Devon Martin

10 Work in pairs. Exchange emails. Check that your partner's email:

- thanks the customer for their enquiry
- sets out the different options clearly
- uses a friendly tone
- suggests the next steps

4% Daydreaming
7% Conducting personal business (banking, etc.)
23% Socializing with colleagues
45% Using the Internet for personal use

21st CENTURY OUTCOMES CREATIVE THINKING Brainstorming solutions

Review 6 | UNITS 11 AND 12

LISTENING

1 Read the article about a company called CHG Healthcare. Then choose the correct option to complete the sentences.

1. CHG is a *relatively young / very old* company.
2. CHG employees do *permanent / temporary* work in other organizations.
3. CHG is recognized for *being a good employer / having good employees*.

2 🎧 74 Listen to part of an interview about what makes CHG Healthcare a great place to work. Tick (✓) the items the speaker mentions.

a job satisfaction
b promotion
c trust (between employer and employee)
d training
e holidays
f home-work balance
g pay
h friendly atmosphere
i well-being

3 🎧 74 Work in pairs. Discuss which words from the interview complete the notes. Then listen again and complete the notes. Use one word per space.

- 98% of staff enjoy the [1]_____ of their work
- Over 90% say CHG [2]_____ them to do their job and gives them [3]_____ when they need it
- Employees get [4]_____ paid days of holiday and [5]_____ unpaid if they want
- In some cases they can work from [6]_____
- Employees are very [7]_____ – it feels like a [8]_____
- The company also pays for [9]_____ days
- Health benefits include free health [10]_____ and an onsite [11]_____ centre

GRAMMAR

4 Complete the sentences about CHG with these modal verbs.

can   don't have to   must
needs to   should   shouldn't

1. Employees _____ do voluntary work, but many choose to. On average the company pays for eight hours of voluntary work per employee per year.
2. If they want, employees _____ work 'compressed work weeks'. This means they work more hours on fewer days.
3. Another interesting idea is the PTO (paid time off) gift programme. If an employee thinks a colleague _____ have some time off, they can give some of their paid holiday to that colleague.
4. CHG believes its workers _____ miss out on exercise, just because they are at work. So the company offers its employees fitness and yoga classes.
5. CHG also believes that companies _____ give employees training to improve their professional skills.
6. If you want to get the best from your employees, you _____ make work a happy place to be.

5 Complete the comments about working conditions. Use the zero, first and second conditional.

1. 38 per cent of the executives at CHG are women. If other companies _____ (have) more women executives, I think there _____ (be) more caring workplaces like CHG.
2. Staff at CHG are well-paid. If they _____ (not / be), perhaps they _____ (not / be) so satisfied.
3. Communication between management and staff is good. Ninety per cent of employees say that if they _____ (ask) a manager a question, they _____ (always / get) an honest answer.
4. One CHG employee said: If I _____ (stay) at CHG, I _____ (use) the fitness centre more. I only use it once a week.

CHG is a healthcare company founded in 1979. It provides healthcare professionals – doctors, nurses, physical assistants, etc. – to communities across the USA. So when a particular hospital or organization needs to fill a temporary position for a healthcare professional, CHG can provide the staff so that the organization doesn't have to employ more permanent staff. CHG has been in *Fortune* magazine's top 30 best companies to work for in the USA for the last five years.

138

VOCABULARY

6 Complete the text about how *Fortune* magazine calculates which are the best companies to work for. Use the correct form of *make* and *do*.

> To find out which are the 100 best places to work, *Fortune* magazine asks the opinions of employees. The employees say what things ¹ _____ the most difference to them. The most important thing for them is trust. In other words, 'Does the organization I work for trust me to ² _____ good decisions and to ³ _____ a good job?' Fairness is also very important. Employees don't necessarily want to ⁴ _____ a lot of money, but they want a fair salary. Next, they want to feel proud of their work, so the company must ⁵ _____ business in a way that benefits society. They also want respect. They will ⁶ _____ their best for their organization, but only if the organization shows them respect in return. Lastly, they want to work in a friendly environment, where there is a sense of community and people are prepared to ⁷ _____ each other a favour now and then.

7 Choose the correct option to complete the statements by employees about the places they work at.

1. I love my new job. It's a very *welcoming / at home* atmosphere and everyone is very *relaxing / relaxed*.
2. The great thing about my company is that even though I have a fairly unimportant job, I feel *valued / appreciative*.
3. I work for a construction company that puts great emphasis on safety. That's great for us because the most *stressed / stressful* thing is the chance of an accident.
4. I work with children. It's a *tiring / tired* job, but it's also very *happy / enjoyable*.

DISCUSSION

8 Work in small groups. Discuss the questions.

1. What did you find most attractive about CHG Healthcare as a place to work?
2. What other things make an organization a great place to work?

SPEAKING

9 Read the conversation about a problem in the workplace. Then complete the conversation using the prompts.

A: Someone complained yesterday that the office was too noisy.
B: ¹ *What / kind / noise / they / complain / about?*
_____
_____

A: Noise from other people. It's an open-plan office. They say they can't concentrate.
B: ² *anyone else / ever / say / this is a problem?*
_____

A: Yes, several people have.
B: OK. ³ *Then we / need / do / something about it.*
⁴ *What / you / suggest?*
_____
_____

A: Perhaps ⁵ *if those people / wear / headphones / they / not / be bothered* by the noise.
_____
_____

B: I'm not sure about that. ⁶ *Another alternative / be / put / partitions up* between the desks.
_____
_____

A: ⁷ *not / that / be expensive?*
_____

B: Perhaps. I don't know.
A: Well, ⁸ *rather than / spend / money / the problem, why / not / we / ask people* to stop talking so much?
_____
_____

B: I think ⁹ *we / be / careful here.* ¹⁰ *If / ask / people not to talk / it / create / a bad feeling.*
_____
_____

WRITING

10 Read the post. Then write a short reply, recommending what the writer should do.

> Hello
>
> I am trying to improve my English, but I don't have much time in the day, because I work full-time. I could go to evening classes, but they are quite expensive. Does anyone have any suggestions for me?
>
> Thanks
>
> Jean-Baptiste

11 Work in pairs. Exchange replies and compare your suggestions. Did you make similar recommendations?

Grammar summary | UNIT 1

PRESENT SIMPLE

Form and use

Affirmative	Negative
I/you/we/they **live**	I/you/we/they **don't live** (don't = do not)
he/she/it **lives**	he/she/it **doesn't live** (doesn't = does not)

Question	Short answer
do I/you/we/they **live**?	Yes, I/you/we/they **do**. No, I/you/we/they **don't**.
does he/she/it **live**?	Yes, he/she/it **does**. No, he/she/it **doesn't**.

We use the present simple to talk about:
- things which are always or generally true
  I'm an architect. I **design** office buildings.
- repeated actions and routines
  He **takes** the children to school and then he **goes** to work.
- permanent situations
  She **works** as an occupational therapist.

To form the third person singular (affirmative), we add -s to the main verb.
  She **helps** people after an injury.

After words ending -s, -ss, -sh, -ch and -o, we add -es.
  He **watches** a lot of sport on TV.

If a verb ends in -y, we replace -y with -i and add -es.
  She **studies** Russian in her free time.

Negatives and questions

To form negative sentences and questions in the present simple, we use *do/don't/does/doesn't* with the main verb.
  She **doesn't like** chicken.   They **don't have** a car.
  Do you **work** here?   **Does** the bank **open** on Saturday?
  What time **does** the film **start**?

We often give short answers to *yes/no* questions using *do, don't, does* and *doesn't*. We don't use the full verb.
  A: **Do** you **work** at weekends? B: No, I **don't**. (not ~~No, I don't work.~~)
  A: **Does** she **live** near here? B: Yes, she **does**. (not ~~Yes, she lives.~~)

Wh- questions start with a question word (e.g. *What, Where, Who, When, How*). The question word is sometimes the subject, and sometimes the object.

In **subject questions,** the question word is the subject of the question. We do not use the auxiliary verb (*do/does*).
  Who manages the company? (subject)
  Which bus goes to the city centre? (subject)

In **object questions,** the question word is not the subject of the verb. We use the auxiliary verb *do/does*.
  Who do you work for? (object)
  Which bus do I take to go to the city centre? (object)

▶ Exercises 1 and 2

EXPRESSIONS OF FREQUENCY

Adverbs of frequency

We often use adverbs of frequency (*always, usually, often, sometimes, rarely, never*) with the present simple to talk about how often we do something.

Adverbs of frequency normally come before the main verb or after the verb *be*.
  I **always** wear a suit to work.   He is **often** late.

Sometimes, usually and *often* can also come at the beginning of a sentence.
  Sometimes I stay at home and read a book.

In negative sentences, adverbs of frequency come between the auxiliary verb and the main verb.
  I don't **often** eat Mexican food.

Adverbial phrases

We use adverbial phrases (*once a week, on Mondays, at the weekend*) with the present simple.

- **every** hour / day / week / month / year / Sunday
- **most** days / weeks / weekends
- **once** a(n) / **twice** a(n) / **three times** a(n) day / week / month
- **at** the weekend / nine o'clock
- **in** the spring / the summer / the autumn / the winter

Adverbial phrases can come at the beginning or the end of a sentence.
  Most days I get home before 6 p.m.
  They go on holiday **twice a year**.

▶ Exercises 3–5

INDIRECT QUESTIONS

When we want to be polite, we ask indirect questions. We start with an expression such as *Can/Could you tell me … , Do you know … , I'd like to know …* In these questions, the word order is the same as in an affirmative sentence.
  Can you tell me how many rooms **your flat has**? (Direct question: *How many rooms does your flat have?*)
  Do you know how old **she is**? (Direct question: *How old is she?*)

For *yes/no* questions, we form indirect questions using *if* or *whether*.
  I'd like to know **if the bus leaves** from here. (Direct question: *Does the bus leave from here?*)

▶ Exercise 6

EXERCISES

1 Complete the text using the present simple form of the verbs.

My children all work now. Chris ¹ _____ (have) a job with a computer games company. He ² _____ (not / get) paid much, but he ³ _____ (love) it. Sarah and Kate ⁴ _____ (work) for a big theatre in London. Sarah ⁵ _____ (do) marketing and Kate ⁶ _____ (design) costumes. Sarah ⁷ _____ (get) us tickets for shows sometimes and then we ⁸ _____ (go) to London to see them. I'm very happy that they ⁹ _____ (have) jobs, because a lot of young people ¹⁰ _____ (not / find) it easy to get work these days.

2 Complete the conversations. Use the notes to write present simple questions and answers.

1 A: Jess / go / to / university?

B: Yes, / she

A: Which / university / go to?

B: Manchester.

2 A: Who / like / cake?

B: I / not

A: you / want / some biscuits instead?

3 A: you / commute / to work / by train?

B: Yes, / I

A: How long / take?

B: An hour, each way.

4 A: Which key / open / the front door?

B: The silver one.

3 Put the words in the right order to make sentences.

1 it / at this time of year / rains / often

2 usually / I / with my tea / milk / take / don't

3 the trains / on time / run / in England / rarely

4 the last / always / is / person / he / to arrive

5 but / sometimes / eat / we / vegetarians / fish / we're

6 never / is / enough time / to do everything / there

4 Complete the text from a travel guidebook with these words.

are	always	every	most
often	once	sell	year

Shopping

The town has several markets. There is a food market ¹ _____ week in the main square. The quality of the food is high, but the prices ² _____ sometimes high too. ³ _____ a month, on Saturdays, there is an antiques market, selling old furniture and art objects. People ⁴ _____ find lots of interesting things here. There is a Christmas market next to the food market ⁵ _____ Saturdays and Sundays in December. These are ⁶ _____ very popular with tourists and visitors, because local traders usually ⁷ _____ traditional Christmas gifts. Finally, there is a big food fair in the town once a ⁸ _____ at the beginning of May. As well as food stalls there are cookery demonstrations and even cookery workshops.

5 Correct the mistake in each sentence.

1 He like Chinese food.

2 Doctors works very long hours.

3 She don't know the answer.

4 He's go to the gym every day after work.

5 Is he look like his father?

6 We eat always takeaway food on Fridays.

6 Rewrite the questions. Rewrite questions 1–3 as direct questions. Rewrite questions 4–6 as indirect questions.

1 Do you know when the bank opens?

2 Can you tell me how far the station is from here?

3 I'd like to know what the job involves.

4 'Which company does she work for?'
Do you know _____.

5 'How do I apply for the job?'
Can you tell me _____.

6 'Do you offer English courses?'
I'd like to know _____.

Grammar summary | UNIT 2

PRESENT SIMPLE AND PRESENT CONTINUOUS

We use the present simple to describe things that are generally true, permanent situations or routines.
   He **lives** in Maastricht. (= that is his permanent or usual home)
   In July it **gets** very hot in the day. (= a generally true situation)

We use the present continuous to describe events which are happening now or around now, and temporary situations.
   He **is staying** with his aunt until he finds a flat. (= temporary situation)
   It**'s getting** colder at night. (= currently changing situation)

For the present simple form, see page 140.

▶ Exercise 1

PRESENT CONTINUOUS

Form and use

Affirmative	Negative
I**'m waiting** ('m = am)	I**'m not waiting**
you/we/they **are waiting**	you/we/they **aren't waiting** (aren't = are not)
he/she/it **is waiting**	he/she/it **isn't waiting** (isn't = is not)

Question	Short answer
am I waiting?	Yes, I **am**. No, I**'m not**.
are you/we/they **waiting**?	Yes, you/we/they **are**. No, you/we/they **aren't**.
is he/she/it **waiting**?	Yes, he/she/it **is**. No, he/she/it **isn't**.

We form the present continuous with the present simple of the verb *be* plus the *-ing* form of the verb.

We use the present continuous to describe:
- events that are happening now or around now
   Jack isn't here. He**'s playing** tennis.
   What **are** you **reading**?
- temporary situations
   The TV **isn't working**. Can you fix it?
- trends (situations that are in a process of change)
   Sales of mobile phones **are increasing** every year.

▶ Exercise 2

Stative verbs

We do not usually use the present continuous with stative verbs: *have, own, know, like, want, understand, think* (when *think* means 'believe').
   I **want** to learn the piano. (not ~~am wanting~~)
   They **own** a beautiful house on the Mediterranean coast.
   She **doesn't have** a driving licence, but she's learning to drive.

▶ Exercise 3

Trends

We often use the present continuous to describe trends because trends are situations which are in the process of change.
   House prices **are going** up and up.
   The summers **are getting** warmer.
   The quality of food in restaurants **is** definitely **improving**.

▶ Exercise 4

Time expressions

The most common time expressions used with the present continuous are: *at the moment, currently, now, today* and expressions with *this* (*this week, this month*, etc.).
   She**'s speaking** to a customer **at the moment**. Can you call back in ten minutes?
   I**'m currently working** on an interesting project in Dubai.
   They**'re selling** all computers at twenty per cent discount **this week**.

▶ Exercises 5–7

EXERCISES

1 Choose the correct options to complete the conversations.

1. A: *Do you smoke / Are you smoking*?
   B: Occasionally. But *I try / I'm trying* to stop.

2. A: What *do you read / are you reading* at the moment?
   B: It's a book by Len Deighton. He *writes / is writing* thrillers.

3. A: *Does anyone sit / Is anyone sitting* here?
   B: Yes, my friend. *He just gets / He's just getting* a coffee from the canteen.

4. A: I *usually take / am usually taking* the train to work, but they *do / are doing* some work on the line at the moment.
   B: Oh, I *never take / am never taking* the train. It's too expensive.

5. A: What *does your company do / is your company doing*?
   B: We *make / are making* parts for helicopters.

2 Complete the conversation using the present continuous form of the verbs.

A: Hello. Can I help you?
B: Yes, ¹ _____ (I / look) for Mr Jarvis' office.
A: Oh, come with me. ² _____ (I / go) in that direction. ³ _____ (he / expect) you?
B: Yes, our meeting's at 2.00 p.m.
A: OK. Here we are. Oh dear, he's not here. Perhaps ⁴ _____ (he / have) lunch. I can phone him if you like.
B: No, that's OK.
A: Well, can I get you a cup of tea while ⁵ _____ (you / wait)? I can't get you a coffee, I'm afraid, because the coffee machine ⁶ _____ (not / work) at the moment.
B: Thanks. Tea is great.

3 Look at the underlined verbs. Are the uses of the present continuous correct? If not, rewrite the verb using the present simple.

I bought a new bed and now I ¹ <u>am trying</u> to build it, but I ² <u>am not understanding</u> the instructions. My wife ³ <u>is working</u> today and I ⁴ <u>am wanting</u> to finish the bed before she comes home. We ⁵ <u>are not having</u> another bed, because we threw the old one away. Normally I like this kind of job, but I ⁶ <u>am not enjoying</u> this one. I ⁷ <u>am knowing</u> that she will be angry if the bed is not finished.

4 Complete the sentences describing trends using the correct form of these verbs.

eat   get (x2)   go   live   increase

1. More and more people _____ abroad for their holidays.
2. The cost of fruit and vegetables _____.
3. It _____ harder to find a job.
4. People _____ healthier food.
5. The weather _____ warmer.
6. More and more people _____ in big cities.

5 Choose the correct time expression to complete the sentences.

1. Sorry, I can't speak. I'm working *at the moment / always*.
2. They clean the room *this week / every day*.
3. We're *currently / this week* looking for a new editor.
4. They're interviewing people for the job *every day / this week*.
5. She *currently / usually* goes for a run on Saturday morning.
6. Where is he living *sometimes / now*?

6 Complete the conversation using the present simple and present continuous form of the verbs.

A: ¹ What / you / do / at the moment?

B: ² Well, currently / I / work / as a chef in a restaurant, but I / look / for a new job.

A: Oh, why's that?
B: ³ Well, I / like / the work generally, but right now I / not / learn / anything new.

A: ⁴ What / you / want / to learn?

B: ⁵ I / hope / to be a pastry chef one day.

A: You mean making cakes and things?
B: Yes, that's right. ⁶ I / currently / do / a French pastry course. ⁷ I / go / to classes every week.

A: Good for you! ⁸ I / often / think / about training to do something different, but I / never / do / anything about it!

7 Correct the mistake in each sentence.

1. We are often eating out in the evenings.

2. I only stay here for a few days.

3. What do you do these days?

4. They are owning a big house in the country.

5. Exam results in schools improve each year.

Grammar summary | UNIT 3

COUNTABLE AND UNCOUNTABLE NOUNS

Form and use

There are two types of noun in English: countable and uncountable. Countable nouns are things we can count (three pens, seven tickets). They have a singular and a plural form. We use them with *a/an*, *the* and numbers.

> I bought **a ticket** for myself and **two tickets** for you and Pete.
> They don't have **a car**.
> Do you have **a mobile phone**?
> Did you see **the programme** about tigers?

Uncountable nouns are things we can't count. They are singular and don't have a plural form. We use uncountable nouns with *the* or no article. You can't use them with *a/an* or numbers. We don't put a final *-s* on an uncountable noun.

> He brought **the money** to pay for our trip.
> I drink **coffee** every day.
> Did you see **the advice** about how to lose weight?

Common uncountable nouns are: *advice, information, meat, money, time*.

▶ Exercises 1 and 2

some, any and no

	Countable nouns	Uncountable nouns
Affirmative	I have **some** books.	I have **some** information.
Negative	I don't have **any** books.	I don't have **any** information. I have **no** information.
Question	Do you have **any** books?	Do you have **any** information?

We use *some, any* and *no* with plural countable and uncountable nouns to talk about quantity. With plural countable nouns and uncountable nouns, we use:

- *some* in affirmative sentences
  I have **some paper**.
  She has **some tickets**.
- *any* in questions
  Do you have **any** brothers or sisters?
- *not ... any* or *no* in negative sentences
  We **don't** have **any** information about the exact date at the moment.
  We have **no information** about the exact date at the moment.

Notice that we use *some* in questions, particularly in requests and offers, when we want or expect the answer 'yes'.
> Would you like **some coffee**? Yes, please.

▶ Exercises 3 and 4

EXPRESSIONS OF QUANTITY: *MUCH, MANY, A LOT OF, A FEW, A LITTLE*

Countable nouns

We use *many, a lot of* and *a few* with plural countable nouns.
We use *a lot of* and *a few* in affirmative sentences.
> I have **a lot of** friends from university.
> There are **a lot of** good places to eat round here.
> There are **a few** eggs in the cupboard.

We use *many* in negative sentences and questions.
> I don't have **many** friends at work.
> How **many** people are coming to the party?

We can also use *a lot of* in negative sentences.
> I don't have **a lot of** friends at work.

Uncountable nouns

We use *much, a lot of* and *a little* with uncountable nouns.
We use *a lot of* and *a little* in affirmative sentences.
> There is **a lot of** information to read.
> There's **a little** milk in the fridge.

We use *much* in negative sentences and questions.
> There isn't **much** time to read the information.
> How **much** money do you need?

We can also use *a lot of* in negative sentences.
> There isn't **a lot of** time to read the information.

▶ Exercises 5–7

EXTENSION: *VERY, TOO AND ENOUGH*

We use *not + very + much/many +* noun to express quantity. *Very* does not change the meaning greatly. With an affirmative verb, we use *very + little/few +* noun to emphasize the small quantity.
> I don't have **very many** friends in London.
> There isn't **very much** milk in the fridge.
> The website gives **very little** information about the club.
> There were **very few** people at the concert.

We use *enough +* noun to say there is the correct or a sufficient quantity of something. We use *not + enough +* noun to say there is less than we need.
> There are **enough** chairs to seat 120 people.
> I do**n't** have **enough** money to buy lunch.

We use *too + much/many +* noun to say there is more than we want or need. We use *too + little/few +* noun to say there is less than we want or need.
> There are **too many** cars in the city centre.
> I've got **too much** work at the moment – I need a holiday.
> I had **too little** time to visit the whole museum.
> There are **too few** women managers in some companies.

▶ Exercise 8

144

EXERCISES

1 Complete the table with these words.

biscuit	chair	dollar	food	fun
furniture	job	money	music	party
river	song	water	work	

Countable: _____, _____, _____, _____, _____, _____, _____

Uncountable: _____, _____, _____, _____, _____, _____, _____

2 Which of these words needs an -s on the end?

1. a lot of information_____
2. three suitcase_____
3. some good suggestion_____
4. some expensive luggage_____
5. a lot of question_____
6. a bowl of banana_____
7. terrible weather_____
8. a lot of work_____

3 Choose the correct options to complete the conversations.

1. A: Do you have ¹ *a / any* news about the job you applied for?
   B: No. They said they would send me ² *a / some* letter, but I haven't received anything.

2. A: Can you help? I need to move ³ *a / some* furniture.
   B: Sure. What do you want to move?
   A: I need to put ⁴ *a / some* table and ⁵ *a / some* chairs into the meeting room.

3. A: Do we have ⁶ *a / any* food for dinner?
   B: There ⁷ *is / are* the meat that I bought yesterday.
   A: I don't want ⁸ *some / any* meat. I'm not very hungry.

4. A: I'm going to the shops. Do you want anything?
   B: We need ⁹ *a / some* fruit – and perhaps ¹⁰ *a / some* newspaper.

4 Complete the sentences with *some, any* and *no*.

1. Can you give me _____ advice?
2. They have _____ flowers in their garden – just two large trees.
3. She made _____ delicious cakes for the party.
4. I need to go to the shop. We don't have _____ milk left.
5. Are there _____ people that you want me to contact?
6. The factory closed down two months ago and now there is _____ work in the area.

5 Choose the correct option to complete the conversations.

A: How ¹ *much / many* money does a lawyer earn?
B: It depends. Big corporate lawyers earn ² *much / a lot of* money. But most lawyers work ³ *many / a lot of* hours and have quite low salaries.

A: Do you speak German?
B: Not really. I know ⁴ *a little / a few* words, but I didn't pay ⁵ *much / many* attention to languages at school.

A: How was your holiday? Did you do ⁶ *much / many* sunbathing?
B: No. It was cloudy most of the time. There was even ⁷ *a little / a few* rain.

A: Are you busy this afternoon? There are ⁸ *a little / a few* emails we need to look at.
B: OK, I can spare ⁹ *a little / a few* moments. How ¹⁰ *much / many* emails are there?

6 Complete the conversation. Use one word in each space.

A: I need ¹ _____ help! I don't have ² _____ time before I have to leave for the airport. I need to find ³ _____ book to read and ⁴ _____ suntan lotion.
B: Suntan lotion? I thought it was ⁵ _____ business trip.
A: It is – but I hope I'll have a ⁶ _____ time for relaxation. I have a ⁷ _____ meetings on Friday morning, but I don't have ⁸ _____ meetings on Saturday.

7 Correct the mistake in each sentence.

1. He gave us a lot of informations in the lecture.
   _____
2. I have an advice for you.
   _____
3. I can't make an omelette. We have any eggs.
   _____
4. There is a few time before we have to leave.
   _____
5. He earns much money as a banker.
   _____
6. Could you pass me any water?
   _____

8 Complete the second sentence so it has the same meaning as the first. Use the words given.

1. There is too little space to put another desk here.
   There _____ to put another desk here. (enough)
2. There weren't many restaurants in the town centre.
   There were _____ in the town centre. (very)
3. It was impossible to understand all the information they gave us.
   They gave _____ to understand. (too)
4. I'm sorry. I'm in a hurry.
   I'm sorry. I don't have _____. (very / time)
5. We can't make a football team with only eight people.
   There are _____ to make a football team. (too / people)

Grammar summary | UNIT 4

PAST SIMPLE AND PAST CONTINUOUS

Past simple: form and use

For regular verbs, we form the past simple with infinitive + -ed:
play ➡ played, want ➡ wanted, walk ➡ walked
I **worked** in Italy in 2014.
He **started** his own company two years ago.

Notice the spelling rules for other regular verbs:
- for verbs ending in -e, we add -d: organize ➡ organized
- for verbs ending in -y, we change the -y to an -i and add -ed: study ➡ studied, try ➡ tried
- for verbs ending in vowel + consonant (not -w, -x or -y), we double the consonant and add -ed: stop ➡ stopped

Some verbs have an irregular affirmative form in the past simple:
be ➡ was/were, do ➡ did, come ➡ came,
go ➡ went, know ➡ knew, write ➡ wrote

We use the past simple:
- to talk about completed actions and events in the past. We often use a time phrase (yesterday, last month, five years ago).
  I **met** James three years ago.
  I **learned** German at school.
- to describe actions and events that happened one after another (often in a story or narrative).
  She **listened** carefully to the arguments and she **thought** for a few moments. Then she **said**, 'Yes, I agree.'
- for a single, repeated action in the past.
  He **walked** to work every day.

Negatives and questions

To form negative sentences and questions in the past simple, we use did/didn't + the main verb.
Did you **see** Pete yesterday?
I **didn't know** that before.
Did she **marry** him? No, she **didn't**.

The past simple of be is I/he/she/it was and we/you/they were. The negative forms are wasn't and weren't. We invert the subject and verb when we ask questions.
I **was** a teacher for ten years.
The students **weren't** at school last week – it was a holiday.
Were you at the concert last weekend?

▶ Exercise 1

Past continuous: form and use

We form the past continuous with the past simple of the verb be (was/were) plus the -ing form of the verb.
She **was waiting** for the train to arrive.
We **were playing** tennis.

We use the past continuous to talk about an activity or event in progress in the past at the same time as the main event (in the past simple).
We **were sitting** at our desks doing some work. Suddenly we **heard** a loud crash.

We often use the past continuous with the past simple to talk about an activity in progress when another action took place. We can join the actions with while or when.
She heard the news while she **was driving** to work.
My colleagues **were waiting** for me when I arrived at the café.

We do not usually use the past continuous with stative verbs: have, own, know, like, want.
I went to Manchester to study medicine. At that time I **wanted** to be a doctor.

▶ Exercise 2

PAST PERFECT

Form and use

We form the past perfect with had ('d) + the past participle.
He **had seen** the aeroplane crash.
They **hadn't visited** London before.
Had she **heard** about the restructuring before she applied for the job?

We use the past perfect to talk about an event or action that happened before another event in the past. We often use the past perfect simple and the past simple together.

main event   main event
↓   ↓
He **went** to the interview, but he **didn't get** the job because he **hadn't prepared** for it.
                                 ↑
                          earlier event

We often use the following time expressions with the past perfect to emphasize that this action happened earlier: already, before, earlier, just, previously, recently

▶ Exercise 3

Comparison of narrative tenses

When we tell a story:
- we use the past continuous to describe the scene or background to the main event
- we use the past simple to describe the main events one after another
- we use the past perfect to refer to an earlier time before the main event
  I **was walking** in the park. The sun **was shining**. I **heard** a scream and **ran** to the lake. I **saw** a boy. He **had fallen** into the water.

▶ Exercises 4–6

EXERCISES

1 Complete the conversation using the past simple form of the verbs.

A: ¹_____ (you / see) the documentary about consumerism on the TV last night?
B: No ²_____ (I / not).
³_____ (be / it) good?
A: Yes, it was very good. It ⁴_____ (explain) why we throw things away and buy new things. Fifty years ago people ⁵_____ (make) things to last. But many companies ⁶_____ (change) that in the 1980s. Also in the programme, they ⁷_____ (interview) people waiting in a queue to buy the latest iPhone. The interviewer ⁸_____ (ask) one man if the new phone ⁹_____ (be) very different. The man ¹⁰_____ (reply) that he ¹¹_____ (not / think) so, but he just ¹²_____ (want) to have the latest phone!

2 Choose the correct option (past simple or past continuous) to complete the sentences.

1 I *was sitting / sat* in the park at lunchtime when a bird *was flying / flew* down and *was stealing / stole* my sandwich.
2 She *had / was having* a brilliant idea while she *was walking / walked* to work this morning.
3 Jaime *was leaving / left* the meeting while they *were still discussing / still discussed* the project.
4 He *was leaving / left* before the meeting *was ending / ended*.
5 They *weren't getting / didn't get* any sleep because the neighbours *were playing / played* loud music all night.
6 Sorry, I *wasn't knowing / didn't know* that you were *waiting / waited* for me.
7 We *were driving / drove* to Vancouver and then we *were taking / took* a ferry to Vancouver Island.
8 *Did you stay / Were you staying* in bed while you *had / were having* a cold?

3 Look at the underlined verbs. Are the uses of the past perfect correct? If not, rewrite the verb using the correct tense.

1 When I arrived at the post office it <u>had closed</u>. So I couldn't buy any stamps.
2 She got up and <u>had eaten</u> breakfast. Then she cleaned her bedroom.
3 The room was cold because someone <u>had left</u> the window open.
4 They went to Rome because they <u>had never visited</u> Italy before.
5 I sent you a message yesterday. <u>Had</u> you <u>got</u> it?
6 When my phone rang, I <u>hadn't answered</u> it.

4 Danny and Sam were invited to dinner at 8 p.m. Say approximately what time they arrived in each case. Give reasons for your answers.

1 When Danny and Sam arrived, we sat down and <u>ate</u> dinner.
_____

2 When Danny and Sam arrived, we <u>were eating</u> dinner.
_____

3 When Danny and Sam arrived, we <u>had already eaten</u> dinner.
_____

5 Complete the story using the past simple, past continuous and past perfect form of the verbs.

A few years ago my wife and I ¹ _____went_____ (go) to Marrakech in Morocco for a short holiday. We ²_____ (want) to see the city and to spend some time relaxing in the warm weather. We ³_____ (know) that Marrakech was famous for its markets, but we ⁴_____ (not / want) to do any shopping. We ⁵_____ (do) lots of sightseeing and we ⁶_____ (have) a great time.

On our last day we ⁷_____ (walk) through a market when my wife ⁸_____ (see) some shoes that she really ⁹_____ (like). Although we ¹⁰_____ (decide) not to do any shopping that day, she ¹¹_____ (go) into the shop to buy them. I ¹²_____ (wait) outside. Twenty minutes later, she ¹³_____ (come) out of the shop. The shopkeeper ¹⁴_____ (sell) her three pairs of shoes, a handbag and a set of six plates!

6 Correct the mistake in each sentence.

1 Where were you training to become a teacher?
_____
2 He broke his leg while he played football.
_____
3 I was thinking it was the best thing to do.
_____
4 Sorry, I had forgotten to buy some milk.
_____
5 When I got to the station, the train already left.
_____
6 Why did you parked the car so far from your house?
_____

147

Grammar summary | UNIT 5

COMPARATIVES AND SUPERLATIVES

Regular adjectives

Adjective	Comparative	Superlative
cheap	cheaper	the cheapest
big	bigger	the biggest
simple	simpler	the simplest
healthy	healthier	the healthiest
expensive	more expensive	the most expensive

We add -er to regular, short adjectives to form the comparative.
We add -est to regular, short adjectives to form the superlative.
    cheap → cheaper → cheapest

We add *more* and *most* to longer adjectives to form the comparative and superlative.
    expensive → more expensive → most expensive

Notice the spelling rules for comparative and superlative adjectives.

- for regular, short adjectives, add -er/-est:
  long → longer → longest
- for adjectives ending in -e, add -r/st:
  large → larger → largest
- for adjectives ending in -y (after a consonant), change the -y to -i and add -er/-est:
  happy → happier → happiest,
  healthy → healthier → healthiest
- for adjectives ending in consonant-vowel-consonant, double the final consonant and add -er/-est:
  big → bigger → biggest

We use the comparative form to compare two things. We use *than* after a comparative adjective.
    London is **bigger** than Paris.
    Life in the country is **more peaceful** than city life.

We use the superlative form to compare one thing with three or more other things. We usually use *the* before a superlative adjective.
    My school days were **the happiest** days of my life.
    The train is **the most comfortable** way to travel.

▶ Exercises 1 and 2

Irregular adjectives

Adjective	Comparative	Superlative
good	better	the best
bad	worse	the worst
many	more	the most
little	less	the least

Some adjectives have irregular comparative forms.
    The weather was **better than** we expected.
    It's a **worse** film **than** the first one.
    He won **the most** votes of all the candidates.
    I want to spend **the least** amount of money possible.

Notice that we can also use *less* and *the least* and *more* and *the most* with an adjective.
    The Acacia hotel is **the least expensive**, but it's also **less convenient than** the other two hotels.

▶ Exercises 3 and 4

(not) as … as

We use *as* + adjective + *as* to compare two things and say they are the same or equal.
    Ewa is **as tall as** her sister.
    Alaska is **as cold as** Canada.

We use *not as* + adjective + *as* to compare two things and say that one is less than the other.
    The Italian restaurant is **not as expensive as** the French restaurant. (= The Italian restaurant is less expensive than the French restaurant.)
    She is **not as young as** she looks!
    The film was **not as good as** the book.

more + noun

We can also make comparisons with *more* + noun.
    There are **more waiters** than customers in this restaurant.
    The bus is cheaper but it takes **more time**.

the same and different

We also use *the same … as* and *different from/to* to compare things.
    He's wearing **the same** shirt **as** you.
    English is **different from** other languages.
    This coat is a **different** colour **to** the other one, but they are the **same** price **as** each other.

▶ Exercises 5 and 6

EXERCISES

1 Complete the sentences using the comparative and superlative form of the adjectives.

1. What is the _____ (quick) way to get to the station from here?
2. Do you have a _____ (cheap) perfume than this one?
3. What do you think is a _____ (rewarding) career – law or banking?
4. He always chooses the _____ (expensive) dish on the menu.
5. I always pay in cash. It's _____ (simple) than using a card.
6. Do you think eating a lot of meat is _____ (healthy) than eating no meat at all?
7. It was the _____ (pretty) dress in the shop.
8. That was the _____ (difficult) interview I have ever had.

2 Put the words in the correct order to make sentences.

1. than / is / gold / less / silver / expensive
   _____
2. is / flying economy / than / more / comfortable / flying business class
   _____
3. the problem / you / than / difficult / think / more / is
   _____
4. of / she's / daughters / oldest / four / the
   _____
5. idea / is / your / best / first / always / not / your
   _____

3

| best | ~~better~~ | least | less |
| more | most | worse | worst |

Most people think it is ¹ _____better_____ to be rich than to be poor. But that is not always true. Winning the lottery was actually the ² _____ thing that ever happened to me! Suddenly I had ³ _____ 'friends' than I had ever had before. But they weren't real friends. They were ⁴ _____ interested in me than in my money. To make things ⁵ _____, my real friends stayed away.

I didn't go crazy with the money. I bought a few new things – the ⁶ _____ thing was a new car – but they didn't really make me any happier. So in the end I gave all the money to a local children's hospital. People often ask me if it was a difficult decision. And I say, 'No, it is probably one of the ⁷ _____ difficult decisions I have made and it also gave me the ⁸ _____ satisfaction'.

4 Look at the underlined comparatives and superlatives. Are they correct? If not, correct the mistake.

1. I'm sorry only two people replied. But two is <u>better</u> than none.
2. What is <u>the more interesting</u> place to visit in the area?
3. Making your own website is <u>simpler</u> than you think.
4. He's a pessimist. He always expects <u>the worse</u> thing to happen.
5. She left work <u>more early</u> than usual.
6. I have <u>the least</u> money than I thought I had.
7. She is <u>the tallest</u> person in the class.
8. He wasn't <u>as angry than</u> I expected.

5 Complete the conversations. Use one word in each space.

1. A: What is ¹ __the__ tallest building in the world?
   B: I think it's the Burj Al Khalifa in Dubai. It's certainly taller ² _____ the Petronas Towers in Malaysia.
2. A: What do you think of the restaurant 'In Shanghai' on Bridge Street? Apparently it's the ³ _____ popular Chinese restaurant in Manchester.
   B: Really? The food is good, but it's not as tasty ⁴ _____ the food at 'China Kitchen'.
3. A: Do you still run every day?
   B: No. I'd like to. I'm not ⁵ _____ fit as I was in the past. The trouble is I'm too busy with work. I need ⁶ _____ time for exercise.
   A: Yes, I'm in the same situation ⁷ _____ you.
4. A: Do you think it's ⁸ _____ difficult for young people to find a job these days ⁹ _____ when we were young?
   B: Yes, I do. But I think the ¹⁰ _____ difficult thing for them is to find somewhere cheap to live in the city. The rents in London are some of ¹¹ _____ highest in the world. It's very different ¹² _____ twenty years ago.
   A: Yes, but London is unusual. Things are ¹³ _____ as bad ¹⁴ _____ that everywhere.

6 Correct the mistake in each sentence.

1. New York is more expensive that Paris.
   _____
2. My wedding day was the happier day of my life.
   _____
3. I find physics a more easier subject than maths.
   _____
4. It is different than how it was twenty years ago.
   _____
5. It is the most bad restaurant in the city.
   _____
6. The interview went the best than I expected.
   _____

Grammar summary | UNIT 6

VERB PATTERNS WITH INFINITIVE AND -ING

verb + to + infinitive	agree, decide, expect, hope, learn (how), manage, need, plan, promise, seem, try, want, would like
verb + object + to + infinitive	ask, encourage, expect, help, need, persuade, teach … (how), tell, want, would like
verb + -ing	avoid, consider, continue, enjoy, finish, hate, like, spend time
verb + -ing OR to + infinitive	continue, like, start

Verb + to + infinitive

After certain verbs we use the to + infinitive form of another verb. This is often to talk about hopes, intentions and decisions.
  We decided **to wait**.
  I tried **to explain** the risks.
  He wants **to come** with us.

> Common verbs which are followed by the to + infinitive form are: agree, decide, expect, hope, learn, manage, need, plan, promise, seem, try, want, would like.

Notice that know and learn are often followed by how before to + infinitive.
  I **know how to write** my name in Japanese.
  She is **learning (how) to swim**.

Verb + object + to + infinitive

Certain verbs can also have an object before the to + infinitive form of another verb. In these cases the object is the object of the main verb but the subject of the to + infinitive verb.
  She **asked me to check** the train times.
  I **would like everyone to concentrate**.
  I **need you to help** me with my homework.

> Common verbs which are followed by object + to + infinitive are: ask, encourage, expect, help, need, persuade, teach, tell, want, would like.

Some verbs must have an object before to + infinitive. The most common are: encourage, persuade, tell, teach.
  I **told him to wait** in reception.
  They **persuaded us to stay** another night.

We don't have to use to with the verb help.
  Coffee **helps me (to) stay** awake.

Notice that teach is often followed by how before to + infinitive.
  He **taught me (how) to play** guitar.

Verb + -ing

We use the -ing form of the verb after certain verbs.
  I enjoy **listening** to music in my car.
  They don't like **watching** football matches.
  Did you consider **saying** 'no'?

> Common verbs which are followed by the -ing form of the verb are: avoid, consider, continue, enjoy, finish, hate, like, spend time.

Verb + -ing or to + infinitive

Some verbs can be followed by either -ing or to + infinitive. The meaning is the same. The most common verbs which can be followed by both forms are: continue, like and start.
  It **continued to rain / raining** for three days.
  I **like to eat / eating** Chinese food from time to time.
  He **started to play / playing** football when he was five.

Negatives in verb patterns

To make the second verb negative in these verb patterns, we use not before to + infinitive or the -ing form.
  I told him **not to wait**.
  We spent a lot of time **not doing** anything.

▶ Exercises 1 and 2

INFINITIVE AND -ING CLAUSES

We can use verbs in two ways to describe how something is.

It + be + adjective + to + infinitive	Verb + -ing + be + adjective
It is easy to find our house.	Finding our house is easy.
It is tiring to commute every day.	Commuting every day is tiring.

▶ Exercises 3–5

150

EXERCISES

1 Complete the conversations using *to* + infinitive or the *-ing* form of the verbs.

1. A: What are you doing?
   B: I'm trying ¹ _____ (fix) my bike.
   A: Would you like me ² _____ (help) you?
   B: Yes, please. Do you know how ³ _____ (make) the brakes work?

2. A: Do you enjoy ⁴ _____ (speak) in public?
   B: I don't mind ⁵ _____ (give) presentations if I have time to prepare.
   A: I hate ⁶ _____ (stand) up in front of large groups of people.
   B: When do you have to do that?
   A: I agreed ⁷ _____ (give) a talk at a conference next month.

3. A: Are you planning ⁸ _____ (do) anything special for your 30th birthday?
   B: Yes. My friend Juan and I have decided ⁹ _____ (have) a big party.
   A: Where?
   B: We considered ¹⁰ _____ (rent) the DanceMania nightclub, but it was too expensive.
   A: How many people do you expect ¹¹ _____ (come)?
   B: About 200. We'll continue ¹² _____ (look) for a venue, but it's not easy.

4. A: What do you think of these companies that avoid ¹³ _____ (pay) their taxes?
   B: I think it's terrible. Someone needs ¹⁴ _____ (do) something about it.
   A: I agree. It seems ¹⁵ _____ (be) the big companies that are the problem.
   B: Why should small companies pay and not big ones? No one likes ¹⁶ _____ (pay) taxes.

2 Put the words in the correct order to make sentences.

1. buy / to / some / need / I / stamps
   I need to buy some stamps.
2. you / him / me / call / can / tell / to
   _____?
3. want / you / go / me / to / do / the bank / to
   _____?
4. not / I / hope / be / late / to
   _____.
5. agreed / her / pay / £12 per hour / I / to
   _____.
6. not / hate / I / the answer / knowing
   _____.
7. me / encouraged / the job / apply / she / for / to
   _____.
8. her / asked / two tickets / to / I / book
   _____.

3 Rewrite the sentences so they have the same meaning.

1. It can be stressful to change jobs.
   _____ stressful.
2. Knowing the right person to contact is essential.
   It _____.
3. Helping people with their problems is very rewarding.
   It _____.
4. It was strange to see him again after so many years.
   _____ strange.
5. Walking downhill is easier than walking uphill.
   It _____.
6. It was embarrassing not to have the right information.
   _____ embarrassing.
7. Planning a big event takes a long time.
   It _____.
8. It was great to spend time with my family.
   _____ great.

4 Write two sentences for each set of prompts.

1. nice / have a picnic / in the summer
   It's nice to have a picnic in the summer.
   Having a picnic in the summer is nice.
2. not easy / write poetry
   _____.
3. tiring / work / twelve hours per day
   _____.
4. bad idea / go for a run / without a bottle of water
   _____.
5. sensible / book tickets / in advance
   _____.
6. not polite / phone people / after 9 p.m.
   _____.

5 Correct the mistake in each sentence.

1. I enjoy to listen to classical music.
2. I don't mind wait.
3. Can you help us finding a new apartment?
4. He told to do my work again.
5. I persuaded him to not leave.
6. To work late at night is a bad idea.

151

Grammar summary | UNIT 7

PRESENT PERFECT SIMPLE

Form and use

Affirmative	Negative
I/you/we/they **have lived**	I/you/we/they **haven't lived** (haven't = have not)
he/she/it **has lived**	he/she/it **hasn't lived** (hasn't = has not)

Question	Short answer
have I/you/we/they **lived?**	Yes, I/you/we/they **have**. No, I/you/we/they **haven't**.
has he/she/it **lived?**	Yes, he/she/it **has**. No, he/she/it **hasn't**.

We form the present perfect simple with the present simple of the verb *have* (*have*/*has*) + past participle. We add *-ed* to regular verbs to form the past participle:
play ➞ played, watch ➞ watched, work ➞ worked

The spelling rules for other regular verbs are the same as for the past simple tense (see page 146).

Some verbs have irregular past participles, e.g.:
do ➞ done, make ➞ made, see ➞ seen

To form negative sentences and questions in the present perfect, we use *have*/*has* and *haven't*/*hasn't* + past participle.
He **hasn't read** any of Hilary Mantel's books.
Have you **met** her before?

We use the present perfect simple to talk about experiences or things that happened at an unspecified time in the past. The present perfect may also suggest that the action may happen again in the future.
I **have visited** many different countries in my life.
Brazil **has won** the World Cup five times.

The verb *go* has two past participle forms: *been* and *gone*. We use *been* to say someone went to a place and came back. We use *gone* to say the person is still in the place.
I**'ve been** to the bank. (And now I'm back.)
He**'s gone** to London for the day. (He's still in London.)

▶ Exercises 1 and 2

PRESENT PERFECT SIMPLE AND PAST SIMPLE

When we use the present perfect simple, we often don't say when the action happened (the time is not specified). We use the past simple to describe a finished action at a specific time in the past. We often say when the action or event happened.
He**'s worked** mostly in the food industry.
He **worked** for Kraft foods from 2011 to 2013.
Yes, I**'ve met** her before. We **met** at Jo's party.

We often use the past simple after a present perfect question to give more information about the experience.
Have you **been** to Greece?
Yes, I have. I **went** there in 2015.

▶ Exercise 3

We often use the present perfect with *ever*, *never*, *already* and *yet*. *Ever* means at any time in the past; *never* means at no time in the past.
Have you **ever** been on a seaplane?
She's **never** lived on her own.

We use *already* and *yet* to talk about actions that happened recently, or actions that have not happened but we think will happen soon. We use *already* in affirmative sentences and *yet* in questions and negative sentences.
I've **already** made the sandwiches, but I haven't prepared any drinks **yet**.
Has he returned **yet**?

▶ Exercise 4

We also use the present perfect simple to talk about things which happened recently, where the present result not the past action is important.
I**'ve lost** my wallet. (= I can't find my wallet.)
He**'s left** the company. (= He doesn't work here anymore.)

▶ Exercises 5 and 6

EXTENSION: PRESENT PERFECT CONTINUOUS

We form the present perfect continuous with *have*/*has* + *been* + *-ing*.
We **have been travelling** since six o'clock this morning.
He **hasn't been watching** the football match.

We use the present perfect continuous to talk about:
- the duration of an action which started in the past and is continuing now.
  We **have been waiting** for them to arrive since 10 a.m.
  We **have been working** on this project for three years.
- how someone has spent their time recently (not the result of their actions).
  Jack**'s been playing** on his computer all day.

We use *for* to introduce the duration of an event or action and *since* to say when the event/action began.
I've been waiting **for** three hours.
I've been waiting **since** nine o'clock.

When we use a stative verb (e.g. *know*, *live*, *belong*) to talk about an event or action that started in the past and is continuing, we use the simple not the continuous form.
I **have known** him for years. (not ~~I have been knowing him for years.~~)

▶ Exercise 7

152

EXERCISES

1 Complete the conversation using the present perfect simple form of the verbs.

A: So, I ¹_____ (look) at your CV. ²_____ (you / have) any experience of working with animals before?

B: A little. I ³_____ (own) a few pets – a dog and some rabbits – and I ⁴_____ (also / help) my uncle on his farm a few times. But I ⁵_____ (not / work) in a zoo before.

A: What animals does your uncle have?

B: He only has cows and pigs now, but he ⁶_____ (also / own) some more exotic animals in the past. He had llamas and ostriches too, but he ⁷_____ (sell) those now.

A: And working with animals: what ⁸_____ (it / teach) you?

B: The most important thing is that I ⁹_____ (learn) to be more patient. It ¹⁰_____ (also / give) me more confidence.

2 Are the sentences with *been* and *gone* correct? If not, correct them.

1 He**'s** just **been** to the shops. He'll be back in a moment.
2 **Have** you **ever been** to the USA?
3 I**'ve gone** to the garage. They said there was nothing wrong with my car.
4 My sister **has been** to Australia to start her new job.

3 Choose the correct option to complete the sentences.

1 Hello. I don't think *we met / we've met*. My name's Paul.
2 The ship *has left / left* the harbour at 3 a.m.
3 John is a well-known portrait painter. He *painted / has painted* many famous people.
4 *I had / I've had* quite a lot of cooking experience.
5 She *didn't see / hasn't seen* our new house – but she's coming next week.
6 She *didn't see / hasn't seen* me when I waved at her.
7 He *broke / has broken* the world record in 1998.
8 *Did you call / Have you called* me last night?

4 Rewrite the sentences. Put the words in brackets in the correct place.

1 Have you seen a whale? (ever)
_____

2 I've eaten breakfast, thank you. (already)
_____

3 He's had a full-time job. (never)
_____

4 Have they replied to your letter? (yet)
_____

5 Has she worked with children? (ever)
_____

6 Sorry, I haven't had time to look at your report. (yet)
_____

5 Complete the conversations using the present perfect simple and past simple form of the verbs.

A: What's the matter?
B: I ¹_____ (lose) my mobile phone.
A: Where ²_____ (you / lose) it?
B: I think I ³_____ (leave) it on the bus this morning. It's really annoying. I ⁴_____ (never / do) that before.

A: Where's John?
B: You ⁵_____ (just / miss) him. He ⁶_____ (go) out to meet someone five minutes ago.
A: ⁷_____ (he / say) if he was coming back?
B: No, but I hope he will. He ⁸_____ (not / finish) the work I asked him to do yet.

B: How's your tooth?
A: It's a bit painful but I ⁹_____ (book) an appointment with the dentist.
B: Oh good. When for?
A: Monday 24th. They ¹⁰_____ (not / have) any appointments before then.

6 Correct the mistake in each sentence.

1 Did you ever have any experience of selling?
_____

2 I have seen him yesterday.
_____

3 I have gone to many countries in my life.
_____

4 She hasn't yet arrived.
_____

5 We have met each other at the 2015 annual conference.
_____

6 Have you wrote this proposal by yourself, or did you write it with a colleague?
_____

7 Complete the conversation using the present perfect continuous form of the verbs.

A: What ¹_____ (you / do) today?
B: I ²_____ (get) ready for my holiday.
A: Oh, where are you going?
B: Japan. My husband does business there sometimes and he ³_____ (try) to persuade me to go there for years.
A: How long ⁴_____ (he / go) there?
B: Well, he ⁵_____ (work) with Mitsubishi Bank since 2005 – so over ten years now.

153

Grammar summary | UNIT 8

PREDICTIONS WITH *WILL* AND *MIGHT*

Predictions with *will*

Affirmative	Negative
I/you/he/she/it/we/they **will live**	I/you/he/she/it/we/they **won't live** (won't = will not)

Question	Short answer
will I/you/he/she/it/we/they **live**?	Yes, I/you/he/she/it/we/they **will**. No, I/you/he/she/it/we/they **won't**.

We use *will* + infinitive (without *to*) to make predictions about the future that we are certain about. We often use *will* with *I think / I hope / I expect / I'm sure / I don't think*.

    The price of petrol **will rise** over the next ten years.
    I expect they **will move** to America, because they have a lot of friends there.
    I'm sure he**'ll phone** us from the airport.

Notice that the verb form remains the same in the third person. (*I think she will takes the job.* ✗)

will: negatives and questions

We form negative sentences with *won't* (= *will not*) + infinitive (without *to*).
    They **won't know** the answer until Tuesday.

We form questions with *will* + subject + infinitive (without *to*).
    Will you **be** home for dinner?
    When **will** you **finish** your report?

Predictions with *might*

We use *might* + infinitive (without *to*) to talk about events in the future which we think are possible, but we are less certain about. *It might* means 'It is possible that it will …'
    Bring an umbrella. It **might rain** later.
    I **might be** home late this evening.
    John **might not be** at the party.

▶ Exercises 1 and 2

DECISIONS WITH *GOING TO*

We use *(be) going to* + infinitive to talk about a future plan or intention which we have already decided to do before we speak.
    I**'m going to visit** my parents next weekend.
    The company **is going to launch** their new website on 1st April.
    We**'re going to go** to France for our summer holidays. (We've already got our tickets.)
    He **isn't going to come** to the party
    Are they **going to watch** the match this evening?

▶ Exercise 3

DECISIONS WITH *WILL*

We use *will* + infinitive (without *to*) to talk about future offers and actions or a decision we make at the moment when we are speaking.
    Jack? One moment. I**'ll see** if he's here. (not *I'm going to see if he's here.*)
    Sorry, I can't speak now. I**'ll call** you later. (not *I'm going to call you later.*)

    A: The train has been cancelled.
    B: OK. In that case, **I'll take** the bus. (I have just decided to do this, at the moment of speaking.)

    A: The train has been cancelled.
    B: That's OK. **I'm going to take** the bus. (I have already decided this and have got a bus ticket.)

▶ Exercises 4 and 5

REPORTED SPEECH

When we report what someone said, we put the verb they used at the time one step 'backwards' in the past

Direct speech	Reported speech
Present simple '**I'm** sorry.'	Past simple He said (that) he **was** sorry.
Present continuous 'We**'re playing** football.'	Past continuous They said (that) they **were playing** football.
Present perfect simple 'I**'ve eaten**, thanks.'	Past perfect simple She said (that) she **had eaten**.
Past simple 'I **visited** New York.'	Past perfect Luc said (that) he **had visited** New York.
will/won't 'I**'ll meet** you at eight.'	would/wouldn't He said (that) he **would meet** me at eight.
can/can't 'I **can** help.'	could/couldn't She said (that) she **could** help.

We often need to make other changes when we report what someone said:

- Pronouns: *I* → *he/she*; *we* → *they*; *my* → *his/her*; *our* → *their*
- Time expressions: *tomorrow* → *the next day*; *yesterday* → *the previous day*

For information about reported (indirect) questions, see page 140.

▶ Exercise 6

EXERCISES

1 Put the words in the correct order to make conversations.

1. A: you / when / home / will / tonight / be
   _____?
   B: hope / home / by 6.30 / I / I / 'll / be
   _____.

2. A: won't / the election / the Green Party / win
   _____.
   B: No, / get / but / might / a lot of votes / they
   No, _____.

3. A: might / this / it / afternoon / rain
   _____.
   B: Oh dear, / very heavily / rain / it / will
   Oh dear, _____?

4. A: think / 'll / do / she / like / her present / you
   _____?
   B: Yes, / she / it / love / 'll
   Yes, _____.

2 Complete the sentences. Use *will*, *won't*, *might* and *might not* with these verbs.

   be   get   go   leave   spend   take

1. They _____ the night in London. It depends how late the show finishes.
2. Please could you complete this short questionnaire? Don't worry – it _____ long.
3. I'm sure she _____ better quickly. She's young and fit.
4. I don't like holidays abroad. I'm always worried that something _____ wrong.
5. It's a risk going skiing in Europe in late March. There _____ any snow.
6. He's overqualified for the job, so I think sooner or later he _____ the company.

3 Complete the list of New Year resolutions (things people are planning to do next year to improve their lives). Use *be going to* and these verbs.

   do   eat   learn   lose
   save   stop   travel   not work

1. Cassie *is going to learn* to speak Arabic.
2. Sarah and Pete _____ money for a new flat.
3. I _____ more exercise.
4. _____ (John) smoking?
5. My brother says he _____ weight.
6. _____ (you) healthier food?
7. Deborah _____ so hard.
8. We _____ to new places.

4 Choose the correct future form to complete the conversations.

A: Hello. Can I speak to Jake Holmes?
B: One minute. ¹ *I'm going to see / I'll see* if he's here. … Sorry, he's out.
A: OK. ² *I'm going to call / I'll call* back later.
B: OK. ³ *I'm going to tell / I'll tell* him you called.

A: The printer is still broken.
B: Yes, I know. ⁴ *I'm going to fix / I'll fix* it. I just haven't had any time.
A: ⁵ *I'm going to call / I'll call* the engineer, if you like.

A: Hi. Are you ready to order?
B: No, not yet.
A: OK. ⁶ *I'm going to / I'll come back* in a moment.
B: Thanks. But ⁷ *we're going to have / we'll have* a drink while we are waiting.

A: Excuse me. Can you tell me the way to the station?
B: Sure. ⁸ *I'm going to take / I'll take* you there.
A: Oh, I don't want to trouble you.
B: No, that's OK. ⁹ *I'm going to catch / I'll catch* a train there myself in ten minutes.
A: OK. Thank you very much.

5 Correct the mistake in each sentence.

1. We'll see a play at the theatre this evening.
2. I think it will rains this afternoon.
3. They might to cancel the meeting next week.
4. That bag looks heavy. I'm going to carry it for you.
5. In the future, we'll to see more electric vehicles on our roads.
6. Marco will move house next month.

6 Rewrite the sentences using reported speech.

1. 'I'll send the email again.'
   He said that he _____.
2. 'Martha hasn't really answered my question.'
   Boris said that Martha _____.
3. 'I can call Barbara back later.'
   Joan called. She said that she _____.
4. 'I'm a bit annoyed about the delay.'
   Kate told me that she _____.
5. 'We posted it on Tuesday by express post.'
   She said that _____.
6. 'I want to check the quote before I send it.'
   James said that he _____.

155

Grammar summary | UNIT 9

ZERO AND FIRST CONDITIONAL

Zero conditional: form and use

If/When-clause	main clause
If/When + present simple	present simple

We form the zero conditional using:
  If/When + present simple, present simple
  If/When they **don't drink** enough water, people **become** dehydrated.
  I **am** always tired **if/when** I **arrive** home from work late.

We can use *if/when* in two positions:
  If/When-clause first: **If** I arrive home from work late, I am always tired..
  Main clause first: I am always tired **if** I arrive home from work late.

When the *if/when*-clause is at the beginning of the sentence, we use a comma to separate it from the main clause.

We use the zero conditional to talk about facts or things which are generally true.
  If you **cool** water to zero degrees, it **freezes**.
  I **ride** my bicycle to college when it**'s** sunny.

When we talk about facts or things which are generally true, we can use *if* or *when*. There's no difference in meaning.

▶ Exercise 1

First conditional: form and use

If-clause	main clause
If + present simple,	will/won't + infinitive (without to)

We form the first conditional using:
  If + present simple, will/won't + infinitive (without *to*)
  If I **have** a lot of work tomorrow, I**'ll stay** late at the office.

We can use *if* in two positions:
  If-clause first: **If** I have a lot of work tomorrow, I'll stay late at the office.
  Main clause first: I'll stay late at the office **if** I have a lot of work tomorrow.

When the *if*-clause is at the beginning of the sentence, we use a comma to separate it from the main clause.

We use the first conditional to talk about a possible future action or situation and its future result.
  If I **have** a lot of work tomorrow, I**'ll stay** late at the office.
  (= it is possible that I will have a lot of work)
  I**'ll ride** my bicycle to college tomorrow **if** it**'s** sunny. (= it is possible that it will be sunny tomorrow)

unless

We can also use *unless* to talk about possible actions and situations in the future. *Unless* means 'if … not'.
  I**'ll ride** my bicycle to college tomorrow **unless** it **rains**.
  (= if it doesn't rain)
  You **won't finish** your essay unless you **start** today.

▶ Exercise 2

when and if

When we talk about possible situations in the future using the first conditional, we can use *if* or *when*, but there is a difference in meaning. We use *when* to talk about a certain future action or situation.
  If I see Anna, I will give her your message. (= it is possible, but not certain that I will see Anna)
  When I see Anna, I will give her your message. (= it is certain that I will see Anna)

▶ Exercise 3

IMPERATIVES IN CONDITIONALS

Imperative	if + present simple

We use an imperative + the present simple in the *if*-clause when we tell or ask people to do things.
  Just ask **if** you need any help.

We can also use *when*, *before*, *as soon as* or *until* instead of *if* when we refer to future events.
  Call me **when** you arrive.
  Please lock the windows **before** you leave.
  Don't leave the house **until** I get there.

▶ Exercises 4–6

EXERCISES

1 Match the two halves of the sentences.

1. People like to be praised
2. We don't go swimming
3. I can't sleep
4. Some plants die
5. I always wear a suit
6. People don't work well

a. when they feel stressed.
b. when I have an important meeting.
c. when they do a good job.
d. if the light is on.
e. if the water is cold.
f. if you water them too much.

2 Choose the correct options to complete the conversations.

1. A: I'm tired.
   B: Then go to bed. You ¹ *feel / will feel* a lot better tomorrow if you ² *get / will get* a good night's sleep.

2. A: Unless you ³ *change / will change* your password regularly, sooner or later someone else ⁴ *discovers / will discover* it.
   B: Yes, but if I ⁵ *change / will change* it, I ⁶ *probably forget / will probably forget* it.

3. A: If you ⁷ *turn / will turn* off your phone, you ⁸ *find / will find* it much easier to concentrate.
   B: Yes, but what if I ⁹ *get / will get* an urgent call?

4. A: Are you going to stay in your job?
   B: Yes, I ¹⁰ *stay / will stay* in my job, unless I ¹¹ *find / will find* a better one.

5. A: I'm so bored. I want my life to change!
   B: Well, you know what people say – if you ¹² *want / will want* things to change, then you ¹³ *have to / will have to* change them yourself.

6. A: Why do you write everything down?
   B: Because if I ¹⁴ *don't write / won't write* things down, I ¹⁵ *always forget / will always forget* it.

3 Complete the sentences with *if* and *when*.

1. We'll start the meeting _____ Jessica arrives.
2. _____ you want me to help you, you'll have to wait a few minutes.
3. _____ my train is late, I will call you.
4. There will be a big celebration _____ he wins the election.
5. I'll go to the bank _____ it opens.
6. _____ I don't take this opportunity now, I'm sure I'll regret it.

4 Put the words in the correct order to make instructions.

1. the food / serve / is / hot / it / when
   _____
2. please / as soon as / arrives / she / let me know
   _____
3. starts making / switch off / a noise / if / the computer / it
   _____
4. always / send / you / check / them / your emails / before
   _____
5. don't / I / do / until / tell / you / anything
   _____
6. operate / before / read / the instructions / you / a new machine / always
   _____

5 Complete the text. Use the correct form of these verbs.

be	begin	come	do	feel
go	hurt	look	stand	switch

If you sit in front of a computer all day, here's some advice to stop you feeling the bad physical effects. When your eyes ¹ _____ to feel tired, ² _____ off the screen for a moment or ³ _____ away from the screen for a minute. If your back ⁴ _____, ⁵ _____ up and walk around the room for a few minutes. Even better, if you ⁶ _____ outside into the fresh air, you ⁷ _____ more refreshed when you ⁸ _____ back to your desk. You may think these things are a waste of your work time, but if you ⁹ _____ them regularly, you ¹⁰ _____ more productive.

6 Correct the mistake in each sentence.

1. I will buy the new version of Microsoft Office if it will come down in price.
   _____
2. Come with me if you will be free.
   _____
3. Unless you will try to do new things, you will never learn anything.
   _____
4. If I see her later, I give her your message.
   _____
5. When I live to be ninety years old, I will be very happy.
   _____
6. Please visit reception as soon as you will arrive.
   _____

Grammar summary | UNIT 10

THE PASSIVE

Passive and active

We use the active form to talk about what the subject does. We use the passive when we want to focus on an action or the object of the action, rather than on the person who is doing the action. The object of the active sentence becomes the subject of the passive sentence.

We form the passive with the verb *be* + past participle.

Active: The farmers **pick** the oranges in November. (subject / object)

Passive: The oranges **are picked** by the farmers in November. (subject / object)

▶ Exercise 1

by + agent

In an active sentence, you know who or what did the action.
   The regulator **fixes** *the prices.*
   Zaha Hadid **designed** *the building.*

In a passive sentence, when we want to say or when it's important to know who does or did the action (the agent), we use the passive verb + *by* + agent.
   The prices **are fixed by** *the regulator.*
   The building **was designed by** *Zaha Hadid.*

It isn't always necessary to use *by* + agent. We often use the passive because we do not know who or what did the action, or when it isn't important to say.
   The bicycle **was stolen** *from right in front of my house.* (I don't know who stole it.)
   Breakfast **is served** *from 7.00 to 9.00 a.m.* (We do not need to say *by the hotel staff*.)

▶ Exercise 2

Present simple passive

Affirmative and negative		
Coffee	is/isn't	produced here.
Plants	are/aren't	cultivated in this garden.

Question		
Is	coffee	produced here?
Are	plants	cultivated in this garden?

We form the present simple passive with the present simple of the verb *be (am/is/are)* + past participle. We use the present simple passive to describe:

- facts which are generally true
  Tea **is grown** *in India.*
- actions which happen regularly
  The Olympic Games **are held** *every four years.*
- steps in a process
  The cars **are assembled** *by robots. When the cars* **are finished***, they* **are loaded** *onto lorries and they* **are transported** *to the docks for shipping.*

▶ Exercise 3

Past simple passive

Affirmative and negative		
Coffee	was/wasn't	produced here.
Plants	were/weren't	cultivated in this garden.

Question		
Was	coffee	produced here?
Were	plants	cultivated in this garden?

We form the past simple passive with the past simple of the verb *be (was/were)* + past participle.

We use the past simple passive:

- to talk about past or historical facts
  The company **was founded** *in 1897 by Thomas Cardew.*
- to describe a past process or series of events
  After the volcano erupted, a lot of ash **was sent** *into the atmosphere. Because of the ash cloud, many flights* **were cancelled***.*

▶ Exercises 4 and 5

PHRASAL VERBS

A phrasal verb is a verb + particle (usually a preposition). The verb + particle create a phrase with a meaning you would not expect from the two separate words, e.g.: *come across* = to find unexpectedly, *take off* = leave the ground.

Phrasal verbs can be transitive (+ object) or intransitive (with no object).
   I **came across** *an interesting article in the newspaper.* (transitive)
   The plane **took off** *three hours late.* (intransitive)

Some transitive phrasal verbs are **inseparable**: the object must go after the particle. Three-part phrasal verbs (verb + two particles) with one object are always inseparable.
   I'm **looking after** *my grandson tomorrow.*
   I'm **looking after** *him tomorrow.*
   He always **comes up with** *good ideas.*

Some transitive phrasal verbs are **separable**: the object can go before or after the particle. But if the object is a pronoun, it must come before the particle.
   They **turned down** *our offer.*
   They **turned** *our offer* **down***.*
   They **turned** *it* **down***.*

▶ Exercise 6

EXERCISES

1 Choose the correct option (active or passive) to complete the sentences.

1. Pasta *makes / is made* from wheat.
2. The Pyramids *built / were built* around 4,500 years ago.
3. The company *promoted / was promoted* John to finance director.
4. They *clean / are cleaned* the windows twice a month.
5. His new book *published / was published* last week.
6. British people *now drink / are now drunk* more coffee than tea.
7. Every schoolchild *gives / is given* a computer tablet from the age of five.
8. *Did they give / Were they given* any training before they started working?

2 Read the sentences. Cross out the agent when it isn't necessary.

1. He was arrested last night by the police.
2. She was taught to ski by her father.
3. Strawberries are grown by farmers in this area.
4. The fire was finally put out by the firefighters after six hours.
5. We were met at the airport by a driver.
6. The teachers are supported by teaching assistants.

3 Complete the description of making yoghurt at home using the verbs in the present simple active or passive form.

Home-made yoghurt tastes much better than yoghurt from the supermarket and it's really easy to make. Basically, yoghurt ¹_____ (make) by adding certain bacteria to milk. The bacteria ²_____ (find) in other yoghurt. Just buy some natural yogurt from the shop with live bacteria and ³_____ (add) a spoonful to the milk. Then ⁴_____ (leave) the milk somewhere at a temperature of between 40 and 46 degrees Celsius. In about four hours, the milk ⁵_____ (transform) into yoghurt. Some people ⁶_____ (use) a yoghurt maker to do this, but my yoghurt ⁷_____ (make) in an old pot.

4 Complete the facts using the past passive form of these verbs.

| build | destroy | hold | invent |
| open | sell | speak | write |

1. The 2014 football World Cup _____ in Brazil.
2. The wheel _____ around 3500 BC.
3. According to archaeologists, the Giza pyramids _____ around 2500 BC.
4. The Panama Canal, which links the Atlantic and Pacific Oceans, _____ in 1914.
5. 'Mr Watson – come here – I want to see you.' These were the first words that _____ on the telephone.
6. The play *Romeo and Juliet* _____ by William Shakespeare.
7. The library of Alexandria _____ in a terrible fire.
8. The first personal computer _____ in 1975 for $400.

5 Correct the mistake in each sentence.

1. The car is Japanese but it produce in the UK.

2. We were offered the students the chance to work with us during the summer vacation.

3. The house was built from my parents.

4. Was he arrest for his crimes?

5. Does she employed by the airline or the airport?

6. Most chopsticks make from wood.

6 Put the words in the correct order. There is sometimes more than one possible order.

1. up / from the airport / I'm / at 10 a.m. / him / picking
   _____ .

2. up / people / how many / turned / for the meeting
   _____ ?

3. working / he / on / late into the night / carried
   _____ .

4. Freddy / get / very well / I / along / and
   _____ .

5. over / the company / they / in 2008 / took
   _____ .

6. I / look / the word / had to / in the dictionary / up
   _____ .

7. It's her own company. it / up / in 2012 / she / set
   It's her own company. _____ .

8. They didn't complain. just / with / on / they / it / got
   They didn't complain. _____ .

159

Grammar summary | UNIT 11

MODAL VERBS (1): MUST, MUSTN'T, HAVE TO, DON'T HAVE TO, NEED TO, DON'T NEED TO, CAN

must, have to and need to

must
You **must** come to the meeting this afternoon.
They **must** arrive on time.

have to
I **have to go** to the airport now to meet Sam.
She **has to speak** Chinese when she works in China.

need to
I **need to finish** my assignment before Thursday.
He **needs to take** the car to the garage to fix the brakes.

Notice these rules for modal verbs:
- there is no third person -s with modal verbs.
  She **must** go.
- there is no *to* before the infinitive which follows.
  They **must stay** there till 9.00.
- *have to* and *need to* are regular verbs, not modal verbs.
  I **have to** go. He/She **has to** help.
  They **need to** be here. He/She **needs to** help set up the conference.

We use *must*, *have to* and *need to* + infinitive to say that something is necessary. We often use *must* and *have to* + infinitive to talk about rules.
You **must** show respect to older people.
Cars **have to** drive on the left in England and Japan.
You **need to** be careful when you cross the road.

There isn't much difference between *must* and *have to*, but we often use *must* to express an obligation that comes from inside us and *have to* to express an external obligation (e.g. a law).
I **must** finish my report today – I'm going on holiday tomorrow.
I **have to** finish my report today – we are meeting to discuss the findings tomorrow.

mustn't, don't have to and don't need to

We use *mustn't* + infinitive to talk about things that are not permitted, i.e. there is an obligation <u>not</u> to do them.
You **mustn't** touch the door until the paint is dry.

We use *don't have to* and *don't need to* + infinitive to say something is not necessary, or there is no obligation to do something.
I **don't have to** go to work tomorrow. It's my day off.
He **doesn't need to** call me first. He can just come when he's ready.

Notice that:
- there is no auxiliary *do* with modal verbs in the negative and question form.
  I **mustn't** lose.
- *have to* and *need to* are regular verbs.
  They **don't have to** wait. He/She **doesn't need to** stay.
  Do I **have to** see him? Does he/she **have to** work till 6.00?
- The negative of *need to* is *don't/doesn't need to*. We can also use *needn't*. The meaning is the same.
  We **don't need to** stay.
  We **needn't stay**.

▶ Exercise 1

can

Can is also a modal verb.
They've finished work for today, so they **can go** home now.
Sorry, I **can't come** to your party this evening.
Can you **bring** your laptop to the meeting, please?

We use *can* + infinitive when we want to say something is possible or permitted.
You **can come** to the film with us, if you want to.
Pedestrians and horses **can use** this track, but not cyclists.

We use *can't* + infinitive when something is not allowed or permitted.
You **can't play** football tomorrow.

As *can* is a modal verb, notice that:
- there is no third person -s.
  He/She/It **can** stay.
- there is no auxiliary *do* in the negative and question form.
  He **can't** play. **Can** I visit her later?

▶ Exercise 2

MODAL VERBS (2): SHOULD AND SHOULDN'T

We use *should* and *shouldn't* + infinitive to give advice or to make a recommendation: to say what is the right or wrong thing to do. We use *should* and *shouldn't* to make suggestions rather than to express an obligation.
You **should** have a break if you're tired.
He **shouldn't** drive so fast. It's dangerous.

▶ Exercises 3–5

EXERCISES

1 Choose the correct option to complete the sentences.

1. You *must / mustn't* park there. It's the director's parking space.
2. He *needs to / mustn't* read more to improve his reading speed.
3. I *need to / don't have to* be there by eight o'clock – that's the time when the film starts.
4. You *have to / mustn't* sign the register every time you enter, so we know who is in the building.
5. You *mustn't / don't have to* get a visa if you are staying less than one month.
6. You *must / don't need to* finish your food or people will think you don't like it.
7. You *mustn't / don't need* to take the lift – you can take the stairs if you prefer.
8. You *have to / don't need to* follow the rules, like everyone else.

2 Put the words in the correct order to make sentences.

The best thing about the holidays is:

1. you / get up / you / want / when / can
2. have / you / worry / don't / being on time / to / about

The best thing about your birthday is:

3. nice / you / to / everyone / must / be
4. choose / want / you / to / do / you / what / can

3 Complete the second sentence giving advice so it has the same meaning as the first. Use *should* or *shouldn't*.

1. Listening to loud music can damage your ears.
   You _____ loud music.
2. Getting a job that you enjoy is important.
   You _____ a job that you enjoy.
3. There's no point worrying too much about the future.
   You _____ too much about the future.
4. Why don't you listen to Sarah? I think her advice is right.
   You _____ to Sarah's advice.
5. Wearing a hat in winter can keep you warm.
   You _____ in winter.
6. Even if you make a wrong decision, don't spend time regretting it.
   You _____ your decisions.

4 Look at the road signs. Complete the meaning of each sentence using *must, mustn't, can* and *should*.

1  2

3  4

5  6

7  8

1. You _____ enter this street.
2. You _____ ride a bicycle on this track.
3. You _____ drive carefully here – the road is slippery.
4. Pedestrians _____ cross the road here.
5. You _____ drive along this street in this direction.
6. You _____ overtake other cars here.
7. You _____ watch out for sheep in the road.
8. You can drive at 20 mph but you _____ drive at more than 20 mph.

5 Correct the mistake in each sentence.

1. You must to pay to see the dentist.
2. You haven't to cook, if you don't want to.
3. He should to see a doctor.
4. You don't have to eat in the library. It's forbidden.
5. We don't must be late.
6. One minute. I need finish writing this letter.

161

Grammar summary | UNIT 12

SECOND CONDITIONAL

Form and use

If-clause	main clause
If + past simple,	*would* + infinitive (without *to*)

We form the second conditional using:
If + past simple, *would* + infinitive (without *to*)
  If I **won** *the lottery, I* **would give** *most of the money to charity.*

We can use *if* in two positions:
  If-clause first: *If he lost the election, I would be very surprised.*
  Main clause first: *I would be very surprised if he lost the election.*

There is no difference in meaning, but when the if-clause is at the beginning of the sentence, we use a comma to separate it from the main clause.

We use the **first conditional** to talk about future events or situations which are a real possibility. We use the **second conditional** to talk about situations which are imaginary or improbable. Notice that even though the verb in the main clause is in the past simple, the sentence refers to the present or future.
  If I **come** *with you, I* **will have** *to take a day off work.*
  (= It's possible that I will come with you)
  If I **came** *with you, I* **'d have** *to take a day off work.*
  (= I probably won't come with you)

Notice that *would* can be contracted to *'d*.

▶ Exercise 1

would and *could*

If-clause	main clause
If + past simple,	*would* / *could* + infinitive (without *to*)

We use *would* in the main clause to say what we think the future outcome of a situation will be. We use *could* to say what the future outcome perhaps will be. *Could* also means 'would be able'.
  If I **left** *work early, I* **would go** *to the cinema.*
  If I **left** *work early, I* **could meet** *you before the film.*
  (= Perhaps I would be able to meet you)
  If that wall **fell** *down, it* **could cause** *a nasty accident.*
  (= it's possible that it would cause)

Notice that *would* can be contracted to *'d*, but *could* cannot be contracted.

Unreal situations

We use the second conditional to talk about situations in the present which are the opposite of reality.
  If I **had** *a bicycle, I* **would cycle** *to work.* (= I don't have a bicycle)
  If I **knew** *her number, I'***d call** *her.* (= I don't know her number)

If I was/were

When we use the verb *be* in the *if*-clause, we can use *was* or *were* after *I, he, she* and *it*. We always use *were* to give advice: *If I were you, I'd … .*
  If he **was/were** *rich, he* **wouldn't need** *to work.*
  If it **was/were** *my house, I'***d sell** *it*
  If I **were** *you, I would get an electrician to mend the cable.*

▶ Exercises 2 and 3

Would without the *if*-clause

Sometimes we talk about hypothetical outcomes using *would*, when there is no *if*-clause.
  Driving **would be** *pointless. I only live ten minutes away.*
  (= If I drove, it would be pointless.)
  I think an umbrella **would be** *a good idea.* (= It would be a good idea if you took an umbrella with you.)

▶ Exercises 4 and 5

EXTENSION: THIRD CONDITIONAL

If-clause	main clause
If + past perfect,	*would have* + past participle

We form the third conditional using:
If + past perfect, *would have* + past participle
  If I **had run,** *I* **would have caught** *the train.* (= I didn't run and so I missed the train.)
  If you **hadn't eaten** *so much, you* **wouldn't have felt** *sick.*
  (= You ate a lot and so you felt sick.)

We use the second conditional to talk about imaginary situations in the present and future. We use the third conditional to talk about imaginary situations in the past.
  If I **left** *work early, I'***d go** *to the cinema.* (= I may leave work early.)
  *If I'***d left** *work early, I* **would have gone** *to the cinema.*
  (I didn't leave work early and so I didn't go to the cinema.)

▶ Exercise 6

EXERCISES

1 Put the words in the correct order to make second conditional sentences.

1. she / a great piano player / would / more / if / practised / she / be

   _____

2. would / to the country / if / moved / have / we / a better quality of life / we

   _____

3. you / get / more quickly / you / the train / there / took / if / would

   _____

4. go to bed / he / feel / didn't / would / feels tired / so late / if / he

   _____

5. so popular / if / it / be / a different presenter / had / the TV programme / wouldn't

   _____

6. 'd / if / lost / the match / I / I / very upset / be

   _____

2 Complete the sentences with the correct form of the verb to make first or second conditional sentences.

1. If the train leaves on time, we _____ (not / be) late.
2. If I _____ (have) £1 for each time someone asked me that question, I'd be rich!
3. I could understand her if she _____ (speak) more slowly.
4. If you _____ (come) to my city, I will be very happy to show you around.
5. If she was an American citizen, she _____ (not / need) a work permit.
6. If it _____ (rain) this afternoon, we'll have to cancel the match.
7. If I _____ (be) taller, my head _____ (touch) the ceiling.
8. I'm expecting Harry at 10.00, but if he _____ (arrive) early, _____ (you / call) me?

3 Complete the conversation with the correct form of the verbs to make second conditional sentences.

A: I've seen a car I want to buy, but I feel nervous about spending so much money.
B: If you ¹_____ (have) more money, ²_____ (you / feel) nervous?
A: No, of course not. If I ³_____ (be) rich, it ⁴_____ (not / be) a problem.
B: Have you spoken to the seller? I'm sure you ⁵_____ (feel) better if the seller ⁶_____ (reduce) the price.

4 Complete the responses using a verb with *would*.

1. A: Shall we ask Pete to join us for supper?
   B: Yes, that _____ nice.
2. A: Shall I send the parcel first or second class?
   B: First. Second class _____ too long.
3. A: Shall we leave in half an hour?
   B: Yes, that _____ me the chance to have something to eat first.
4. A: Shall I put the cat in the bedroom?
   B: No, that _____ a good idea.

5 Correct the mistake in each sentence.

1. If I would have his number, I would call him.
2. I would tell you the answer if I know it.
3. If I was you, I would drive.
4. We went to the Caribbean for our holiday if we had more money.
5. Emily really wants that job. She'll be upset if she didn't get it.

6 Rewrite the sentences so they have the same meaning. Use the third conditional.

1. I didn't practise and so I failed my driving test.
   If I'd practised, I wouldn't have failed my driving test.
2. I wasn't at the meeting and so I didn't say anything.
3. The food was so bad that I asked for a refund.
4. I stayed out late so I didn't get much sleep.
5. They insisted that we stay for dinner, so we did.
6. I bought the jacket because it was half price.

Audioscripts

Unit 1

🎧 3

I = Interviewer, T = Occupational therapist

I: So, what do you do exactly?
T: Well, I work as an occupational therapist. We work with people who have disabilities or when they're recovering after an accident. They just want to have normal lives and to work again. So we help them to do everyday tasks for their jobs or around the house.
I: I see, and the patient comes to your clinic, or do you go to them?
T: Most days I visit people in their homes and see what they can do and what they can't. I usually advise them about equipment that can help them in the home. People in these situations often have no confidence – they feel anxious. So I always try to make them feel more confident.
I: And does that give you a lot of satisfaction?
T: Yes, making people feel more confident is the really rewarding part of my job. But I don't spend all my time with patients. You know, as with every job, there are more routine tasks to do. I write reports and attend meetings with other healthcare professionals every day. I rarely get home before 6.30 in the evening, but I love my job.

🎧 4

1 I'm usually at work by 8.00 in the morning.
2 My boss rarely checks my work.
3 He sometimes works on the train.
4 I always check my emails before I send them.
5 People in my country don't usually work late.
6 People often wear casual clothes on Fridays.
7 I tidy my desk once a month.
8 I never take work home with me in the evenings.

🎧 6

J = Jake, M = Martha

J: So what do you do?
M: I'm an acoustics engineer.
J: What's that? Like a sound engineer?
M: No, not exactly. We help design spaces like concert halls or conference centres or theatres – spaces where the quality of sound is important.
J: So who do you work for?
M: I'm a trainee with an international firm of architects.
J: Where are you based?
M: I'm on a one-year training programme in Frankfurt.
J: Wow! What does your job involve then?
M: Well, I work on different projects. On each project I work on a different area, like buying materials or budgeting and planning or design.
J: Is it a big firm then?
M: Yes, very big but there are only ten of us in the Frankfurt office.
J: Do you mind me asking – what kind of contract are you on?
M: Well, as I say, it's a one-year contract, but hopefully at the end of the year, they'll give me a permanent job. But I have to do well this year.
J: Do you like the job?
M: Yeah, it's great. I learn something new every day.
J: Oh, well, good luck. I hope you get the job.
M: Thanks.

🎧 7

1 What do you do?
2 Who do you work for?
3 Where are you based?
4 What does your job involve?
5 Is it a big firm then?
6 What kind of contract are you on?
7 Do you like the job?

Unit 2

🎧 9

2 So let's watch a movement happen, start to finish, in under three minutes and dissect some lessons from it.

🎧 10

J = Jim, T = Theresa, F = Franco

J: Hello, Theresa. Good to see you. How are you doing?
T: Yeah, things are going very well, thanks. What brings you here?
J: We're here to present our new product.
T: Oh, well, good luck with that. By the way, this is Franco, my marketing assistant.
J: Hi, Franco. Good to meet you. I'm Jim Hyland.
F: Pleased to meet you, Jim.
J: Is it your first conference?
F: Yes, I'm doing an internship at NYT, in Theresa's department.
J: How's it going? Is Theresa working you very hard?
F: Well, yes and no, but I love the job.
T: When's your presentation, Jim?
J: It's tomorrow at 4.30. Please come along.
T: Yes, I'd love to. Well, we have a meeting to go to now, but great to see you and see you tomorrow.
J: Great! See you then. Have a good day.

🎧 11

J = Jim, T = Theresa, F = Franco

1 J: How are you doing?
2 T: Things are going very well, thanks.
3 T: This is Franco.
4 J: Hi, Franco. Good to meet you.
5 F: Pleased to meet you, Jim.
6 J: How's it going?
7 T: Great to see you.

Review 1 (Units 1 and 2)

🎧 12

I = Interviewer, E = Eleanor

I: So, first of all, can you just explain what Broken Spoke does?
E: Well, we do three things: we run training courses – how to ride bikes and how to repair them, we sell bicycle parts and we have drop-in workshops where people repair their own bikes with our tools and our help.
I: And is it a business or a charity?
E: It's a non-profit business.
I: Which activity makes the most money?
E: Actually, we got equal income from each of the three activities.
I: And why did you start it? Did you want people to have a more healthy form of transport? Was it because you love cycling? Or …
E: Yes, it's partly about physical health. Cycling is healthy. But also it's about building a community and people sharing what they know with each other. We live in a world where people don't have the skills or knowledge to repair things when they break. I wanted to do something practical and direct about that, something that brings people together, teaches them a skill and helps the environment at the same time.
I: And is this a model that you can repeat – it'll work in other places?
E: Oh, yes. There are lots of similar projects – in the UK, the USA and around the world. The problem for us here in Oxford is that renting a workshop is so expensive. The business model works, but the difficulty is finding a place with a reasonable rent. We're renting this place now at a low rent but it's only temporary.
I: Well, I hope you find somewhere more permanent. I think what you're doing is fantastic.
E: Thank you.

Unit 3

🎧 15

P = Presenter, L = Professor Long

P: Now we haven't had any good news about the economy lately, but here *is* some positive information – some facts that will perhaps make you feel better about the money in your pocket. In the studio today, we have an economist, Professor David Long, who claims that we are lucky compared to people living one hundred years ago – people who didn't have any hopes of buying the things that we can afford today. So we should be grateful, Professor.
L: Absolutely. Most middle-class people in Europe now have a better standard of living than a king living 300 years ago or a rich person 120 years ago. Most people were poor 120 years ago. They didn't have many possessions. They didn't have much food. They worked long hours and only had a little time for leisure. For example, in 1895 a person had to work 24 hours to earn the money to buy an office chair. Now a person only has to work two hours to do the same. Of course there are still a lot of poor people in the world and a few countries have very low economic growth, but even in these less developed countries the standard of living is rising fast compared to 120 years ago.

🎧 16

L = Professor Long

L: Absolutely. Most middle class people in Europe now have a better standard of living than a king living 300 years ago or a rich person 120 years ago. Most people were poor 120 years ago. They didn't have many possessions. They didn't have much food. They worked long hours and only had a little time for leisure. For example, in 1895 a person had to work 24 hours to earn the money to buy an office chair. Now a person only has to work two hours to do the same. Of course there are still a lot of poor people in the world and a few countries have very low economic growth, but even in these less developed countries the standard of living is rising fast compared to 120 years ago.

🎧 17

1 A: I'd like $200 in Swiss Francs, please. What's the rate today?
   B: OK. $200 buys you 181 Swiss Francs.
   A: Do you charge commission?
   B: No, it's commission-free.
2 A: OK. That's $16.80, please
   B: Thanks. Here's $20. Please keep the change.
   A: Thank you.
   B: Oh, and can I have a receipt, please?
3 A: Excuse me. Do you have change for a £10 note?
   B: Sorry, I don't, but you can get coins from the change machine.
   A: OK, thanks.
4 A: Thanks, that was delicious. Could you bring us the bill?
   B: Certainly … Here you are.
   A: Thanks. Is service included?
   B: No, it isn't.
5 A: Could you lend me £5 to get some lunch?
   B: Sure.
   A: I'll pay you back when I go to the bank.
   B: OK, no hurry.

🎧 19

1 Could you bring me a glass of water?
2 Do you have her address?
3 Could you lend me your pen for a moment?
4 Do you charge a fee for registration?

Unit 4

🎧 23

I = Interviewer, Y = Yvonne Cortez

I: So, Yvonne. Why did you decide to leave school at seventeen? Why didn't you go on to college at that point?
Y: Well, I guess like a lot of kids I had studied for long enough. I wanted to get out and see life and earn some money.
I: And did you hope to become a professional singer then?
Y: Um, well, yes and no. I had done some concerts at school and a lot of people had said I was good, but for me, I hadn't thought about it as a career – it was still just a hobby. I didn't think I was ready to be a professional. So I took a job as a door-to-door salesperson. I hadn't had any sales experience – it was just to earn money, really.

🎧 25

Conversation 1
A: Did you post my letter?
B: Oh, I'm sorry. I was having an off day yesterday. I forgot.

Conversation 2
A: Can I just ask – why did you book a table for only four people? There are six of us.
B: Oh, sorry. You were on a call and I did it without checking with you first.

Conversation 3
A: Did you finish writing the report for Sarah?
B: No, sorry. I had a day off yesterday and I didn't realize it was urgent.

Conversation 4
A: Did you translate the letter to Hans Ulrich?
B: I did my best. But I'm a bit out of practice with my German, I'm afraid.

Conversation 5
A: Why did you order so much paper? We have nowhere to put it.
B: Oh, sorry. It seemed like a good idea at the time. It was really cheap.

Conversation 6
A: Did you book our plane tickets?
B: No, sorry. I was in a hurry and I forgot.

Unit 5

🎧 27

1 A recent survey said that 27 per cent of bosses believe their employees are inspired by their firm. However, in the same survey, only four per cent of employees agreed.
2 Companies are losing control of their customers and their employees. But are they really?

🎧 28

3 Buyers could determine the price, but the offer was exclusive.
4 It may have jeopardized short-term sales, but it built lasting, long-term loyalty.

🎧 30

Conversation 1
A: Do you know the new Thai restaurant round the corner?
B: Olly's Thai? Yeah, we went there last week.
A: What do you think of it?
B: Yeah, I'd recommend it. The menu's very limited, but the food is fantastic.

Conversation 2
A: Is Brighton a good town for shopping?
B: I don't know. But I imagine it's more interesting than many places, because it has a lot of independent shops.

Conversation 3
A: I'm thinking of buying a new bike. Do you know anything about Giant bikes?
B: Yes. I've got one myself. I love it, but it depends on what you're looking for.
A: What do you mean?
B: Well, they're generally quite heavy bikes, but they're really strong. That's important for me, because I'm quite hard on bikes.

Conversation 4
A: We're going to a Vietnamese restaurant tonight. Do you know if the food is good?
B: I couldn't tell you, really.
A: Is it spicy?
B: In my experience, in most Asian restaurants you can just ask the waiter to make the dish less spicy.

Conversation 5
A: What do you think of Tarantino's new film?
B: It's OK. I don't think it's anything special.

Unit 6

🎧 33

5 … when she went down that rabbit hole …
6 Our scientists and engineers are the ones that are tackling our grandest challenges …
7 … the engineers that I've worked with …

🎧 34

1 A: Do you come from Spain?
   B: Yes, I do. How did you know?
   A: It was your accent. Whereabouts in Spain are you from?
   B: From Madrid. Do you know it?
2 A: Is it your first time in Vienna?
   B: Yes, it is. I really like it.
   A: Have you visited the Schönbrunn Palace yet?
   B: No, I haven't, but it's on my to do list.
3 A: Can you believe this weather we're having?
   B: I know, it's amazing. A bit hot for work, though.
   A: That's true. Do you have a holiday coming up soon?
   B: No, unfortunately not.

4 A: I love the food in this hotel.
   B: Yes, it's great.
   A: I know. I have to be careful I don't eat too much.
   B: Oh, I don't worry about that.
5 A: I like your jacket. It's a really nice colour.
   B: Thanks. I just bought it yesterday, actually.
   A: Oh, where did you get it?
   B: At Mango.
6 A: Oh, you're reading *Wonder*. I really enjoyed that book.
   B: Yes, I've only just started it, but I can't put it down.
   A: Have you read her other book?
   B: No, what's that called?

35

1 A: Are you here on business?
   B: No, we're on holiday, actually.
2 A: Are you enjoying the party?
   B: Yes, it's great.
3 A: I'd really like to visit the city centre.
   B: Yes, so would I.
4 A: Do you speak Portuguese?
   B: No, not really. Just a few words.
5 A: Don't you love the food here?
   B: Yes, I do. It's fantastic.

Review 3 (Units 5 and 6)

36

1 A: Where are you from?
   B: I'm from Italy.
   A: Whereabouts in Italy?
   B: Milan. Do you know it?
2 A: I like your jacket.
   B: Thanks.
   A: Where did you get it?
   B: From a vintage clothes shop in Brighton.
3 A: Is it your first time here?
   B: Yes, it is. It's great.
   A: Have you visited the Rijks museum?
   B: Not yet, but I'd like to.
4 A: I can't believe this hot weather we're having.
   B: I know. It's incredible.
   A: What's the weather like in England at the moment?
   B: It's the same, actually.

Unit 7

40

Meanwhile back at home, new statistics just published show that while unemployment is down, there are still six per cent of people in the UK who have never had a job. London remains the highest skilled workforce – sixty per cent of people working in London have been to university. In technology, 73 per cent of us now use the Internet every day, but eleven per cent of Britons have never used it. Other highlights show that eighty per cent of Britons have travelled abroad at some time in their lives and one in six households has been the victim of a crime. Lastly, in our relationships it seems that we can't make up our minds if we want to be with someone who is similar or very different. Fifty per cent of people say the partner they have chosen is their complete opposite. In a few minutes …

44

I = Interviewer, H = Harry

I: Hi, please come in and take a seat. Sorry to keep you waiting.
H: That's all right.
I: So, I understand you graduated recently and you're looking for work with a charitable organization. What attracted you to this job in particular?
H: Well, the main thing is that I'm very interested in working in the field, in countries where animals are in danger. I mean, I understand that the job also involves desk work …
I: Well, that depends on the job …
H: OK and well, I love what RSQ is doing too.
I: Thank you. We're very proud of our work too. You're a graduate in economics. What are your long-term ambitions – to work in a bank, perhaps?
H: No. A lot of my friends have taken jobs in the City but as I said – I'm keen on doing something practical and more useful, I guess. I'd like to do a job where I'm helping the environment.
I: OK and what *can* you do, practically?
H: I'm good with my hands. I help my father a lot with building jobs.
I: Do you have experience of foreign countries?
H: Mm, I haven't worked abroad before, but, I've travelled a lot and I'm very willing to learn.
I: Uh-huh, I see. Do you have any experience of working with animals?
H: Yes, horses and cows and pigs. I've worked on a farm most of my life. My parents are farmers.
I: OK. And what other experience do you have that's relevant to this position?
H: Well, at uni I worked on a campaign, an environmental campaign, helping to save a local green area from development. There was a lot of wildlife there – birds and so on – and the council was going to build some flats there.
I: Oh, that's interesting. Did the campaign succeed?
H: Yes, we persuaded the council to use only thirty per cent of the land for development. So we saved the rest. I think I'm good at persuading people. Also, I really love a challenge and I'm not afraid of taking risks.
I: OK, and what about …

Unit 8

46

Today I'm going to show you an electric vehicle that weighs less than a bicycle …

47

Today I'm going to show you an electric vehicle that weighs less than a bicycle, … that you can carry with you anywhere, that you can charge off a normal wall outlet in fifteen minutes, and you can run it for 1,000 kilometres on about a dollar of electricity.

48

1. I want to help.
2. They won't wait.
3. They want to go by car.
4. I won't know the answer before Tuesday.
5. I won't tell him.
6. They want to leave here before eleven o'clock.
7. She won't come.
8. They want to do business with us.

49

I = Interviewer, C = Councillor

I: Look – I think everyone agrees that the traffic situation in our city can't continue as it is. What are you planning to do about it?
C: You're right. There's already too much traffic congestion and, without action, the problem will just get worse. So we have to get people out of their cars and onto other forms of transport.
I: OK. How are you going to do that?
C: Well, first we have to make other forms of transport more attractive. We're going to introduce a City Bicycle scheme – a fleet of bicycles that people can pick up and drop off at different locations around the city. Also, we're going to create special Park and Ride car parks around the city where car drivers will be able to park their car for free and then travel into the city by bus.
I: OK – that sounds very positive. Anything else?
C: Yes, we're going to make parking in the city easier, but much more expensive, because …
I: I'm not sure that will be popular.
C: Maybe not, but it's necessary. We're going to introduce smart parking meters so you can pay for your parking with your phone. It will cost you significantly more than before. However, you won't have to worry always about having the right change or about going back to the meter to put more money in.
I: OK, thank you. And just on another subject while you're here …

50

J: This is the voicemail of John Waterfield. I'm sorry I'm not available to take your call. Please leave a message. Speak after the tone.

Message 1
P: Oh, hi, John. This is Pete. I'm just calling about the film later. What time are we going to meet? Let me know. You can just send a text, if you like. OK. See you later.

Message 2
T: Hello. It's Thomas Clark here from KM Digital. I'm calling about the proposal that you asked for. No need to call back. I'll send you all the information in an email.

Message 3
W: Hi, it's me again. Sorry to bother you at work. The dog's not well. I'm going to take him to the vet. I'll let you know what happens.

Message 4
B: John. Hi, it's Bianca from HSBC. Sorry I missed your call. I was in a meeting. Um, yes, please call me back on this number. I'll be in the office this afternoon.

Review 4 (Units 7 and 8)

52

I = Interviewer, J = Journalist

I: So where did the idea for the One World Play Project come from?
J: Well, it started as the One World Futbol project. Back in 2006, a guy called Tim Jahnigen was watching a TV report about refugees in Darfur, Sudan. He saw some boys playing football with a ball they had made from old bits of rubbish tied together with string. He could see that they needed something better.
I: So he designed the One World football. What's it made of?
J: It's plastic and it can be used in any conditions – on roads, on beaches, on grass. The important thing is that it's very strong and never breaks or needs pumping up.
I: And how many of these footballs have they delivered to poor communities?
J: Over one million.
I: Wow! That's a lot. But who pays for them?
J: The project is sponsored by Chevrolet, the car brand – the balls have Chevrolet's name on them. They've supported the project since its launch at the 2010 football World Cup. One World Play Project sells the balls too. They promise that for each ball they sell, they will give another one free to a poor community.
I: That's interesting. So, where do you see …

Unit 9

55

1. I think you've got your shoes on the wrong way round.
2. I think your T-shirt is on inside out. I can see the label.
3. If you turn the bottle upside down, then the shampoo will run to the top.
4. He always wears his baseball cap back to front.

56

So – here's some advice for all those people who travel to meetings and conferences and have to pack a smart suit or jacket in their bags. If you're like me, then you probably spend ages trying to get the jacket flat so that it looks OK and uncreased when you unpack it at the other end. But here's a trick to avoid all that trouble.

Firstly, turn one half of the jacket inside out. Then fold the jacket in half, putting the sleeve that's not inside out into the inside out sleeve. Now roll the jacket, like you would do with a towel. But before you do that, put some other clothes – some socks, for example – inside the shoulder of the jacket. By doing this, you'll make sure that there are no lines or creases in the jacket when you unroll it. Finally, just to be sure, hang your jacket in the bathroom when you arrive at your hotel.

Unit 10

🎧 57

This is where I come from, Todmorden. It's a market town in the north of England, 15,000 people, between Leeds and Manchester, fairly normal market town. It used to look like this, and now it's more like this, with fruit and veg and herbs sprouting up all over the place. We call it propaganda gardening.

🎧 58

We've even invented a new form of tourism. It's called vegetable tourism, and believe it or not, people come from all over the world to poke around in our raised beds.

🎧 59

So today I'm going to talk a little about Transition towns and what they are. The great thing about Transition towns is that they focus on simple, practical actions. Different ideas are tried and if they work, they're put into action. I'll give you some examples of Transition town projects.

There's a group in Brixton in London which has its own community power station. Electricity is produced by solar panels on top of people's houses.

In Deventer in the Netherlands, a group has set up 'repair cafés', where people teach each other how to mend broken household objects. In the past, broken things were often thrown away.

Then in Oxford, in the UK, volunteers collect food that isn't wanted by supermarkets. Before, this food was put in the rubbish. Now it's taken by the volunteers to poorer members of the community.

In many Transition towns, street parties and festivals are organized by local residents. These are occasions when communities can get to know each other better. In the past events like these weren't organized unless it was a special national holiday.

🎧 61

Conversation 1

A: So what are you going to have?
B: Um, there are a few things I'm thinking of, but what's this: 'Bigos'? Can you explain?
A: It's a kind of stew, made with meat and sauerkraut.
B: Sauer what?
A: Sauerkraut. You know pickled cabbage.
B: Oh, OK. So is it a local dish?
A: Not especially. But it is a traditional Polish dish. It means 'hunter's stew'.
B: Do you recommend it?
A: Well, how hungry are you?
B: Quite hungry.
A: Then yes, it's good. It's not a light dish.
B: You mean, it's very filling.
A: Yes it is …

Conversation 2

W = Waiter, C = Customer

W: Are you ready to order?
C: Yes I'd like the pepper steak, please. Is it spicy?
W: Yes, it is quite spicy, but we can make it less spicy if you like.
C: No, that's OK. And, er, do any vegetables come with it?
W: Yes, french fries and a small salad.
C: OK.
W: And how would you like your steak?
C: Er, medium, please.
W: And can I get you anything to drink?
C: No, thanks. Just a jug of water would be great.

Unit 11

🎧 63

No, I mean, I think I learned early on that if you can run one company, you can really run any companies. I mean, companies are all about finding the right people, inspiring those people, you know, drawing out the best in people. And I just love learning and I'm incredibly inquisitive and I love taking on the, you know, the status quo and trying to turn it upside down. So I've seen life as one long learning process. And if I see – you know, if I, you know, if I fly on somebody else's airline and find the experience is not a pleasant one, which it wasn't 21 years ago, then I'd think, well, you know, maybe I can create the kind of airline that I'd like to fly on. And so, you know, so got one second-hand 747 from Boeing and gave it a go.

🎧 64

And if I see – you know, if I, you know, if I fly on somebody else's airline and find the experience is not a pleasant one, which it wasn't 21 years ago, then I'd think, well, you know, maybe I can create the kind of airline that I'd like to fly on.

🎧 65

So what does this data tell us about our business leaders? Well, first it's clear that we must get more women running companies. Ten per cent is a very low figure. In Germany company boards have to be at least thirty per cent female. We also need to have more ethnic diversity. If there are so few women and people from different backgrounds at the top, how can you expect to find diversity in other parts of the company? But it's good that a quarter of CEOs are under 35. You must involve young people, if you want things to change.

Secondly CEOs work too much. Eight per cent of them never take a day off! I'm not saying you mustn't work hard. But you don't have to work all the time to be efficient. The information about parents is interesting. It seems you can run a business if your parents weren't entrepreneurs – that is, had no experience of running a business – but it certainly helps if they did. Forty-nine per cent of CEOs have parents who are or were entrepreneurs. And if you're interested in the other findings …

🎧 66

A: So how's work these days?
B: Well, it's OK, but I work really hard and I don't see much benefit from it. I'm thinking about leaving, actually. In fact I think I should start my own consultancy business. Do you reckon that's a good idea?
A: Well, hang on a minute. You really need to ask yourself why, first. You shouldn't start a business just because you don't like the company that you're working for.

B: No, that's not it. I've got a lot of contacts and I think I can make it work.
A: OK, well, good. But remember that it'll probably be more work and more stress too. The most stressful thing is not having the money to give your business a chance of success. Do you have any savings?
B: Well, I've got a bit of money, but perhaps not enough.
A: Right. So the first thing you should do is to write a business plan. Then you should find a financial backer – maybe go and see the bank. You know, if you start with that …

67

C = Colleague, R = Roberto

C: Hi, Roberto. Philip just called me. He hasn't received the programme for the open day.
R: No, that's right. I didn't send it to him.
C: Really? Why not?
R: It isn't finished.
C: Why isn't it finished?
R: I didn't feel confident about my English.
C: Why don't you get some English lessons?
R: Well, I want to, but it's too expensive.
C: You should ask the university to pay. Or, another solution is to ask someone else to check it. You know, it's OK to ask for help.

68

1 Why didn't you ask me for some help?
2 Why weren't the books sent here?
3 Did you get the train tickets?
4 Why was the talk cancelled?

Unit 12

69

1 There is now a kind of sleep deprivation one-upmanship – especially here in Washington …
2 … we, at the moment, have had brilliant leaders in business, in finance, in politics, making terrible decisions. So a high IQ does not mean that you're a good leader.
3 In fact, I have a feeling that if Lehman Brothers was Lehman Brothers and Sisters, they might still be around.

70

So I urge you to shut your eyes and discover the great ideas that lie inside us, to shut your engines and discover the power of sleep.

72

A = Andy, L = Leanne

A: OK. So, Leanne, I think you wanted to say something?
L: Well, yeah, just briefly, 'cos I was at a management conference last week and I went to a talk about productivity – how much time people spend working productively, and how much time they waste. And, actually, some really interesting points were made – points which I thought, maybe … some ideas that could be applicable here.
A: OK, great. Let's hear them.

L: OK, well, the main point the speaker made – and it seems like a simple thing, really – was that most people aren't aware of their own level of productivity. They don't really know how much time they're wasting. And the idea is that if you make them more aware of this, they will become more productive.
A: I see. And how would you do that?
L: OK, well, one way would be to ask them to keep a record of how they spend their time. So, the time they spend at their desk working, the time they spend at their desk looking at other things on the Internet, the time they spend away from their desk – at the coffee machine or going outside to have a cigarette. So you could give them a kind of time sheet and they could fill it in.
A: Would that work? I mean, most people wouldn't answer honestly, would they? Rather than telling them, why don't we just watch them without telling them? Then you'd really find out how much time they were wasting.
L: No, no – that's not the point. We're not checking on people. The point is that we just want people to think about how they're using their time. If people are aware, they waste less time. You don't actually have to spy on anyone. Apparently, if you …

Review 6 (Units 11 and 12)

74

I = Interviewer, E = Employee

I: So what makes CHG a good company to work for?
E: Wow! There are so many things. Obviously the nature of the work is important. When your job is to help people who are in bad health to get better, then naturally you get a lot of job satisfaction. Ninety-eight per cent of the staff say they enjoy the challenge of their work and feel that it's making a difference to society. And over ninety per cent say that CHG gives them responsibility for their work – in other words, trusts them to do their job – and supports them when they need training or professional development.
I: OK – and what about benefits for employees?
E: Employees get eleven paid days of holiday in the year, which sounds very little but this is pretty normal for the USA. However, after one year of working, they can take a further eighteen days a year unpaid if they want or need to. The company is very sensitive to workers' home-work balance. So if an employee's child was sick, for example, they would either help them with time off or allow them to work from home, if that was possible. There is also a very friendly atmosphere among the staff – almost like a family, so employees often help each other out in this kind of situation. Oh, and the company pays for employees to do volunteer days in the community too – like helping out in a local school.
I: And well-being? I guess as it's a healthcare company, they promote employee health too?
E: Oh sure, absolutely. There are free health checks, there's an onsite fitness centre and massage therapy is available. They also have a lot of onsite services at the headquarters such as pharmacies and a wellness clinic that mean that staff can easily access …

Communication activities | STUDENT A

Unit 3.1 Exercise 12, page 33

Read and memorize the two facts. Then introduce your talk: *The increasing gap between the world's rich and poor.*

Fact 1: The world's 85 richest people own as much as the world's poorest 50 per cent.

Fact 2: The income of the world's richest one per cent grew by 30 per cent in the last three years.

Unit 5.2 Exercise 11, page 57

	FIVE PALMS HOTEL white sand beaches	ASTRA HOTEL quiet historic retreat
Stars	★★★★	
Customer rating	#8 of 52 hotels in area	
Location	on seafront; two minutes from beach	
Number of rooms	106	
Amenities	swimming pool, beach bar, two restaurants, nightclub	
Activities	watersports, boat hire	
Cost	$100 per night	

Unit 7.1 Exercise 13, page 77

Autism in adults

A lot of adults don't realize that they have autism because they think it is a condition that only affects children. However, autism affects a lot of adults as well. Sometimes adults discover they have autism because their doctor tells them. Sometimes they read about autism on the Internet and think they perhaps are autistic. Adults who think they are autistic want to know if they can find a cure of some kind. But autism is not an illness. It is a condition that affects the way you see the world. One way to help understand it is to meet other people who have autism.

Unit 8.3 Exercise 8, page 90

G-Form XTREME Protective iPad cover

Product specifications:

- Fits iPad
- Colour: Yellow and black
- Size: 20.5 × 26 cm
- Material: thick rubber
- Absorbs 94% impact when dropped
- Cost: $79.99

Unit 8.4 Exercise 7, page 92

Message 1: You are a friend. Call and invite Student B to dinner on Friday. Ask them to let you know if they can come.

Message 2: Your name is Asha Lamb. You are calling from an insurance company. You want to arrange a meeting with Student B. You will send an email with more information.

Unit 9.4 Exercise 9, page 105

How to take the elevator to your floor without stopping at other floors

1. Get in the elevator.
2. Press the 'close door' button.
3. As you press the 'close door' button, press the button for your floor.
4. When the elevator starts to move, release both buttons.
5. You will arrive at your floor without stopping.

Unit 11.4 Exercise 5, page 126

Problem 1

Read the description of what happened. Then prepare to answer questions your partner asks.

- An office computer was destroyed.
- Someone in the office sprayed water from a fire extinguisher on it and it exploded.
- She did this because she saw smoke from the back of the computer and then picked up the wrong fire extinguisher.
- There were two fire extinguishers in the office – one for electrical fires and one for other fires, but they weren't labelled.

Problem 2

Ask Student B questions about the problem. Begin like this: *What's the problem?*

Communication activities | STUDENT B

Unit 3.1 Exercise 12, page 33

Read and memorize the two facts. Then introduce your talk: *The amount of food people waste.*

Fact 1: Every year we throw away one third of the food we produce in the world.
Fact 2: The United States throws away $43 billion of food each year.

Unit 5.2 Exercise 11, page 57

	ASTRA HOTEL quiet historic retreat	FIVE PALMS HOTEL white sand beaches
Stars	★★★★	
Customer rating	#7 of 52 hotels in area	
Location	quiet location in hills; twenty minutes from beach	
Number of rooms	32	
Amenities	swimming pool, restaurant, gym, large gardens	
Activities	golf, tennis	
Cost	$120 per night	

Unit 7.1 Exercise 13, page 77

Understanding what it is like to be autistic

One of the most difficult things for a person without autism to understand about people with autism is that their senses seem to be under attack all the time. For example, most of us are able to block out the sounds that surround us (e.g. music, machines, traffic or other people talking), but an autistic person's brain often does not have this ability. They are almost in pain trying to deal with all the noises at the same time. The same is true of the other senses: smell and vision and so on. The world seems to be attacking them with strange and unpleasant sights and smells. It is not surprising that autistic people often seem angry or upset. It's important for those without autism to understand what autistic people are experiencing and to be patient and sympathetic with them.

Unit 8.3 Exercise 8, page 90

Polaroid Socialmatic Instant camera

Product specifications:

- Prints small photo stickers
- 14 megapixel camera
- Available in black and white
- Photos are 5 cms × 7.5 cms
- Weight: less than 300 g
- Cost: approx $200

Unit 8.4 Exercise 7, page 92

Message 1: You are calling from the Regency Hotel. You want to know if Student A made a reservation for a single or a double room.

Message 2: You are a colleague of Student A. You have a meeting with them at 3.00 p.m. this afternoon, but you are going to be thirty minutes late.

Unit 9.4 Exercise 9, page 105

How to stop cables that are attached to each other from coming unplugged

1. Unplug the two cables from each other.
2. Tie the two cables together, making a knot about 5cms from the end of each one.
3. Plug the two cables back together.
4. If you pull the cables the knot will get tighter, but the cables will not come unplugged.

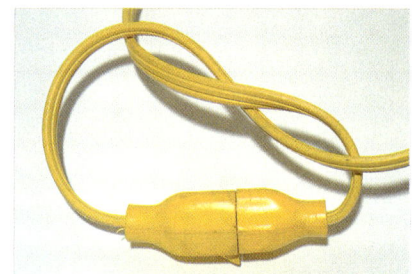

Unit 11.4 Exercise 5, page 126

Problem 1

Ask Student A questions about the problem. Begin like this: *What's the problem?*

Problem 2

Read the description of what happened. Then prepare to answer questions your partner asks.

- The rubbish in bins outside people's houses smells very bad.
- The weather has been hot and no one has collected the rubbish for twelve days.
- This is because the council has decided to collect people's rubbish every two weeks, not every week.
- The council has done this to save money.

TED Talk transcripts

The transcripts use British English for all the talks, irrespective of the nationality of the speaker.

Any grammatical inaccuracies in the talks have been left uncorrected in the transcripts.

Unit 1 A life lesson from a volunteer firefighter

0.13 Back in New York, I am the head of development for a non-profit called Robin Hood. When I'm not fighting poverty, I'm fighting fires as the assistant captain of a volunteer fire company. Now in our town, where the volunteers supplement a highly skilled career staff, you have to get to the fire scene pretty early to get in on any action.

0.32 I remember my first fire. I was the second volunteer on the scene, so there was a pretty good chance I was going to get in. But still it was a real footrace against the other volunteers to get to the captain in charge to find out what our assignments would be. When I found the captain, he was having a very engaging conversation with the homeowner, who was surely having one of the worst days of her life. Here it was, the middle of the night, she was standing outside in the pouring rain, under an umbrella, in her pyjamas, barefoot, while her house was in flames.

1.06 The other volunteer who had arrived just before me – let's call him Lex Luthor – (*Laughter*) got to the captain first and was asked to go inside and save the homeowner's dog. The dog! I was stunned with jealousy. Here was some lawyer or money manager who, for the rest of his life, gets to tell people that he went into a burning building to save a living creature, just because he beat me by five seconds. Well, I was next. The captain waved me over. He said, 'Bezos, I need you to go into the house. I need you to go upstairs, past the fire, and I need you to get this woman a pair of shoes.' (*Laughter*) I swear. So, not exactly what I was hoping for, but off I went – up the stairs, down the hall, past the 'real' firefighters, who were pretty much done putting out the fire at this point, into the master bedroom to get a pair of shoes.

2.06 Now I know what you're thinking, but I'm no hero. (*Laughter*) I carried my payload back downstairs where I met my nemesis and the precious dog by the front door. We took our treasures outside to the homeowner, where, not surprisingly, his received much more attention than did mine. A few weeks later, the department received a letter from the homeowner thanking us for the valiant effort displayed in saving her home. The act of kindness she noted above all others: someone had even gotten her a pair of shoes.

2.46 (*Laughter*)

2.48 In both my vocation at Robin Hood and my avocation as a volunteer firefighter, I am witness to acts of generosity and kindness on a monumental scale, but I'm also witness to acts of grace and courage on an individual basis. And you know what I've learned? They all matter. So as I look around this room at people who either have achieved, or are on their way to achieving, remarkable levels of success, I would offer this reminder: don't wait. Don't wait until you make your first million to make a difference in somebody's life. If you have something to give, give it now. Serve food at a soup kitchen. Clean up a neighbourhood park. Be a mentor.

3.30 Not every day is going to offer us a chance to save somebody's life, but every day offers us an opportunity to affect one. So get in the game. Save the shoes.

3.41 Thank you.

3.42 (*Applause*)

Unit 2 How to start a movement

0.12 So, ladies and gentlemen, at TED we talk a lot about leadership and how to make a movement. So let's watch a movement happen, start to finish, in under three minutes and dissect some lessons from it.

0.23 First, of course you know, a leader needs the guts to stand out and be ridiculed. But what he's doing is so easy to follow. So here's his first follower with a crucial role; he's going to show everyone else how to follow.

0.36 Now, notice that the leader embraces him as an equal. So, now it's not about the leader anymore; it's about them, plural. Now, there he is calling to his friends. Now, if you notice that the first follower is actually an underestimated form of leadership in itself. It takes guts to stand out like that. The first follower is what transforms a lone nut into a leader. (*Laughter*) (*Applause*)

1.02 And here comes a second follower. Now it's not a lone nut, it's not two nuts – three is a crowd, and a crowd is news. So a movement must be public. It's important to show not just the leader, but the followers, because you find that new followers emulate the followers, not the leader.

1.19 Now, here come two more people, and immediately after, three more people. Now we've got momentum. This is the tipping point. Now we've got a movement. So, notice that, as more people join in, it's less risky. So those that were sitting on the fence before, now have no reason not to. They won't stand out, they won't be ridiculed, but they will be part of the in-crowd if they hurry. (*Laughter*) So, over the next minute, you'll see all of those that prefer to stick with the crowd because eventually they would be ridiculed for not joining in. And that's how you make a movement.

1.55 But let's recap some lessons from this. So first, if you are the type, like the shirtless dancing guy that is standing alone, remember the importance of nurturing your first few followers as equals so it's clearly about the movement, not you. OK, but we might have missed the real lesson here.

2.13 The biggest lesson, if you noticed – did you catch it? – is that leadership is over-glorified. That, yes, it was the shirtless guy who was first, and he'll get all the credit, but it was really the first follower that transformed the lone nut into a leader. So, as we're told that we should all be leaders, that would be really ineffective.

2.33 If you really care about starting a movement, have the courage to follow and show others how to follow. And when you find a lone nut doing something great, have the guts to be the first one to stand up and join in. And what a perfect place to do that, at TED.

Thanks. (*Applause*)

Unit 3 An escape from poverty

0.12 I've been working on issues of poverty for more than twenty years, and so it's ironic that the problem that and question that I most grapple with is how you actually define poverty. What does it mean? So often, we look at dollar terms – people making less than a dollar or two or three a day. And yet the complexity of poverty really has to look at income as only one variable. Because really, it's a condition about choice, and the lack of freedom.

0.40 And I had an experience that really deepened and elucidated for me the understanding that I have. It was in Kenya, and I want to share it with you. I was with my friend Susan Meiselas, the photographer, in the Mathare Valley slums. Now, Mathare Valley is one of the oldest slums in Africa. It's about three miles out of Nairobi, and it's a mile long and about two-tenths of a mile wide, where over half a million people live crammed in these little tin shacks, generation after generation, renting them, often eight or ten people to a room.

1.10 And it was here that I met Jane. I was struck immediately by the kindness and the gentleness in her face, and I asked her to tell me her story. She started off by telling me her dream. She said, 'I had two. My first dream was to be a doctor, and the second was to marry a good man who would stay with me and my family, because my mother was a single mom, and couldn't afford to pay for school fees. So I had to give up the first dream, and I focused on the second.' She got married when she was eighteen, had a baby right away. And when she turned twenty, found herself pregnant with a second child, her mom died and her husband left her – married another woman. So she was again in Mathare, with no income, no skill set, no money.

1.53 In 2001, her life changed. She had a girlfriend who had heard about this organization, Jamii Bora, that would lend money to people no matter how poor you were, as long as you provided a commensurate amount in savings. And so she spent a year to save 50 dollars, and started borrowing, and over time she was able to buy a sewing machine. She started tailoring. And that turned into what she does now, which is to go into the second-hand clothing markets, and for about three dollars and 25 cents she buys an old ball gown. Some of them might be ones you gave. And she repurposes them with frills and ribbons, and makes these frothy confections that she sells to women for their daughters' Sweet 16 or first Holy Communion – those milestones in a life that people want to celebrate all along the economic spectrum. And she does really good business. In fact, I watched her walk through the streets hawking. And before you knew it, there was a crowd of women around her, buying these dresses.

2.55 And I reflected, as I was watching her sell the dresses, and also the jewellery that she makes, that now Jane makes more than four dollars a day. And by many definitions she is no longer poor. But she still lives in Mathare Valley. And so she can't move out.

3.12 Jamii Bora understands that and understands that when we're talking about poverty, we've got to look at people all along the economic spectrum. And so with patient capital from Acumen and other organizations, loans and investments that will go the long term with them, they built a low-cost housing development, about an hour outside Nairobi central. And they designed it from the perspective of customers like Jane herself, insisting on responsibility and accountability. So she has to give ten per cent of the mortgage – of the total value, or about 400 dollars in savings. And then they match her mortgage to what she paid in rent for her little shanty. And in the next couple of weeks, she's going to be among the first 200 families to move into this development.

4.00 I said, 'Well what about your dreams?' And she said, 'Well, you know, my dreams don't look exactly like I thought they would when I was a little girl. But if I think about it, I thought I wanted a husband, but what I really wanted was a family that was loving. And I fiercely love my children, and they love me back.' And she said, 'I thought I wanted to be a doctor, but what I really wanted to be was somebody who served and healed and cured. And so I feel so blessed with everything that I have, that two days a week I go and I counsel HIV patients. And I say, "Look at me. You are not dead. You are still alive. And if you are still alive you have to serve."' And she said, 'I'm not a doctor who gives out pills. But maybe me, I give out something better because I give them hope.'

4.49 And in the middle of this economic crisis, where so many of us are inclined to pull in with fear, I think we're well suited to take a cue from Jane and reach out, recognizing that being poor doesn't mean being ordinary. Because when systems are broken, like the ones that we're seeing around the world, it's an opportunity for invention and for innovation. It's an opportunity to truly build a world where we can extend services and products to all human beings, so that they can make decisions and choices for themselves. I truly believe it's where dignity starts. We owe it to the Janes of the world. And just as important, we owe it to ourselves.

5.33 Thank you.

5.34 (*Applause*)

Unit 4 Don't eat the marshmallow!

0.12 I'm here because I have a very important message: I think we have found the most important factor for success. And it was found close to here, Stanford. Psychology professor took kids that were four years old and put them in a room all by themselves. And he would tell the child, a four-year-old kid, 'Johnny, I am going to leave you here with a marshmallow for fifteen minutes. If, after I come back, this marshmallow is here, you will get another one. So you will have two.' To tell a four-year-old kid to wait fifteen minutes for something that they like, is equivalent to telling us, 'We'll bring you coffee in two hours.' (*Laughter*) Exact equivalent.

1.01 So what happened when the professor left the room? As soon as the door closed … two out of three ate the marshmallow. Five seconds, ten seconds, 40 seconds, 50 seconds, two minutes, four minutes, eight minutes. Some lasted fourteen-and-a-half minutes. (*Laughter*) Couldn't do it. Could not wait. What's interesting is that one out of three would look at the marshmallow and go like this … Would look at it. Put it back. They would walk around. They would play with their skirts and pants.

1.42 That child already, at four, understood the most important principle for success, which is the ability to delay gratification. Self-discipline: the most important factor for success. fifteen years later, fourteen or fifteen years later, follow-up study. What did they find? They went to look for these kids who were now eighteen and nineteen. And they found that 100 per cent of the children that had not eaten the marshmallow were successful. They had good grades. They were doing wonderful. They were happy. They had their plans. They had good relationships with the teachers, students. They were doing fine.

2.23 A great percentage of the kids that ate the marshmallow, they were in trouble. They did not make it to university. They had bad grades. Some of them dropped out. A few were still there with bad grades. A few had good grades.

2.35 I had a question in my mind: Would Hispanic kids react the same way as the American kids? So I went to Colombia. And I reproduced the experiment. And it was very funny. I used four, five and six years old kids. And let me show you what happened.

4.44 So what happened in Colombia? Hispanic kids, two out of three ate the marshmallow; one out of three did not. This little girl was interesting; she ate the inside of the marshmallow. (*Laughter*) In other words, she wanted us to think that she had not eaten it, so she would get two. But she ate it. So we know she'll be successful. But we have to watch her. (*Laughter*) She should not go into banking, for example, or work in a cash register. But she will be successful.

5.13 And this applies for everything. Even in sales. The sales person that – the customer says, 'I want that.' And … 'OK, here you are.' That person ate the marshmallow. If the sales person says, 'Wait a second. Let me ask you a few questions to see if this is a good choice.' Then you sell a lot more. So this has applications in all walks of life.

5.35 I end with – the Koreans did this. You know what? This is so good that we want a marshmallow book for children. We did one for children. And now it is all over Korea. They are teaching these kids exactly this principle. And we need to learn that principle here in the States, because we have a big debt. We are eating more marshmallows than we are producing. Thank you so much.

Unit 5 3 ways to (usefully) lose control of your brand

0.13 Companies are losing control. What happens on Wall Street no longer stays on Wall Street. What happens in Vegas ends up on YouTube. (*Laughter*) Reputations are volatile. Loyalties are fickle. Management teams seem increasingly disconnected from their staff. (*Laughter*) A recent survey said that 27 per cent of bosses believe their employees are inspired by their firm. However, in the same survey, only four per cent of employees agreed. Companies are losing control of their customers and their employees. But are they really?

0.53 I'm a marketer, and as a marketer, I know that I've never really been in control. Your brand is what other people say about you when you're not in the room, the saying goes. Hyperconnectivity and transparency allow companies to be in that room now, 24/7. They can listen and join the conversation. In fact, they have more control over the loss of control than ever before. They can design for it. But how?

1.23 First of all, they can give employees and customers more control. They can collaborate with them on the creation of ideas, knowledge, content, designs and product. They can give them more control over pricing, which is what the band Radiohead did with its pay-as-you-like online release of its album *In Rainbows*. Buyers could determine the price, but the offer was exclusive, and only stood for a limited period of time. The album sold more copies than previous releases of the band.

The Danish chocolate company Anthon Berg opened a so-called 'generous store' in Copenhagen. It asked customers to purchase chocolate with the promise of good deeds towards loved ones. It turned transactions into interactions, and generosity into a currency.

2.11 The ultimate empowerment of customers is to ask them not to buy. Outdoor clothier Patagonia encouraged prospective buyers to check out eBay for its used products and to resole their shoes before purchasing new ones. In an even more radical stance against consumerism, the company placed a 'Don't Buy This Jacket' advertisement during the peak of shopping season. It may have jeopardized short-term sales, but it built lasting, long-term loyalty based on shared values.

2.44 Research has shown that giving employees more control over their work makes them happier and more productive. The Brazilian company Semco Group famously lets employees set their own work schedules and even their salaries.

3.00 Companies can give people more control, but they can also give them less control. Take the travel service Nextpedition. Nextpedition turns the trip into a game, with surprising twists and turns along the way. It does not tell the traveller where she's going until the very last minute, and information is provided just in time. Similarly, Dutch airline KLM launched a surprise campaign, seemingly randomly handing out small gifts to travellers en route to their destination.

3.36 Is there anything companies can do to make their employees feel less pressed for time? Yes. Force them to help others. A recent study suggests that having employees complete occasional altruistic tasks throughout the day increases their sense of overall productivity. At frog, the company I work for, we hold internal speed-meet sessions that connect old and new employees, helping them get to know each other fast. By applying a strict process, we give them less control, less choice, but we enable more and richer social interactions.

4.15 At the end of the day, as hyperconnectivity and transparency expose companies' behaviour in broad daylight, staying true to their true selves is the only sustainable value proposition. Or as the ballet dancer Alonzo King said, 'What's interesting about you is you.' For the true selves of companies to come through, openness is paramount, but radical openness is not a solution, because when everything is open, nothing is open. 'A smile is a door that is half open and half closed,' the author Jennifer Egan wrote. Companies can give their employees and customers more control or less. They can worry about how much openness is good for them, and what needs to stay closed. Or they can simply smile, and remain open to all possibilities. Thank you. (*Applause*)

Unit 6 Talk nerdy to me

0.13 Five years ago, I experienced a bit of what it must have been like to be Alice in Wonderland. Penn State asked me, a communications teacher, to teach a communications class for engineering students. And I was scared. (*Laughter*) Really scared. Scared of these students with their big brains and their big books and their big, unfamiliar words. But as these conversations unfolded, I experienced what Alice must have when she went down that rabbit hole and saw that door to a whole new world. That's just how I felt as I had those conversations with the students. I was amazed at the ideas that they had, and I wanted others to experience this wonderland as well. And I believe the key to opening that door is great communication.

1.00 We desperately need great communication from our scientists and engineers in order to change the world. Our scientists and engineers are the ones that are tackling our grandest challenges, from energy to environment to health care, among others, and if we don't know about it and understand it, then the work isn't done, and I believe it's our responsibility as non-scientists to have these interactions. But these great conversations can't occur if our scientists and engineers don't invite us in to see their wonderland. So scientists and engineers, please, talk nerdy to us.

1.36 I want to share a few keys on how you can do that to make sure that we can see that your science is sexy and that your engineering is engaging. First question to answer for us: so what? Tell us why your science is relevant to us. Don't just tell me that you study trabeculae, but tell me that you study trabeculae, which is the mesh-like structure of our bones because it's important to understanding and treating osteoporosis.

2.04 And when you're describing your science, beware of jargon. Jargon is a barrier to our understanding of your ideas. Sure, you can say 'spatial and temporal' but why not just say 'space and time', which is so much more accessible to us? And making your ideas accessible is not the same as dumbing it down. Instead, as Einstein said, make everything as simple as possible, but no simpler. You can clearly communicate your science without compromising the ideas. A few things to consider are having examples, stories and analogies. Those are ways to engage and excite us about your content. And when presenting your work, drop the bullet points. Have you ever wondered why they're called bullet points? (*Laughter*) What do bullets do? Bullets kill, and they will kill your presentation. A slide like this is not only boring, but it relies too much on the language area of our brain, and causes us to become overwhelmed. Instead, this example slide by Genevieve Brown is much more effective. It's showing that the special structure of trabeculae are so strong that they actually inspired the unique design of the Eiffel Tower. And the trick here is to use a single, readable sentence that the audience can key into if they get a bit lost, and then provide visuals which appeal to our other senses and create a deeper sense of understanding of what's being described.

3.33 So I think these are just a few keys that can help the rest of us to open that door and see the wonderland that is science and engineering. And because the engineers that I've worked with have taught me to become really in touch with my inner nerd, I want to summarize with an equation. (*Laughter*) Take your science, subtract your bullet points and your jargon, divide by relevance, meaning share what's relevant to the audience, and multiply it by the passion that you have for this incredible work that you're doing, and that is going to equal incredible interactions that are full of understanding. And so, scientists and engineers, when you've solved this equation, by all means, talk nerdy to me. (*Laughter*) Thank you. (*Applause*)

Unit 7 What I've learned from my autistic brothers

0.14 Today I have just one request. Please don't tell me I'm normal.

0.20 Now I'd like to introduce you to my brothers. Remi is 22, tall and very handsome. He's speechless, but he communicates joy in a way that some of the best orators cannot. Remi knows what love is. He shares it unconditionally and he shares it regardless. He's not greedy. He doesn't see skin colour. He doesn't care about religious differences, and get this: He has never told a lie. When he sings songs from our childhood, attempting words that not even I could remember, he reminds me of one thing: how little we know about the mind, and how wonderful the unknown must be.

1.09 Samuel is sixteen. He's tall. He's very handsome. He has the most impeccable memory. He has a selective one, though. He doesn't remember if he stole my chocolate bar, but he remembers the year of release for every song on my iPod, conversations we had when he was four, weeing on my arm on the first ever episode of Teletubbies, and Lady Gaga's birthday.

1.37 Don't they sound incredible? But most people don't agree. And in fact, because their minds don't fit into society's version of normal, they're often bypassed and misunderstood.

1.52 But what lifted my heart and strengthened my soul was that even though this was the case, although they were not seen as ordinary, this could only mean one thing: that they were extraordinary – autistic and extraordinary.

2.11 Now, for you who may be less familiar with the term 'autism', it's a complex brain disorder that affects social communication, learning and sometimes physical skills. It manifests in each individual differently, hence why Remi is so different from Sam. And across the world, every twenty minutes, one new person is diagnosed with autism, and although it's one of the fastest-growing developmental disorders in the world, there is no known cause or cure.

2.40 And I cannot remember the first moment I encountered autism, but I cannot recall a day without it. I was just three years old when my brother came along, and I was so excited that I had a new being in my life. And after a few months went by, I realized that he was different. He screamed a lot. He didn't want to play like the other babies did, and in fact, he didn't seem very interested in me whatsoever. Remi lived and reigned in his own world, with his own rules, and he found pleasure in the smallest things, like lining up cars around the room and staring at the washing machine and eating anything that came in between. And as he grew older, he grew more different, and the differences became more obvious. Yet beyond the tantrums and the frustration and the never-ending hyperactivity was something really unique: a pure and innocent nature, a boy who saw the world without prejudice, a human who had never lied. Extraordinary.

3.51 Now, I cannot deny that there have been some challenging moments in my family, moments where I've wished that they were just like me. But I cast my mind back to the things that they've taught me about individuality and communication and love, and I realize that these are things that I wouldn't want to change with normality. Normality overlooks the beauty that differences give us, and the fact that we are different doesn't mean that one of us is wrong. It just means that there's a different kind of right. And if I could communicate just one thing to Remi and to Sam and to you, it would be that you don't have to be normal. You can be extraordinary. Because autistic or not, the differences that we have – We've got a gift! Everyone's got a gift inside of us, and in all honesty, the pursuit of normality is the ultimate sacrifice of potential. The chance for greatness, for progress and for change dies the moment we try to be like someone else.

5.04 Please – don't tell me I'm normal. Thank you. (*Applause*)

Unit 8 A skateboard, with a boost

0.14 Today I'm going to show you an electric vehicle that weighs less than a bicycle, that you can carry with you anywhere, that you can charge off a normal wall outlet in fifteen minutes, and you can run it for 1,000 kilometres on about a dollar of electricity. But when I say the word electric vehicle, people think about vehicles. They think about cars and motorcycles and bicycles, and the vehicles that you use every day. But if you come about it from a different perspective, you can create some more interesting, more novel concepts.

0.50 So we built something. I've got some of the pieces in my pocket here. So this is the motor. This motor has enough power to take you up the hills of San Francisco at about twenty miles per hour, about 30 kilometres an hour, and this battery, this battery right here has about six miles of range, or ten kilometres, which is enough to cover about half of the car trips in the US alone.

1.16 But the best part about these components is that we bought them at a toy store. These are from remote control airplanes. And the performance of these things has gotten so good that if you think about vehicles a little bit differently, you can really change things.

1.30 So today we're going to show you one example of how you can use this. Pay attention to not only how fun this thing is, but also how the portability that comes with this can totally change the way you interact with a city like San Francisco.

1.44 (*Music*) [6 Mile Range] [Top Speed Near 20 mph] [Uphill Climbing] [Regenerative Braking]

2.51 (*Applause*) (*Cheers*)

3.02 So we're going to show you what this thing can do. It's really manoeuvrable. You have a hand-held remote, so you can pretty easily control acceleration, braking, go in reverse if you like, also have braking. It's incredible just how light this thing is. I mean, this is something you can pick up and carry with you anywhere you go.

3.29 So I'll leave you with one of the most compelling facts about this technology and these kinds of vehicles. This uses twenty times less energy for every mile or kilometre that you travel than a car, which means not only is this thing fast to charge and really cheap to build, but it also reduces the footprint of your energy use in terms of your transportation. So instead of looking at large amounts of energy needed for each person in this room to get around in a city, now you can look at much smaller amounts and more sustainable transportation.

4.02 So next time you think about a vehicle, I hope, like us, you're thinking about something new.

4.07 Thank you.

4.08 (*Applause*)

Unit 9 How to tie your shoes

0.12 I'm used to thinking of the TED audience as a wonderful collection of some of the most effective, intelligent, intellectual, savvy, worldly and innovative people in the world. And I think that's true. However, I also have reason to believe that many, if not most, of you are actually tying your shoes incorrectly.

0.30 (*Laughter*)

0.31 Now I know that seems ludicrous. I know that seems ludicrous. And believe me, I lived the same sad life until about three years ago. And what happened to me was I bought, what was for me, a very expensive pair of shoes. But those shoes came with round nylon laces, and I couldn't keep them tied. So I went back to the store and said to the owner, 'I love the shoes, but I hate the laces.' He took a look and said, 'Oh, you're tying them wrong.' Now up until that moment, I would have thought that, by age 50, one of the life skills that I had really nailed was tying my shoes. But not so – let me demonstrate.

1.12 This is the way that most of us were taught to tie our shoes. Now as it turns out – thank you. Wait, there's more. As it turns out, there's a strong form and a weak form of this knot, and we were taught to tie the weak form. And here's how to tell. If you pull the strands at the base of the knot, you can see that the bow will orient itself down the long axis of the shoe. That's the weak form of the knot.

1.42 But not to worry. If we start over and simply go the other direction around the bow, we get this, the strong form of the knot. And if you pull the cords under the knot, you will see that the bow orients itself along the transverse axis of the shoe. This is a stronger knot. It will come untied less often. It will let you down less, and not only that, it looks better.

2.09 We're going to do this one more time. (*Applause*) Start as usual, go the other way around the loop. This is a little hard for children, but I think you can handle it. Pull the knot. There it is: the strong form of the shoe knot.

2.31 Now, in keeping with today's theme, I'd like to point out – and something you already know – that sometimes a small advantage someplace in life can yield tremendous results someplace else.

2.45 Live long and prosper.

2.46 (*Applause*)

Unit 10 How we can eat our landscapes

0.13 The will to live life differently can start in some of the most unusual places. This is where I come from, Todmorden. It's a market town in the north of England, 15,000 people, between Leeds and Manchester, fairly normal market town. It used to look like this, and now it's more like this, with fruit and veg and herbs sprouting up all over the place. We call it propaganda gardening. (*Laughter*)

0.42 Corner of our railway station car park, front of our health centre, people's front gardens, and even in front of the police station. (*Laughter*) We've got edible canal towpaths, and we've got sprouting cemeteries. The soil is extremely good. (*Laughter*)

1.04 We've even invented a new form of tourism. It's called vegetable tourism, and believe it or not, people come from all over the world to poke around in our raised beds, even when there's not much growing. (*Laughter*) But it starts a conversation. (*Laughter*)

1.20 And, you know, we're not doing it because we're bored. (*Laughter*) We're doing it because we want to start a revolution.

1.28   We tried to answer this simple question: Can you find a unifying language that cuts across age and income and culture that will help people themselves find a new way of living, see spaces around them differently, think about the resources they use differently, interact differently? Can we find that language? And then, can we replicate those actions? And the answer would appear to be yes, and the language would appear to be food.

1.58   So, three and a half years ago, a few of us sat around a kitchen table and we just invented the whole thing. (*Laughter*) (*Applause*) We came up with a really simple game plan that we put to a public meeting. We did not consult. We did not write a report. Enough of all that. (*Laughter*) And we said to that public meeting in Todmorden, look, let's imagine that our town is focused around three plates: a community plate, the way we live our everyday lives; a learning plate, what we teach our kids in school and what new skills we share amongst ourselves; and business, what we do with the pound in our pocket and which businesses we choose to support.

2.39   We put that proposition to the meeting, two seconds, and then the room exploded. I have never, ever experienced anything like that in my life. And it's been the same in every single room, in every town that we've ever told our story. People are ready and respond to the story of food. They want positive actions they can engage in, and in their bones, they know it's time to take personal responsibility and invest in more kindness to each other and to the environment.

3.08   And since we had that meeting three and a half years ago, it's been a heck of a roller coaster. We started with a seed swap, really simple stuff, and then we took an area of land, a strip on the side of our main road, which was a dog toilet, basically, and we turned it into a really lovely herb garden. We took the corner of the car park in the station that you saw, and we made vegetable beds for everybody to share and pick from themselves. We went to the doctors. We've just had a six-million-pound health centre built in Todmorden, and for some reason that I cannot comprehend, it has been surrounded by prickly plants. (*Laughter*) So we went to the doctors, said, 'Would you mind us taking them up?' They said, 'Absolutely fine, provided you get planning permission and you do it in Latin and you do it in triplicate,' so we did — (*Laughter*) — and now there are fruit trees and bushes and herbs and vegetables around that doctor's surgery. And there's been lots of other examples, like the corn that was in front of the police station, and the old people's home that we've planted up with food that they can pick and grow.

4.11   And then there's the second plate, the learning plate. Well, we're in partnership with a high school. We've created a company. We are designing and building an aquaponics unit in some land that was spare at the back of the high school, like you do, and now we're going to be growing fish and vegetables in an orchard with bees, and the kids are helping us build that, and the kids are on the board, and because the community was really keen on working with the high school, the high school is now teaching agriculture.

4.39   And then there's the third plate, because if you walk through an edible landscape, and if you're learning new skills, and if you start to get interested in what's growing seasonally, you might just want to spend more of your own money in support of local producers, not just veg, but meat and cheese and beer and whatever else it might be.

4.55   But then, we're just a community group, you know. We're just all volunteers. What could we actually do? So we did some really simple things. We fundraised, we got some blackboards, we put 'Incredible Edible' on the top, we gave it to every market trader that was selling locally, and they scribbled on what they were selling in any one week. Really popular. People congregated around it. Sales were up.

5.13   And then, we had a chat with the farmers, and we said, 'We're really serious about this,' but they didn't actually believe us, so we thought, OK, what should we do? I know. If we can create a campaign around one product and show them there is local loyalty to that product, maybe they'll change their mind and see we're serious.

5.29   So we launched a campaign – because it just amuses me – called Every Egg Matters. (*Laughter*) And what we did was we put people on our egg map. It's a stylized map of Todmorden. Anybody that's selling their excess eggs at the garden gate, perfectly legally, to their neighbours, we've stuck on there. We started with four, and we've now got 64 on, and the result of that was that people were then going into shops asking for a local Todmorden egg, and the result of that was, some farmers upped the amount of flocks they got of free-range birds, and then they went on to meat birds, and although these are really, really small steps, that increasing local economic confidence is starting to play out in a number of ways, and we now have farmers doing cheese and they've upped their flocks and rare breed pigs, they're doing pasties and pies and things that they would have never done before. We've got increasing market stalls selling local food, and in a survey that local students did for us, 49 per cent of all food traders in that town said that their bottom line had increased because of what we were actually doing. And we're just volunteers and it's only an experiment. (*Laughter*)

6.31   Now, none of this is rocket science. It certainly is not clever, and it's not original. But it is joined up, and it is inclusive. This is not a movement for those people that are going to sort themselves out anyway. This is a movement for everyone. We have a motto: If you eat, you're in. (*Laughter*) (*Applause*) Across age, across income, across culture.

7.02 Through an organic process, through an increasing recognition of the power of small actions, we are starting, at last, to believe in ourselves again, and to believe in our capacity, each and every one of us, to build a different and a kinder future, and in my book, that's incredible.

7.25 Thank you. (*Applause*) Thank you very much. (*Applause*)

Unit 11 Life at 30,000 feet

0.12 Chris Anderson: So, we're going to put up some slides of some of your companies here. You've started one or two in your time. So, you know, Virgin Atlantic, Virgin Records – I guess it all started with a magazine called *Student*. And then, yes, all these other ones as well. I mean, how do you do this?

0.33 Richard Branson: I read all these sort of TED instructions: you must not talk about your own business, and this, and now you ask me. So I suppose you're not going to be able to kick me off the stage, since you asked the question. (*Laughter*)

0.43 CA: It depends what the answer is though.

0.46 RB: No, I mean, I think I learned early on that if you can run one company, you can really run any companies. I mean, companies are all about finding the right people, inspiring those people, you know, drawing out the best in people. And I just love learning and I'm incredibly inquisitive and I love taking on, you know, the status quo and trying to turn it upside down. So I've seen life as one long learning process. And if I see – you know, if I, you know, if I fly on somebody else's airline and find the experience is not a pleasant one, which it wasn't, 21 years ago, then I'd think, well, you know, maybe I can create the kind of airline that I'd like to fly on. And so, you know, so got one second-hand 747 from Boeing and gave it a go.

1.40 CA: Well, that was a bizarre thing, because you made this move that a lot of people advised you was crazy. And in fact, in a way, it almost took down your empire at one point. I had a conversation with one of the investment bankers who, at the time when you basically sold Virgin Records and invested heavily in Virgin Atlantic, and his view was that you were trading, you know, the world's fourth biggest record company for the twenty-fifth biggest airline and that you were out of your mind. Why did you do that?

2.12 RB: Well, I think that there's a very thin dividing line between success and failure. And I think if you start a business without financial backing, you're likely to go the wrong side of that dividing line. We had – we were being attacked by British Airways. They were trying to put our airline out of business, and they launched what's become known as the dirty tricks campaign. And I realized that the whole empire was likely to come crashing down unless I chipped in a chip. And in order to protect the jobs of the people who worked for the airline, and protect the jobs of the people who worked for the record company, I had to sell the family jewellery to protect the airline.

3.02 CA: Now, you use the Virgin brand a lot and it seems like you're getting synergy from one thing to the other. What does the brand stand for in your head?

3.10 RB: Well, I like to think it stands for quality, that you know, if somebody comes across a Virgin company, they –

3.15 CA: They are quality, Richard. Come on now, everyone says quality. Spirit?

3.19 RB: No, but I was going to move on this. We have a lot of fun and I think the people who work for it enjoy it. As I say, we go in and shake up other industries, and I think, you know, we do it differently and I think that industries are not quite the same as a result of Virgin taking them on.

3.40 CA: So, now, you've always had this exploration bug in you. Have you ever regretted that?

3.47 RB: Many times. I mean, I think with the ballooning and boating expeditions we've done in the past. Well, I got pulled out of the sea I think six times by helicopters, so – and each time, I didn't expect to come home to tell the tale. So in those moments, you certainly wonder what you're doing up there or –

4.10 CA: Your companies have had incredible PR value out of these heroics. The years – and until I stopped looking at the polls, you were sort of regarded as this great hero in the UK and elsewhere. And cynics might say, you know, this is just a smart business guy doing what it takes to execute his particular style of marketing. How much was the PR value part of this?

4.40 RB: Well, of course, the PR experts said that as an airline owner, the last thing you should be doing is heading off in balloons and boats, and crashing into the seas. (*Laughter*)

4.59 CA: They had a point, Richard.

5.01 RB: In fact, I think our airline took a full page ad at the time saying, you know, come on, Richard, there are better ways of crossing the Atlantic. (*Laughter*)

5.11 CA: So seriously, is there a dark side? A lot of people would say there's no way that someone could put together this incredible collection of businesses without knifing a few people in the back, you know, doing some ugly things. You've been accused of being ruthless. There was a nasty biography written about you by someone. Is any of it true? Is there an element of truth in it?

5.35 RB: I don't actually think that the stereotype of a businessperson treading all over people to get to the top, generally speaking, works. I think if you treat people well, people will come back and come back for more. And I think all you have in life is your reputation and it's a very small world. And I actually think that the best way of becoming a successful business leader is dealing with people fairly and well, and I like to think that's how we run Virgin.

6.16 CA: Well, Richard, when I was starting off in business, I knew nothing about it and I also was sort of – I thought that business people were supposed to just be ruthless and that that was the only way you could have a chance of succeeding. And you actually did inspire me. I looked at you, I thought, well, he's made it. Maybe there is a different way. So I would like to thank you for that inspiration, and for coming to TED today. Thank you. Thank you so much. (*Applause*)

Unit 12 How to succeed? Get more sleep

0.13 My big idea is a very, very small idea that can unlock billions of big ideas that are at the moment dormant inside us. And my little idea that will do that is sleep.

0.28 (*Laughter*)

0.30 (*Applause*)

0.35 This is a room of type-A women. This is a room of sleep-deprived women. And I learned the hard way, the value of sleep. Two and a half years ago, I fainted from exhaustion. I hit my head on my desk. I broke my cheekbone, I got five stitches on my right eye. And I began the journey of rediscovering the value of sleep. And in the course of that, I studied, I met with medical doctors, scientists, and I'm here to tell you that the way to a more productive, more inspired, more joyful life is getting enough sleep.

1.19 (*Applause*)

1.23 And we women are going to lead the way in this new revolution, this new feminist issue.

1.33 I was recently having dinner with a guy who bragged that he had only gotten four hours' sleep the night before. And I felt like saying to him – but I didn't say it – I felt like saying, 'You know what? If you had gotten five, this dinner would have been a lot more interesting.'

1.47 (*Laughter*)

1.51 There is now a kind of sleep deprivation one-upmanship – especially here in Washington – if you try to make a breakfast date, and you say, 'How about eight o'clock?' they're likely to tell you, 'Eight o'clock is too late for me, but that's OK, I can get a game of tennis in and do a few conference calls and meet you at eight.' And they think that means that they are so incredibly busy and productive, but the truth is they're not, because we, at the moment, have had brilliant leaders in business, in finance, in politics, making terrible decisions. So a high IQ does not mean that you're a good leader, because the essence of leadership is being able to see the iceberg before it hits the Titanic. And we've had far too many icebergs hitting our Titanics.

2.42 In fact, I have a feeling that if Lehman Brothers was Lehman Brothers and Sisters, they might still be around. (*Applause*) While all the brothers were busy just being hyperconnected 24/7, maybe a sister would have noticed the iceberg, because she would have woken up from a seven-and-a-half or eight-hour sleep and have been able to see the big picture.

3.09 So as we are facing all the multiple crises in our world at the moment, what is good for us on a personal level, what's going to bring more joy, gratitude, effectiveness in our lives and be the best for our own careers is also what is best for the world. So I urge you to shut your eyes and discover the great ideas that lie inside us, to shut your engines and discover the power of sleep.

3.43 Thank you.

Keynote Intermediate
Student's Book with the Spark platform
Paul Dummett

Publisher: Gavin McLean
Publishing Consultant: Karen Spiller
Development Editor: Jess Rackham
Editorial Manager: Alison Burt
Head of Strategic Marketing ELT: Charlotte Ellis
Senior Content Project Manager: Nick Ventullo
Manufacturing Manager: Eyvett Davis
Cover design: Brenda Carmichael
Text design: Keith Shaw
Compositor: MPS North America LLC
National Geographic Liaison: Leila Hishmeh
Audio: Tom Dick and Debbie Productions Ltd
DVD: Tom Dick and Debbie Productions Ltd

Cover Photo Caption: Host June Cohen speaks on stage during TED University at TEDGlobal 2012 - June 25–29, 2012, Edinburgh, Scotland. © James Duncan Davidson/TED.

© 2016 National Geographic Learning, a Cengage Learning Company

ALL RIGHTS RESERVED. No part of this work covered by the copyright herein may be reproduced or distributed in any form or by any means, except as permitted by U.S. copyright law, without the prior written permission of the copyright owner.

"National Geographic", "National Geographic Society" and the Yellow Border Design are registered trademarks of the National Geographic Society ® Marcas Registradas

For product information and technology assistance, contact us at
Cengage Learning Customer & Sales Support, cengage.com/contact
For permission to use material from this text or product,
submit all requests online at **cengage.com/permissions**
Further permissions questions can be emailed to
permissionrequest@cengage.com

ISBN-13: 979-8-214-33431-8

National Geographic Learning
Cheriton House, North Way,
Andover, Hampshire, SP10 5BE
United Kingdom

National Geographic Learning, a Cengage Learning Company, has a mission to bring the world to the classroom and the classroom to life. With our English language programs, students learn about their world by experiencing it. Through our partnerships with National Geographic and TED Talks, they develop the language and skills they need to be successful global citizens and leaders.

Locate your local office at **international.cengage.com/region**

Visit National Geographic Learning online at **ELTNGL.com**
Visit our corporate website at **www.cengage.com**

CREDITS

The publishers would like to thank TED Staff for their insightful feedback and expert guidance, allowing us to achieve our dual aims of maintaining the integrity of these inspirational TED Talks, while maximising their potential for teaching English.

The publisher would like to thank all the reviewers who took part in the piloting and development of the material.

Although every effort has been made to contact copyright holders before publication, this has not always been possible. If contacted, the publisher will undertake to rectify any errors or omissions at the earliest opportunity.

The publishers would like to thank the following for permission to use copyright material:

Cover: © James Duncan Davidson/TED.

Photos: 6 (tl, tr, bl, br) © James Duncan Davidson/TED; 6 (ml, mr) © Asa Mathat/TED; 7 (tl) © TED Conferences, LLC; 7 (tr) © James Duncan Davidson/TED; 7 (ml) © Asa Mathat/TED; 7 (mr) © Dafydd Jones/TED; 7 (bl) © Robert Leslie/TED; 7 (br) © Michael Brands/TED; 8–9 © Johnathan Hodgson; 8 © James Duncan Davidson/TED; 10 © James Duncan Davidson/TED; 15 © Ellagrin/Shutterstock.com; 16 (tl) © lightpoet/Shutterstock.com; 16 (tr) © Michelangelo Gratton/Iconica/Getty Images; 16 (ml) © Juice Images/Alamy; 16 (mr, bl) © Image Source/Alamy; 16 (br) © ZUMA Press, Inc/Alamy; 18–19 © isifa/Getty Images; 18 © James Duncan Davidson/TED; 20 © James Duncan Davidson/TED; 21 © Rex Features via AP Images; 25 © Alex Oakenmen/Shutterstock.com; 26 © Image Source Plus/Alamy; 28 © Björn Eiben; 30 © Christophe Viseux; 31 © Asa Mathat/TED; 32 © Asa Mathat/TED; 37 © The Augusta Chronicle/ZUMAPRESS.com; 38 (tl) © Greg Balfour Evans/Alamy; 38 (tr) © UpperCut Images/Alamy; 38 (ml) © Kumar Sriskandan/Alamy; 38 (mr) © Photographee.eu/Shutterstock.com; 38 (b) © altrendo images/Getty Images; 40 © Cory Richards/National Geographic Creative; 41 © Asa Mathat/TED; 42 © Asa Mathat/TED; 43 © Asa Mathat/TED; 44 © John Parra/Stringer/Getty Images; 47 © Blend Image/Getty Images; 48 © allesalltag/Alamy; 50 © Benedicte Desrus/Sipa USA (Sipa via AP Images); 52 © JR/Agence VU/Aurora Photos; 53 © James Duncan Davidson/TED; 54 © James Duncan Davidson/TED; 55 © James Duncan Davidson/TED; 59 © Diane Bondareff/Invision/AP; 60 © Alex Segre/Alamy; 62–63 © Rehahn Photo; 62 © James Duncan Davidson/TED; 64 © James Duncan Davidson/TED; 65 © James Duncan Davidson/TED; 69 © Ingram Publishing/Alamy; 70 (l) © Terry Vine/Getty Images; 70 (r) © Casarsa/iStockphoto; 72 © imageBROKER/Alamy; 74 © YASSER AL-ZAYYAT/AFP/Getty Images; 75 © TED Conferences, LLC; 76 (all) © TED Conferences, LLC; 77 © TED Conferences, LLC; 81 © Rawpixel Ltd./Getty Images; 82 © Ethan Daniels/Shutterstock.com; 84–85 © David McNew/Reuters; 84 © James Duncan Davidson/TED; 85 © pumkinpie/Alamy; 86 © James Duncan Davidson/TED; 87 © AsiaDreamPhoto/Alamy; 90 (l) © Gene Blevins/LA DailyNews/Corbis; 90 (r) © Gene Blevins/ZUMA Wire/Alamy Live News; 91 (microwave) © MrGarry/Shutterstock.com; 91 (telephone) © nyasha/Shutterstock.com; 91 (dishwasher) © dio5050/Shutterstock.com; 91 (vacuum) © tale/Shutterstock.com; 91 (router) © Konstantin Faraktinov; 91 (radio) © Joseph Branston/Tap Magazine via Getty Images; 91 (console) © JOHANNES EISELE/AFP/Getty Images; 91 (kettle) © Petr Malyshev/Shutterstock.com; 91 (bottom: t) © David Paul Morris/Bloomberg via Getty Images; 91 (bottom: m) © Steve Marcus/Reuters; 91 (bottom: b) © Britta Pedersen/picture-alliance/dpa/AP Images; 92 © Hero images/Getty Images;

Printed in Greece by Bakis SA
Print Number: 03 Print Year: 2025

94 (l, r) © Kirby Trapolino; 96 © xPACIFICA/Aurora Photos; 97 (t) © Asa Mathat/TED; 97 (bl) © Sergio Stakhnyk/Shutterstock.com; 97 (bml) © goldenjack/Shutterstock.com; 97 (bmr) © Bayanova Svetlana/Shutterstock.com; 97 (br) © Africa Studio/Shutterstock.com; 98 © Asa Mathat/TED; 99 (tl) © Digital Vision/Getty Images; 99 (tr) © bork/Shutterstock.com; 99 (bl) © EpicStockMedia/Shutterstock.com; 99 (br) © Andy Smith/Cultura/Getty Images; 101 © maxkabakov/iStock/Getty Images Plus; 103 © yamix/Shutterstock.com; 104 © Andrey Kekyalyaynen/Alamy; 106 © Diane Cook, Len Jenshel/National Geographic Creative; 107 (t) © Dafydd Jones/TED; 107 (bl) © Zeljko Radojko/Shutterstock.com; 107 (bml) © LiliGraphie/Shutterstock.com; 107 (bmr) © somyot pattana/Shutterstock.com; 107 (br) © johnandersonphoto/Getty Images; 108 © Dafydd Jones/TED; 113 © AP Photo/Martin Meissner, File; 114 (tl) © taboga/Shutterstock.com; 114 (tr) © monticello/Shutterstock.com; 114 (ml) © Igor Dutina/Shutterstock.com; 114 (mr) © pumnaruk/Shutterstock.com; 114 (bl) © GrigoryL/Shutterstock.com; 114 (br) © Subbotina Anna/Shutterstock.com; 116 © WENN Ltd/Alamy; 118–119 © Randy Olson/National Geographic Creative; 118 © Jo Hale/Getty Images; 120 © Robert Leslie/TED; 125 (Roddick) © Andrew Hasson/Photoshot/Getty Images; 125 (Branson) © Mario Fourmy/Redux; 125 (Charles) © newsphoto/Alamy; 125 (Ford) © Hulton Archive/Getty Images; 125 (Darwin) © Bob Thomas/Popperfoto/Getty Images; 125 (Ash) © AP Photo/Tommy Hultgren; 125 (Edison) © Mondadori Portfolio via Getty Images; 125 (Bethune) © Ken Cedeno/Bloomberg via Getty Images; 126 © Martin Barraud/Caiaimage/ Getty Images; 128 © XPACIFICA/National Geographic Creative; 129 © Michael Brands/TED; 130 © Michael Brands/TED; 133 (l) © Print Collector/Getty Images; 133 (r) © David Cole/Alamy; 135 © Teri Virbickis/Shutterstock.com; 138 © PlusONE/Shutterstock.com; 161 (tl, tr, mtl, mtr, mbr) © designalldone/Getty Images; 161 (bl) © nickylarson974/Getty Images; 161 (br) © Orca/Shutterstock.com; 171 (l) © LOOK Die Bildagentur der Fotografen GmbH/Alamy; 171 (r) © Sandy Jones/Getty Images; 172 (l) © Art Directors & TRIP/Alamy; 172 (r) © Oote Boe Photography/Alamy.

Illustrations & Infographics: 12, 22, 34, 44, 56, 57, 66, 78, 88, 100, 110, 122, 132, 136–137 emc design; 104, 161 (mbl) MPS North America LLC.

Infographics: 22 Sources: Statistic Brain Research Institute; CashSherpa.com; Craig Smith/DMR; 34 Source: *Standards of Living and Modern Economic Growth* by John V. C. Nye, Library of Economics and Liberty; 56 Source: Gravytrain; 66 Based on: circle.cspire.com/thread/6552; 88 Source: EU Infrastructure; 100 Source: elearninginfographics; 110 Source: Transition Network; 122 Source: Inc.com/2012 CEO survey; 132 Source: *The Guardian/Live* Better Challenge; 136–137 Sources: Davidsonstaffing.com; 247wallst.com